LITURGY AND TH
IN BYZAN

C000060243

This book explores the liturgical experience of emotions in Byzantium through the hymns of Romanos the Melodist, Andrew of Crete and Kassia. It reimagines the performance of their hymns during Great Lent and Holy Week in Constantinople. In doing so, it understands compunction as a liturgical emotion, intertwined with paradisal nostalgia, a desire for repentance and a wellspring of tears. For the faithful, liturgical emotions were embodied experiences that were enacted through sacred song and mystagogy. The three hymnographers chosen for this study span a period of nearly four centuries and had an important connection to Constantinople, which forms the topographical and liturgical nexus of the study. Their work also covers three distinct genres of hymnography: *kontakion, kanon* and *sticheron idiomelon*. Through these lenses of period, place and genre this study examines the affective performativity hymns and the Byzantine experience of compunction.

ANDREW MELLAS is a Senior Lecturer in Byzantine Studies at St Andrew's Theological College and an Honorary Associate of the Medieval and Early Modern Centre at the University of Sydney.

LITURGY AND THE EMOTIONS IN BYZANTIUM

Compunction and Hymnody

ANDREW MELLAS

St Andrew's Greek Orthodox Theological College

CAMBRIDGE
UNIVERSITY PRESS

CAMBRIDGE
UNIVERSITY PRESS

University Printing House, Cambridge CB2 8BS, United Kingdom

One Liberty Plaza, 20th Floor, New York, NY 10006, USA

477 Williamstown Road, Port Melbourne, VIC 3207, Australia

314-321, 3rd Floor, Plot 3, Splendor Forum, Jasola District Centre, New Delhi - 110025, India

103 Penang Road, #05-06/07, Visioncrest Commercial, Singapore 238467

Cambridge University Press is part of the University of Cambridge.

It furthers the University's mission by disseminating knowledge in the pursuit of
education, learning and research at the highest international levels of excellence.

www.cambridge.org
Information on this title: www.cambridge.org/9781108720670
DOI: 10.1017/9781108767361

© Andrew Mellas 2020

This publication is in copyright. Subject to statutory exception
and to the provisions of relevant collective licensing agreements,
no reproduction of any part may take place without the written
permission of Cambridge University Press.

First published 2020
First paperback edition 2022

A catalogue record for this publication is available from the British Library

Library of Congress Cataloging in Publication data
Names: Mellas, Andrew, author.
TITLE: Liturgy and the emotions in Byzantium : compunction and hymnody / Andrew Mellas,
St Andrew's Greek Orthodox Theological College, NSW.
DESCRIPTION: Cambridge, United Kingdom ; New York, NY, USA : Cambridge University Press,
2020. | Includes bibliographical references and index.
IDENTIFIERS: LCCN 2019060134 (print) | LCCN 20190601335 (ebook) | ISBN 9781108487597
(hardback) | ISBN 9781108720670 (paperback) | ISBN 9781108767361 (epub)
SUBJECTS: LCSH: Hymns, Greek–History and criticism. | Orthodox Eastern Church–Liturgy–
History. | Lenten hymns–Turkey–Istanbul–History and criticism. | Repentance–Orthodox
Eastern Church. | Emotions–Religious aspects–Orthodox Eastern Church. | Romanos, Melodus,
Saint, active 6th century. | Andrew, of Crete, Saint, approximately 660-740. |
Kassianē, approximately 810–
CLASSIFICATION: LCC BV467 .M45 2020 (print) | LCC BV467 (ebook) | DDC 264/.019023–dc23
LC record available at https://lccn.loc.gov/201906134
LC ebook record available at https://lccn.loc.gov/2019060135

ISBN 978-1-108-48759-7 Hardback
ISBN 978-1-108-72067-0 Paperback

Cambridge University Press has no responsibility for the persistence or
accuracy of URLs for external or third-party internet websites referred to in
this publication, and does not guarantee that any content on such websites is,
or will remain, accurate or appropriate.

Οὐ δάκρυα, οὐδὲ μετάνοιαν ἔχω, οὐδὲ κατάνυξιν,
αὐτός μοι ταῦτα Σωτήρ, ὡς Θεὸς δώρησαι.
Μέγας Κανών

Contents

Figures

Acknowledgements

Several years ago, the desire to embark on an exploration of Byzantine hymnody kindled in my heart. Thence began my Cavafean voyage to Byzantium. Along the way I met many fantastic people whom I owe a debt of gratitude and wish to acknowledge. In many ways they are my Ithaka or, in this case, my Constantinople.

Soon after the voyage began, I encountered Dr Juanita Ruys. Juanita was intrigued by an aspiring Byzantinist who wished to explore compunction as an emotion in liturgical hymns and guided me through the travails of a doctorate. I wholeheartedly thank her and my examiners, Professor Georgia Frank, Professor Constant Mews and Professor Bissera Pentcheva, for their perspicacity and wisdom. I also acknowledge the Australian Research Council Centre for the History of Emotions for its support.

A regular caravanserai along this journey has been St Andrew's Theological College, where Fr Dr Doru Costache and Dr Philip Kariatlis had the vision to convene annual symposia. It is at these symposia that I first met eminent academics such as Pauline Allen, Paul Blowers, David Bradshaw, Fr John Chryssavgis, Adam Cooper, Bronwen Neil, Wendy Mayer and Aristotle Papanikolaou. And it is there that the first Dean of the College, the late Archbishop Stylianos, kindly provided me with insights into compunction and tears.

In 2015 (and again in 2017), I journeyed to Finland for the International Society for Orthodox Church Music conference. There I met many eminent scholars and wonderful singers. I could not possibly list them all here, but I must acknowledge the illumination and encouragement that Mary Cunningham, Daniel Galadza, Alexander Lingas, and Fr Damaskinos Olkinuora kindly gave me.

Later in 2015, not long after I landed in Oxford for the International Conference on Patristic Studies, I sat in Christ Church across the breakfast table from a stranger who seemed oddly familiar. Glancing at his name tag – Derek Krueger – I suddenly realised that this was the author of

Liturgical Subjects and inelegantly exclaimed, 'I've read your book!' Derek's kind support in the years that followed has been inspirational. In Oxford I also met other distinguished scholars such as Fr John Behr, Reuben Demetrios Harper, Elizabeth Jeffreys, Dimitrios Skrekas and Alexis Torrance.

Towards the end of my journey, I was fortunate to take part in the 19th Conference of the Australasian Association for Byzantine Studies. There I rekindled conversations with familiar faces and began new dialogues with eminent Byzantinists such as Eva Anagnostou-Laoutides, Michael Champion, Sarah Gador-Whyte, Meaghan McEvoy, Ken Parry and Roger Scott.

During my doctorate at the University of Sydney, I had the pleasure of several fruitful discussions with Professor Vrasidas Karalis, Professor Daniel Anlezark, Professor Jonathan Wooding and Dr Kimberley-Joy Knight. I humbly thank them for their wit and wisdom. I especially wish to thank the Medieval and Early Modern Centre at the University of Sydney, which kindly supported me to publish this book by welcoming me as an honorary associate in 2018.

Last but certainly not least, I am incredibly grateful to Stella, Niki and Nektarios. Their patience, faith and love have never faltered. Although they may not realise it, they have been my companions on this journey. Even when the night was dark, we found a bright star that smiled upon us. His name is Romanos. He was not with us at the beginning of the voyage, but he has come to us now 'at the turn of the tide'.

Abbreviations

BZ	*Byzantinische Zeitschrifte*
CCSG	Corpus Christianorum Series Graeca
CSCO	Corpus Scriptorum Christianorum Orientalium
GNO	*Gregorii Nysseni Opera*, ed. Wernerus Jaeger et al., 10 vols. (Leiden: Brill, 1952–2014)
DOP	*Dumbarton Oaks Papers*
JECS	*Journal of Early Christian Studies*
JÖB	*Jahrbuch der Österreichischen Byzantinistik*
MLN	*Modern Language Notes* (1886–1961); *MLN* (1962–2017)
MMB	Monumenta Musicae Byzantinae
OCA	Orientalia Christiana Periodica
ODB	*Oxford Dictionary of Byzantium*, ed. Alexander P. Kazhdan et al., 3 vols. (New York, NY: Oxford University Press, 1991)
PG	*Patrologia Graeca*, ed. J. P. Migne et al., 161 vols. (Paris: Garnier, 1867–1912)
SC	Sources Chrétiennes

The Greek text of the Old Testament cited throughout is the Septuagint edited by Alfred Rahlfs, *Septuaginta: Id est Vetus Testamentum Graece iuxta LXX interpretes* (Stuttgart: Privilegierte Württembergische Bibelanstalt, 1935). English translations are based on or follow the translations in Albert Pietersma and Benjamin G. Wright, *A New English Translation of the Septuagint* (New York, NY: Oxford University Press, 2007). The Greek text of the New Testament cited throughout is the fourth revised edition of *The Greek New Testament*, ed. Barbara Aland et al. (Stuttgart: Deutsche Bibelgesellschaft, 1994). English translations are my own, though I have consulted *The Orthodox Study Bible* (Nashville: Thomas Nelson, 2008).

CHAPTER I

Introduction

Today, the word 'compunction' conveys a sense of remorse, though usually in a weakened sense. Its significance for Christianity in Late Antiquity and Byzantium was more profound. The feeling of compunction was intertwined with the experience of paradisal nostalgia and an outpouring of tears. It was portrayed as a feeling that befell the faithful and yet was an emotion that could not be felt unless it was earnestly sought. Responding to a question from an ascetic on why, from time to time, 'compunction falls upon the soul without much effort' and, on other occasions, the soul 'cannot feel any compunction', Basil the Great (c. 330–379) declared:

> Ἡ μὲν τοιαύτη κατάνυξις Θεοῦ ἐστι δῶρον, ἢ εἰς ἐρεθισμὸν τῆς ἐπιθυμίας, ἵνα γευσαμένη ἡ ψυχὴ τῆς γλυκύτητος τοῦ τοιούτου πόνου, σπουδάσῃ τοῦτον ἐξομαλίσαι· ἢ εἰς ἀπόδειξιν τοῦ δύνασθαι τὴν ψυχὴν διὰ σπουδαιοτέρας ἐπιμελείας ἐν κατανύξει εἶναι πάντοτε.[1]

> Such a compunction is a gift from God in order to stir up desire, so that the soul, having tasted the sweetness of such compunction or sorrow might be stirred up to foster it, or as proof that the soul is able through more zealous application to be always in such compunction.[2]

This book explores how this dialectical relationship was embodied in the interpersonal dynamics of Byzantine liturgical hymns, which opened an affective space where compunction could be perceived and felt. It examines the emotion of compunction by reimagining the liturgical performance of the hymns that mobilised and enacted κατάνυξις.[3]

[1] *Asketikon: The Shorter Responses*, 16. PG 31, 1092D.
[2] The English translation is from Anna M. Silvas, trans. *The Asketikon of St Basil the Great* (Oxford: Oxford University Press, 2005), 282–83.
[3] Κατάνυξις is the Greek word for compunction in Byzantium. See G. W. H. Lampe, *Patristic Greek Lexicon* (Oxford: Clarendon Press, 1961), 713. Secondary literature has sometimes transliterated it as *katanyxis* or *katanuxis*. The Greek word is not found in any writings from antiquity but makes its

The compunctious hymns of Romanos the Melodist (c. 490–560), Andrew of Crete (c. 660–740) and Kassia (c. 810–865), which were performed during Great Lent and Holy Week, are my focus.[4] The choice of these three hymnographers allows for a diachronic exploration of compunction from the sixth century until the ninth century. Moreover, all three of these hymnographers had a connection to Constantinople, which is the topographical nexus of this study. Finally, the hymns of each hymnographer provide an opportunity to examine three different genres of Byzantine hymnography – *kontakion*, *kanon* and *sticheron idiomelon*.[5]

Experiencing hymns in Byzantium was a liturgical event. Hymns were performed during sacred rituals that were infused with meaning. The Byzantines saw the order of their highly ritualised society as images of the celestial world.[6] Even a simple procession around the church traced the circle of eternity and consecrated time in their eyes. Language, music and ritual were inextricable, and interiority was not merely an allegorical construct; the performance of hymns evoked godly passions and embodied a liturgical world for the faithful. In reimagining the performance of Byzantine hymns that sought to arouse compunction, I explore the relationships between these modalities and the liturgical world they created.

This will be the first diachronic exploration of compunction as an emotion that was liturgically experienced in Eastern Christendom.

---

first appearance in the Septuagint. See, for example, Isaiah 29:10 or Psalm 59:5. See also T. Muraoka, *A Greek–English Lexicon of the Septuagint* (Leuven: Peeters, 2009), xiii, 378. Its verbal form (κατανύσσω) is usually given a metaphorical meaning rather than a literal one – 'to affect mentally and profoundly', ibid. Likewise, in the New Testament, the noun is imbued with an unfavourable sense and translated as 'bewilderment' or 'stupor' – Johannes P. Louw and Eugene A. Nida, *Greek–English Lexicon of the New Testament: Based on Semantic Domains* (New York, NY: United Bible Societies, 1988). Yet its verbal form retained the metaphorical sense of being pricked in or cut to the heart. See also the interesting translation of κατάνυξις as 'astonishment' in Johann Lust, Erik Eynikel and Katrin Hauspie, *A Greek–English Lexicon of the Septuagint* (Stuttgart: Deutsche Bibelgesellschaft, 1992), 240. On the biblical understanding of compunction and its transformation into a Christian concept, see Marguerite Harl, 'Les origines grecques du mot et de la notion de "componction" dans la Septante et chez ses commentateurs', *Revue des Études Augustiniennes* 32 (1986): 3–21.

[4] I use 'compunctious' (a translation of the Greek adjectival form of 'compunction' – κατανυκτικόν) in a broad sense to describe a hymn or event that evokes, arouses or is characterised by compunction. For an exploration of the term κατανυκτικόν and its meanings in Byzantine religious poetry, see Antonia Giannouli, 'Catanyctic Religious Poetry: A Survey', in *Theologica Minora: The Minor Genres of Byzantine Theological Literature*, ed. Antonio Rigo, Pavel Ermilov and Michele Trizio (Turnhout: Brepols, 2013), 86–109.

[5] These three genres and other technical terms are defined in the Glossary. More detailed definitions and contexts of each of these three genres (*kontakion*, *kanon* and *sticheron idiomelon*) will be explored in Chapters 3, 4 and 5.

[6] Robert F. Taft, *Through Their Own Eyes: Liturgy as the Byzantines Saw It* (Berkeley, CA: InterOrthodox Press, 2006), 134.

However, this is not a history of crying or a study of spiritual weeping.[7] While hymns often linked compunction with tears, this points to the affective mysticism that shaped its experience in Byzantium. The existing literature on compunction has largely overlooked the hymns that dramatised it. Favouring the patristic writings that defined it as a concept or doctrine, scholarship has either presented compunction as synonymous with πένθος (mourning, *penthos*) or neglected its affective dimension. First published in 1944, Irénée Hausherr's study of compunction remains an invaluable point of departure.[8] However, his methodology is deficient. The reference to compunction as a 'doctrine' in the title of the book betrays the Western scholasticism that defines Hausherr's approach. Moreover, his study of *penthos* in patristic literature does not adequately differentiate it from compunction. Indeed, he devotes only four pages to discussing the latter.[9]

Although Hausherr's investigation of *penthos* drew on an array of patristic texts and evidence, it becomes difficult to discern a coherent argument amidst his disparate sources. This did not prevent Sandra McEntire – who in 1990 responded to Hausherr's seminal work with an exploration of compunction in medieval England – from praising Hausherr's book as 'the best study of its kind, unequaled by a comparable examination of the concept of spiritual mourning in the West'.[10] A notable contrast is Hannah Hunt's thorough criticism of Hausherr's methodology.[11] Hunt's main concerns are 'the cavalier attitude' to scholarly material, the imposition of a scholastic reasoning on patristic literature that belongs to the mystical tradition of Byzantine theology and the insensitive approach to the context of patristic texts.[12]

---

[7] On this topic, see Piroska Nagy, *Le don des larmes au Moyen Âge. Un instrument en quête d'institution (V^e–XIIIe siècle)* (Paris: Albin Michel, 2000), 125–42; Kimberley Christine Patton and John Stratton Hawley, eds., *Holy Tears: Weeping in the Religious Imagination* (Princeton, NJ: Princeton University Press, 2005); Elina Gertsman, ed., *Crying in the Middle Ages: Tears of History* (Abingdon: Routledge, 2011); Tomás Fernández, 'Byzantine Tears: A Pseudo-Chrysostomic Fragment on Weeping in the *Florilegium Coislinianum*', in *Encyclopedic Trends in Byzantium? Proceedings of the International Conference Held in Leuven 6–8 May 2009*, ed. Peter van Deun and Caroline Macé (Leuven: Peeters, 2011), 125–42.

[8] Irénée Hausherr, *Penthos: The Doctrine of Compunction in the Christian East* (Kalamazoo, MI: Cistercian Publications, 1982).

[9] Ibid., 7–11.

[10] Sandra J. McEntire, *The Doctrine of Compunction in Medieval England: Holy Tears* (Lewiston, NY: The Edwin Mellen Press, 1990), 3. Given McEntire explores compunction and weeping in medieval England, I have not undertaken a critique of her work.

[11] Hannah Hunt, *Joy-Bearing Grief: Tears of Contrition in the Writings of the Early Syrian and Byzantine Fathers* (Leiden: Brill, 2004), 25–32.

[12] Ibid., 28.

While Hausherr asserted that compunction is 'an emotion which plants deep in the soul a feeling, an attitude, or a resolution' and 'denotes a shock which comes from without' whereas *penthos* is 'the psychological reaction', he concluded that compunction and *penthos* are 'virtual equivalents'.[13] Despite noting their lexicographic differences, Tomáš Špidlík echoed Hausherr's view of the synonymy of the two terms in his own handbook of Eastern Christian spirituality.[14] It was not until John Chryssavgis' consideration of compunction within the context of his broader interest in a theology of tears that a subtle but important distinction between *penthos* and compunction was delineated.[15]

Chryssavgis acknowledged the difficulty in categorising *penthos* and compunction as two disparate states, especially when a prima facie reading of some patristic texts may suggest they coinhere, but insisted on the need for a distinction without defining rationally what is essentially an existential experience:

> Compunction or *katanyxis* is not identical with either *penthos* or tears. *Penthos* is a general term describing the precondition of tears, whether as a gift of God or not ... Compunction, on the other hand, is a state preceding both *penthos* and tears, and is the cause of joyful sorrow.[16]

Hunt also distinguished *penthos* from compunction, suggesting the latter 'tends to refer to a particular moment of awakening, the physical sensation of the heart being pricked—whereas mourning is more of a continuous movement'.[17] This study draws on the distinction articulated by Chryssavgis and developed by Hunt, but explores how compunction emerged in the hymnody of Byzantium and as a chapter in the history of emotions.[18] Chryssavgis and Hunt viewed compunction through the lens of patristic texts and did so only fleetingly. Compunction was a minor consideration within broader studies of the theology of tears and *penthos* respectively.

---

[13] Hausherr, *Penthos*, 8–9.

[14] Tomáš Špidlík, *La spiritualité de l'Orient chrétien* (Roma: Pontificium Institutum Orientalium Studiorum, 1978), 195.

[15] John Chryssavgis, 'Κατάνυξις: Compunction as the Context for the Theology of Tears in St John Climacus', Κληρονομία 17, no. 2 (1985): 131–36; *Ascent to Heaven: The Theology of the Human Person According to Saint John of the Ladder* (Brookline, MA: Holy Cross Orthodox Press, 1989), 125–61; 'A Spirituality of Imperfection: The Way of Tears in Saint John Climacus', *Cistercian Studies Quarterly* 37, no. 4 (2002); *John Climacus: From the Egyptian Desert to the Sinaite Mountain* (Aldershot: Ashgate, 2004), 131–62.

[16] *Ascent to Heaven*, 127.   [17] Hunt, *Joy-Bearing Grief*, 16.

[18] On the history of emotions, see Jan Plamper, *The History of Emotions: An Introduction*, trans. Keith Tribe (Oxford: Oxford University Press, 2015).

While these themes and the associated patristic literature are vital contexts, neither Hunt nor Chryssavgis considered the liturgical context of compunction and the hymns that embodied this emotion.

This study builds on Derek Krueger's exploration of the liturgical self in Byzantium.[19] Krueger acknowledges that 'access to the interior religious experience of Byzantine Christians proves difficult', but contends that their sacred rituals and liturgical hymns 'produce, articulate, and maintain norms for self-understanding and self-presentation'.[20] Similarly, this book does not go in search of what the Byzantine faithful were feeling; it probes how liturgical hymns embodied, mobilised and enacted the emotion of compunction. After all, emotions in Byzantium were socially situated, historically fashioned and shaped by liturgical ritual. Indeed, the 'mapping of biblical narrative into liturgical time' did not simply define the Christian self but also the 'Christian "we"'.[21] This notion lends itself to the concept of an emotional community where the faithful embraced 'the same norms of emotional expression' and valued particular emotions.[22]

The primary texts framing Krueger's exploration of Christian interiority were principally Byzantine hymns and his study raises important methodological considerations. These considerations marry well with those posited by Sarah McNamer in relation to the history of emotions, which I will discuss later in this introduction.[23] Indeed, Krueger acknowledges that 'the history of emotions in Byzantium deserves further investigation',[24] but this topic was not his ultimate objective. Building on Robert Taft's *Through Their Own Eyes*, which examines how the Byzantines experienced liturgy, Krueger probes 'how Byzantine Christians came to view themselves through the liturgy' and how this ritual shaped selfhood.[25]

---

[19] Derek Krueger, *Liturgical Subjects: Christian Ritual, Biblical Narrative and the Formation of Self in Byzantium* (Philadelphia, PA: University of Pennsylvania Press, 2014).

[20] Ibid., 7.   [21] Ibid., 72.

[22] Barbara H. Rosenwein, *Emotional Communities in the Early Middle Ages* (Ithaca, NY: Cornell University Press, 2006), 2.

[23] Sarah McNamer, 'Feeling', in *Oxford Twenty-First Century Approaches to Literature: Middle English*, ed. Paul Strohm (Oxford: Oxford University Press, 2007), 241–57; *Affective Meditation and the Invention of Medieval Compassion* (Philadelphia, PA: University of Pennsylvania Press, 2010), 1–21; 'The Literariness of Literature and the History of Emotion', *PMLA* 130, no. 5 (2015): 1436.

[24] Krueger, *Liturgical Subjects*, 167. However, see Derek Krueger, 'The Transmission of Liturgical Joy in Byzantine Hymns for Easter', in Brouria Bitton-Ashkelony and Derek Krueger, eds., *Prayer and Worship in Eastern Christianities, 5th to 11th Centuries* (New York, NY: Routledge, 2017), 132–50.

[25] Krueger, *Liturgical Subjects*, 3.

Compunction in Patristic Literature

While this book is not a systematic exploration of how compunction evolves as a concept in patristic literature, the writings of church fathers and mothers offer an overarching theological and spiritual framework for understanding how this emotion emerged in a liturgical context. Therefore, from time to time, my exploration of hymns evoking compunction will also reflect on excerpts from these writings. This will shed light on the relationship between the more philosophical musings of church fathers and mothers, and the subtle theology of the liturgical hymns the faithful would hear and sing. Although patristic literature often considered compunction as an element that formed part of a complex concept, it also portrayed compunction as being kindled following a divine encounter, a heartbreaking event that engenders tears – and the visitation of Christ who heals the heart – or within the context of spiritual counsel on themes such as the remembrance of death. Tears of compunction may break the heart, but they are also a divine gift that provokes repentance, mercy and consolation.[26]

In response to a question on how compunction can be acquired through prayer and psalmody, the sixth-century Palestinian monks Barsanuphios and John advised that it is through the remembrance of one's sinfulness and the prospect of divine judgment that the feeling of compunction and desire for repentance will come.[27] However, their spiritual counsel is not as dark as it may first seem and its message is filled with hope, not despair. Psalmody that arouses compunction can elicit divine mercy. In singing to God, 'one must keep one's intellect alert to the words of the text and assume within one's soul the meaning concealed in them' so that the good deeds portrayed are cause for emulation.[28] Likewise, the evil actions depicted in sacred song should encourage asceticism and repentance. The monks suggest the sacred drama that unfolds in the performance of psalmody is not a source of amusement, but the personal adventure of human freedom experienced by the singer. When psalmody is performed

---

[26] See, for example, the patristic references in Chryssavgis, 'Κατάνυξις', 132–34. On the theme of repentance in patristic literature, see Alexis Torrance, *Repentance in Late Antiquity. Eastern Asceticism and the Framing of the Christian Life* (Oxford: Oxford University Press, 2012), 88–175.

[27] Letter 428 in *Barsanuphius and John: Letters*, trans. John Chryssavgis, vol. 2 (Washington, DC: Catholic University of America Press, 2007), 54. For the Greek text, see *Barsanuphe et Jean de Gaza: Correspondance*, ed. François Neyt and Paula de Angelis-Noah. SC 450 (Paris: Éditions du Cerf, 2002).

[28] *Barsanuphius and John*, vol. 2, 55.

in this way, the gift of compunction and ascetic struggle is the benevolence of God.

Another gift of compunction is described in Athanasius of Alexandria's (c. 298–373 AD) exploration of how dreaming could be a vehicle for divine revelation. In his letter *On Sickness and Health*, after citing the visions that Elisha and Daniel experienced whilst asleep and briefly alluding to the five senses of the body and soul, Athanasius describes a divine sense that is awakened by compunction:

> There is, after these, also another sixth sense, with which we who are able to touch partake of the untouchable, about which Solomon said, 'you will discover a divine sense perception' and which often comes to pass in compunction of heart.[29]

Athanasius suggests a threefold framework for these kinds of dreams to occur: a vigilant mind, a spiritual sensorium and the emotion of compunction. While the experiences of dreaming and liturgical worship are not entirely analogous, the potential of the former to participate in the divine illuminates the mystical significance of the latter. As we will see, the singing of hymns activated liturgical memory, which did not interpret the biblical events of salvation and its protagonists through the prism of history, but as realities that become present as part of the mystery of worship, as images resembling what they signified.

The Psalms and Compunction

Throughout this book, I consider the performance of the Psalms in Byzantine worship and how this would have created an atmosphere of compunction in the liturgical cycle. The Psalms of David formed part of the worship of the earliest Christian communities and evolved in elaborate ways over the centuries as a cornerstone of prayer and liturgical song.[30] As early as the fourth century, Psalm 50 was a recurring song of repentance that the faithful would hear, recite or sing during the prayers of the daybreak office and, over time, other parts of the Byzantine divine office.[31] In voicing the words of Psalm 50, the faithful prayed daily for divine mercy

---

[29] Chapter 8. F. Diekamp, *Analecta Patristica*, OCA 117 (Rome: Pontificium Institutum Orientalium Studiorum, 1938), 7. The English translation is my own.

[30] For an overview, see Robert F. Taft, 'Christian Liturgical Psalmody: Origins, Development, Decomposition, Collapse', in *Psalms in Community: Jewish and Christian Textual, Liturgical, and Artistic Traditions*, ed. Harold W. Attridge and Margot Elsbeth Fassler (Leiden: Brill, 2004), 7–32.

[31] Krueger, *Liturgical Subjects*, 19; Kallistos Ware, '"Forgive Us . . . As We Forgive": Forgiveness in the Psalms and the Lord's Prayer', in *Meditations of the Heart: The Psalms in Early Christian Thought*

and asked for the grace of forgiveness, comforted by the promise that their entreaty would not remain unheard: 'a broken and humbled heart God will not despise'.[32] However, this penitential plea for forgiveness was by no means the only song of the Psalter they would have experienced. All 150 Psalms of the Septuagint were interspersed in various arrangements throughout the weekly cycle of worship, and the set of six Psalms known as the *Hexapsalmos* was chanted at the beginning of matins.[33] Moreover, beyond the use of the Psalms in communal worship, the vast majority of extant Byzantine Psalters appear to have been intended for personal devotion, which suggests the Psalms were also read outside of the divine office as a form of prayer by those who were literate.[34]

The *Hexapsalmos*, which consisted of Psalms 3, 37, 62, 87, 102 and 142, narrated a poignant tale of despair coloured with the hope of salvation. The pain of persecution and the sense of fallenness one feels in the descent to the darkest places of the underworld eventually give way to glimmers of hope, mercy and compassion. At the nadir of despair appears the Lord:

> who is very merciful toward all your acts of lawlessness,
> who heals all your diseases,
> who redeems your life from corruption,
> who crowns you with mercy and compassion,
> who satisfies your desire with good,
> your youth will be renewed like an eagle's.[35]

What hitherto was a melancholy voyage where the congregation was invited to identify with the afflicted voice of the Psalmist – 'my life drew near to Hades, I was counted among those who go down into a pit'[36] – suddenly becomes a journey of restoration. Although the rubrics are not always consistent on the question of whether the *Hexapsalmos* was sung by the entire congregation or recited by one person, there was certainly a desire for the words of these psalms to be heard by the faithful.[37] As an integral part of sacred ritual, they became a familiar story that guided listeners and singers alike, teaching them how to feel and how to pray.

---

and Practice. Essays in Honour of Andrew Louth, ed. Andreas Andreopoulos, Augustine Casiday and Carol Harrison (Turnhout: Brepols, 2011), 58.

[32] Psalm 50:19.

[33] Archimandrite Job Getcha, *The Typikon Decoded: An Explanation of Byzantine Liturgical Practice* (Yonkers, NY: St Vladimir's Seminary Press, 2012), 15–23; Eugen J. Pentiuc, *The Old Testament in Eastern Orthodox Tradition* (Oxford: Oxford University Press, 2014), 216–21.

[34] Georgi R. Parpulov, 'Psalters and Personal Piety in Byzantium', in *The Old Testament in Byzantium*, ed. Paul Magdalino and Robert Nelson (Washington, DC: Dumbarton Oaks, 2010), 82.

[35] Psalm 102:3–5.   [36] Psalm 87:4–5.   [37] Krueger, *Liturgical Subjects*, 20–21.

Amidst an array of blessed emotions and depraved feelings, the faithful could yearn for the former while learning to despise the latter. The chapters that follow will show how the Psalms, together with the broader corpus of liturgical hymns, became affective scripts that cultivated holy emotions such as compunction.

Compunction as an Emotion in Byzantium

Looking closely at the history of emotions, it is not a case of false friends to loosely equate the modern word 'emotion' with the Greek word πάθος. Caution is warranted given that scholars have been anxious to employ precise emotion terminology and carefully trace semantic change in concepts of emotion.[38] Contemporary scholars often use 'passion' and 'emotion' interchangeably when discussing antiquity and late antiquity.[39] Although I follow these scholars in translating the Greek word πάθος as 'emotion', I acknowledge that the shift from passions to emotions in the early modern period psychologised and secularised the philosophical and theological dimensions of the former.[40] Thomas Dixon has argued that it was only in the nineteenth century that the passions of the soul gave way to a secular psychological category – emotions.[41] However, this shift in emotional vocabulary occurred centuries earlier.[42] While calling compunction an emotion may be somewhat anachronistic inasmuch as emotions in Byzantium were often called passions, this is not a lexical barrier provided we begin with an understanding of the significance of emotions for Byzantine Christianity and the classical philosophy it inherited.

Πάθος is often translated as 'passion' but it does not suggest extreme emotions in the modern sense of the word. It literally means something that befalls someone or the soul – an event or calamity – and is linked to

---

[38] Ute Frevert, 'Defining Emotions: Concepts and Debates over Three Centuries', in *Emotional Lexicons: Continuity and Change in the Vocabulary of Feeling 1700–2000*, ed. Ute Frevert et al. (Oxford: Oxford University Press, 2014), 1–31.

[39] See, for example, Richard Sorabji, *Emotion and Peace of Mind: From Stoic Agitation to Christian Temptation* (New York, NY: Oxford University Press, 2002); David Konstan, *The Emotions of the Ancient Greeks: Studies in Aristotle and Classical Literature* (London: University of Toronto Press, 2006).

[40] Thomas Dixon, 'Revolting Passions', *Modern Theology* 27, no. 2 (2011): 298–312.

[41] Dixon, *From Passions to Emotions: The Creation of a Secular Psychological Category* (Cambridge: Cambridge University Press, 2003), passim.

[42] Kirk Essary, 'Passions, Affections, or Emotions? On the Ambiguity of 16th-Century Terminology', *Emotion Review* 9, no. 4 (2017): 367–74.

the verb πάσχω ('I suffer' or 'I experience').[43] Diachronically, the word πάθος displays a semantic continuity in denoting what modern scholarship understands as emotion. In the New Testament, the Greek noun πάθος, which appears only on three occasions, bespeaks 'lustful passion'.[44] While Liddell and Scott's primary definition of the ancient Greek word πάθος is 'anything that befalls one', 'a passion, emotion' comes in as a close second.[45] In modern Greek, πάθος is 'the intensity of emotions' or a 'fiery desire'.[46]

Of course, theories of emotion go as far back as Plato, Aristotle and the Stoics. Their ideas influenced Byzantium's culture and theology. Plato thought that emotions, seated as they were in the spirited part of the soul, have a cognitive element, and Aristotle held they are connected with action, belief and judgment. Even Epicurus agreed with Plato and Aristotle on their rational dimension, portraying emotions as 'not simply blind surges of affect, stirrings or sensations' but as 'ways of interpreting the world'.[47] The Stoics, on the other hand, generally argued that emotions were unnatural and therefore should be eliminated.[48] Modern investigations into emotion by philosophers, historians and psychologists have leaned considerably on the ancients in an effort to rehabilitate its intellectual dimension and liberate it from the tyranny of moralism.[49]

The theology of the Alexandrian and Cappadocian Fathers was pivotal in shaping the Byzantine understanding of passions against the backdrop of Hellenism and classical philosophy.[50] Likewise, the Eastern monastic

---

[43] Lampe, *Patristic Greek Lexicon*, 992, 1049–50. See also Alexander P. Kazhdan and Anthony Cutler, 'Emotions', in *ODB*, 691–92.

[44] The three occasions are: Romans 1:26, Colossians 3:5 and 1 Thessalonians 4:5. See Kallistos Ware, 'The Meaning of "Pathos" in Abba Isaias and Theodoret of Cyrus', *Studia Patristica* 20 (1989): 316–17.

[45] H. G. Liddell and R. Scott, *An Intermediate Greek–English Lexicon* (Oxford: Clarendon Press, 2002), 584.

[46] George D. Babiniotis, Λεξικό της Νέας Ελληνικής Γλώσσας [*Dictionary of the Modern Greek Language*] (Athens: Centre of Lexicology, 1998), 1311.

[47] Martha C. Nussbaum, *The Therapy of Desire: Theory and Practice in Hellenistic Ethics* (Princeton, NJ: Princeton University Press, 2009), 369.

[48] See Sorabji, *Emotion and Peace of Mind*, 1–13.

[49] See Martha C. Nussbaum, *Upheavals of Thought: The Intelligence of Emotions* (Cambridge: Cambridge University Press, 2001); William M. Reddy, *The Navigation of Feeling: A Framework for the History of Emotions* (Cambridge: Cambridge University Press, 2001); Daniel M. Gross, *The Secret History of Emotion: From Aristotle's Rhetoric to Modern Brain Science* (Chicago, IL: University of Chicago Press, 2006).

[50] Simo Knuuttila, *Emotions in Ancient and Medieval Philosophy* (Oxford: Clarendon, 2004), 111–76.

tradition influenced Christianity's view of emotions and thoughts.[51] For Byzantium, passion was a far more expansive category than a restrictive definition of emotion would presume. The passions included appetites, such as hunger and thirst, and forms of human behaviour, such as rudeness or loquaciousness.[52] Clement of Alexandria (c. 150–215) referred to sleep and death as πάθη and Gregory the Theologian (329–390) described the phases of the moon using the same term.[53] However, when employed in a spiritual context, πάθος refers to an emotion felt by the soul.[54]

Although passions were a preoccupation of ascetic theology, it was not always a case of differentiating between good and bad passions and making the latter the target of spiritual warfare. More than half of the thirty rungs on John Klimakos' *Ladder of Divine Ascent* are about the struggle against the passions; however, it is important to examine what this struggle signified. The passions were not necessarily evil distortions of human nature. As impulses, passions were neutral, but could become good or bad depending on their use.[55] In the fifth century, Theodoret of Cyrus and Abba Isaias propounded a positive view of the passions that followed the position of Plato and Aristotle rather than the view of the Stoics. Theodoret and Isaias argued that passions were a natural part of human nature since it was none other than God who created them.[56] For example, they argued that anger can be directed against the devil and mingled with desire to engender the harmony of virtue.[57] Even pride, which is often the cause of human downfall in asceticism, when it is in accordance with nature can help in the fight against one's enemies:

---

[51] See Columba Stewart, 'Evagrius Ponticus and the "Eight Generic *Logismoi*"', in *In the Garden of Evil: The Vices and Culture in the Middle Ages*, ed. Richard Newhauser (Toronto: Pontifical Institute of Medieval Studies, 2005), 3–34; Kevin Corrigan, *Evagrius and Gregory: Mind, Soul and Body in the 4th Century* (Farnham: Ashgate, 2009), 73–101; Columba Stewart, 'Evagrius Ponticus and the Eastern Monastic Tradition on the Intellect and the Passions', *Modern Theology* 27, no. 2 (2011): 263–75.

[52] See the chapter entitled 'Concerning the Natural and Innocent Emotions' in the third book of John of Damascus' *Exposition on the Orthodox Faith*. Bonifatius Kotter, ed., *Die Schriften des Johannes von Damaskos II. Expositio fidei* (Berlin: De Gruyter, 1973), 162–63 (chapter 64). It is chapter 20 in PG 94, 1081–84.

[53] *Protrepticus* 10 and Oration 27 respectively. Cited in Ware, 'The Meaning of "Pathos"', 315.

[54] Although Byzantine literature referred to the mind and the soul as discrete categories, its monastic and hesychastic tradition regarded the heart as the centre of the human person. The modern dichotomy between emotion and reason does not accurately reflect how Byzantine literature portrayed the passions. See John Meyendorff, *Byzantine Theology: Historical Trends and Doctrinal Themes* (New York, NY: Fordham University Press, 1983), 69–72; David Bradshaw, 'The Mind and the Heart in the Christian East and West', *Faith and Philosophy* 26, no. 5 (2009): 576–98.

[55] Ware, 'The Meaning of "Pathos"', 315.   [56] Ibid., 319.   [57] Ibid., 320.

when Job found this pride, he reviled his enemies, calling them 'dishonourable men of no repute, lacking everything good, whom I would not consider fit to dwell with the dogs that guard my flocks'.[58]

Thus, human passibility for some church fathers was not a curse but part of divine providence. According to Gregory the Theologian, '[the passions of the soul] are gifts from God, being moved by the guidance and rule of the Logos' (Δωρήματ' ἐστὶν ἐκ Θεοῦ, κινούμενα Λόγου ποδηγίᾳ τε καὶ στρατηγίᾳ).[59] Emotions were not necessarily targeted for extirpation but for healing, reorientation and transformation. In similar fashion to Theodoret and Isaias, Gregory suggested anger and desire, when used properly, could be positive passions:

Ζήλου μὲν ὅπλον θυμὸς ἐμμέτρως πνέων·
Πόθου δὲ χωρὶς οὐχ ἁλώσιμος Θεός.[60]

For anger that seethes according to measure is a weapon against zeal, and without desire God is not attainable.[61]

For Philo of Alexandria (c. 25 BC–50 AD), the emotion of fear could be an ally in spiritual warfare, 'warning the soul to treat nothing carelessly'.[62] And for Maximus the Confessor (c. 580–662 AD), the 'blessed passion of holy love'[63] was a sacred emotion, though the love of self was the very first passion.[64]

This way of viewing emotions is also present in the Latin tradition. Lactantius (c. 250–325 AD) repudiated the Stoic avowal of *apatheia* (freedom from emotion) and the Peripatetic fondness of *metriopatheia* (the moderation of emotion), arguing that 'God would not have endowed human beings with emotions if they served no useful purpose'.[65] Similarly, Gregory of Nyssa (c. 335–395 AD) defended the emotions as integral aspects of human nature that play a role in the spiritual ascent. In his dialogue with Macrina, *On the Soul and the Resurrection*, Gregory

---

[58] Abba Isaias, *Logoi* II, 1–2, quoted by Ware in 'The Meaning of "Pathos"', 315.
[59] Gregory of Nazianzus, *Against Anger*, in *Gregory Nazianzus, Poems on Scripture*, trans. Brian Dunkle (New York, NY: St Vladimir's Seminary Press, 2012), 107. For the Greek text of this poem, see PG 37, 838A.
[60] Ibid.   [61] Dunkle, trans., *Gregory Nazianzus, Poems on Scripture*, 107.
[62] *Allegorical Interpretation*, II, 8. Quoted in Ware, 'The Meaning of "Pathos"', 217.
[63] Maximus the Confessor, *Centuries on Love*, III, 67. The English translation is from G. E. H. Palmer, Philip Sherrard, and Kallistos Ware, trans. *The Philokalia: The Complete Text*, vol. 2 (London: Faber and Faber, 1981), 93. For the Greek text, see Aldo Ceresa-Gastaldo, ed. *Capitoli sulla carità* (Rome: Editrice Studium, 1963), 176.
[64] Maximus the Confessor, *To Thalassius*, prol. PG 90, 253D–256D.
[65] Lactantius, *Divine Institutes*, trans. Anthony Bowen and Peter Garnsey (Liverpool: Liverpool University Press, 2003), 364–68.

(or rather his sister) presents the emotions as neutral forces; neither inherently evil nor good but judged according to their mode of use:

οὐκοῦν εἰ μέν τις τούτοις κατὰ τὸν δέοντα χρῆσαι λόγον, ἐν αὐτῷ λαμβάνηται ἐκεῖνα, καὶ μὴ αὐτὸς ἐν ἐκείνοις, ἀλλ'οἷόν τις βασιλεὺς τῇ πολυχειρίᾳ τῶν ὑπηκόων συνεργῷ χρώμενος, ῥᾷον κατορθώσει τὸ κατ' ἀρετὴ σπουδαζόμενον.[66]

Therefore, if a person uses these emotions according to their right principle, receiving them into himself without falling into their power, he will be like some king who, by using the many hands of his servants for assistance, will easily accomplish his virtuous purpose.[67]

Indeed, Gregory's *On the Formation of the Human Being* argues that emotions do not constitute a postlapsarian aspect of humanity; they are another instance of how God formed human nature as the midpoint between the earthly and the divine.[68] Anger may be a brutish impulse, but it is only a depraved emotion through 'the evil cultivation of the mind' (τῆς πονηρᾶς τοῦ νοῦ γεωργίας).[69] However, Gregory argues that every emotion, when 'exalted by the loftiness of mind' (τῷ ὑψηλῷ τῆς διανοίας συνεπαιρόμενον), can be 'conformed to the beauty of the divine image' (τῷ κατὰ τὴν θείαν εἰκόνα κάλλει συσχηματίζεται).[70] Macrina, Gregory and the Cappadocian Fathers reworked the Stoic notion of good and bad use (χρῆσις) of emotions, marrying it with the Aristotelian view of virtue as essentially teleological.[71]

To be sure, the abiding influence of Stoicism lingered in the writings of Sarapion of Thmuis (bishop of Thmuis, c. 329–370 AD), Nemesios of Emesa (fl. c. 390 AD) and Synesios of Cyrene (c. 373–414 AD), to mention

---

[66] *Gregorii Nysseni. De anima et resurrectione: opera dogmatica minora, pars III*, ed. Andreas Spira. GNO 3 (Leiden: Brill, 2014), 46, lines 6–9 (PG 46, 65C).

[67] The translation is from Gregory of Nyssa, *On the Soul and the Resurrection*, trans. Catharine P. Roth (Crestwood, NY: St Vladimir's Seminary Press, 1993), 59–60.

[68] A critical edition of Gregory's *On the Formation of the Human Being* has been foreshadowed by the editors of *Gregorii Nysseni Opera*. In the meantime, I have used the Greek text in PG 44, 124–256. Although the title of Gregory's treatise, Περί Κατασκευῆς Ἀνθρώπου, is commonly translated as *On the Making of Man*, this is neither an accurate translation nor a reflection of Gregory's main theme. Gregory's view of humanity as the intermediate between the earthly and divine elements of creation is elaborated in chapter 16 of his treatise.

[69] *On the Formation of the Human Being* 18, PG 44, 193B. The English translation is my own.

[70] PG 44, 193C.

[71] Paul M. Blowers, 'Hope for the Passible Self: The Use and Transformation of the Human Passions in the Fathers of the Philokalia', in *The Philokalia: A Classic Text of Orthodox Spirituality*, ed. Brock Bingaman and Bradley Nassif (New York, NY: Oxford University Press, 2012), 216–29; J. Warren Smith, *Passion and Paradise: Human and Divine Emotion in the Thought of Gregory of Nyssa* (New York, NY: The Crossroad Publishing Company, 2004).

only a few.[72] These writers condemned the emotions, describing them as an irrational movement (κίνησις) of the soul.[73] Indeed, Synesios of Cyrene identified emotion with the very nature of the devil who is 'passion alive and in movement'.[74]

Maximus the Confessor echoed the Cappadocian thinking on passions, emphasising their transformation through the ascetic life and placing them within an eschatological context. It is through the participation of the entire human person, including the passible faculties, in the grace of the Incarnation that passion can become a receptacle for the divine to dwell.[75] Indeed, Maximus' Christological framework perceives the very deification of the human person to be a mystical emotion, describing it as a 'supernatural passion, without boundaries' (ὑπὲρ φύσιν πάθος, ἀόριστον).[76]

In the Alexandrian milieu, Cyril (c. 375–444 AD) considered the question of Christ's emotions in his commentary on the Gospel according to John, who was the Evangelist that most profoundly narrated Jesus' feelings. However, Cyril did not follow Gregory of Nyssa or Athanasius of Alexandria in ascribing Christ's emotions to his human nature. Interpreting the Johannine account of such events as the raising of Lazarus and Christ praying in the garden of Gethsemane, Cyril of Alexandria presented the emotions Christ experiences without enforcing a sharp distinction between his flesh and divine nature. When Jesus wept before the tomb of his friend, his 'holy flesh' inclined to tears but in such a way that the 'ever undisturbed and calm' divinity ensured the grief was not excessive and 'taught [the flesh] to feel things beyond its nature' (τὰ ὑπὲρ φύσιν ἰδίαν διδασκομένη φρονεῖν).[77] Ultimately, for Cyril, the question of the Logos' emotions was a soteriological one:

> Moreover, just as death was brought to naught in no other way than by the death of the Saviour, so also with regard to each of the passions of the flesh. For unless [Christ] had felt cowardice, human nature could not be freed from cowardice; unless He had experienced grief there would never have been any deliverance from grief; unless He had been troubled and alarmed,

---

[72] On Sarapion, see Oliver Herbel, *Sarapion of Thmuis: Against the Manicheans and Pastoral Letters.* Early Christian Studies 14 (Strathfield, NSW: St Paul's Publications, 2011).

[73] Knuuttila, *Emotions in Ancient and Medieval Philosophy*, 111–19.

[74] *Providentia* 1.10. Quoted in Ware, 'The Meaning of "Pathos"', 317.

[75] Adam G. Cooper, *The Body in St Maximus the Confessor: Holy Flesh, Wholly Deified* (Oxford: Oxford University Press, 2005); Paul M. Blowers, 'Gentiles of the Soul: Maximus the Confessor on the Substructure and Transformation of Human Passions', *JECS* 4, no. 1 (1996): 57–85.

[76] Maximus the Confessor, *To Thalassius*, 22, scholion 6, PG 90, 324B.

[77] Cyril of Alexandria, *Commentary on the Gospel of John* 7, on John 11:33, PG 74, 53A. For an introduction to Cyril, see Norman Russell, *Cyril of Alexandria* (London: Routledge, 2000).

no escape from these feelings could have been found. And with regard to every human experience, you will find exactly the corresponding thing in Christ. The passions of His flesh were aroused, not that they might have the upper hand as they do in us, but in order that when aroused they might be thoroughly subdued by the power of the Word dwelling in the flesh, the nature thus undergoing a change for the better.[78]

Christ's emotions were not attributed simply to his human nature but ascribed to the one incarnate Logos.

Martin Hinterberger and Antonia Giannouli have undertaken important research into Byzantine emotions and have begun to explore tears of compunction in Byzantium.[79] Analysing an assortment of texts, Hinterberger argued that the Byzantines considered compunction to be a blessed emotion and a gift from God, but it could be manipulated by imperial figures such as Emperor Leo VI, who in the tenth century publicly wept to make amends for his fourth marriage and restore his communion with the Church.[80] While Giannouli surveyed an array of religious poetry that urges compunction, she did not draw on the history of emotions. I acknowledge the substantial groundwork these scholars have laid but explore the emotion of compunction from another perspective.

Unlike Hinterberger and Giannouli, I examine the liturgical experience of compunction diachronically. I explore dimensions of liturgy, such as sacred space and soundscape, which have been studied in their own right but have been neglected in previous studies of compunction. Moreover, I eschew Hinterberger's methodology, which approaches emotions in Byzantium as 'ideational' constructs rather than embodied phenomena.[81] This bespeaks 'the primacy of the Cartesian dichotomy' and 'relies on strict definitions of specifically Byzantine emotions' for understanding the

---

[78] Cyril of Alexandria, *Commentary on the Gospel of John* 8, on John 12:27, PG 74, 92D. The English translation is my own.

[79] Martin Hinterberger, 'Tränen in der Byzantinischen Literatur. Ein Beitrag zur Geschichte der Emotionen', *JÖB* 56 (2006): 27–51; Antonia Giannouli, 'Die Tränen der Zerknirschung. Zur Katanyktischen Kirchendichtung als Heilmittel', in *'Doux remède . . .' Poésie et poétique à Byzance. Actes du Quatrième Colloque International Philologique 'EPMHNEIA' Paris, 23–24–25 février 2006 organisé par l'E.H.E.S.S. et l'Université de Chypre*, ed. Paolo Odorico, Panagiotis A. Agapitos and Martin Hinterberger (Paris: Centre d'études byzantines, néo-helléniques et sud-est européennes, 2009), 141–55; Martin Hinterberger, 'Emotions in Byzantium', in *A Companion to Byzantium*, ed. Liz James (Chichester: Wiley-Blackwell, 2010), 123–34; Giannouli, 'Catanyctic Religious Poetry', 86–109.

[80] Hinterberger, 'Tränen', 35–36.

[81] Sophie V. Moore, 'Experiencing Mid-Byzantine Mortuary Practice: Shrouding the Dead', in *Experiencing Byzantium: Papers from the 44th Spring Symposium of Byzantine Studies, Newcastle and Durham, April 2011*, ed. Claire Nesbitt and Mark Jackson (Farnham: Ashgate, 2013), 197.

textual expression of feeling.[82] Precise definitions of any emotional lexeme are 'relational' and cannot preclude the interplay of other emotions: 'links between word and meaning are rarely 1:1' in any given semantic field.[83] Indeed, psalmody and hymnody 'offered an affective itinerary, not so much a single state of mind as a sequence of dispositions'.[84]

Byzantine Hymnography and Its Ritual Dynamics

Some scholars have scorned Byzantine hymns as the populist theology of the masses.[85] To this day, an authoritative and comprehensive monograph on Byzantine hymnography is yet to be published. Moreover, the only anthology of Greek hymns that is still a useful resource was first published in 1871.[86] Panagiotes Trembelas' Greek study of Orthodox hymnology is an important historical overview, but it traces the development of hymnography without sufficiently examining its significance, unearthing its theology or analysing its contexts.[87] Egon Wellesz, Dimitri Conomos and Alexander Lingas have illuminated the musical and liturgical dimensions of Byzantine hymns.[88] However, modern scholarship comprises either a historical introduction that is helpful but generic, or an insightful contribution that focuses on one dimension of hymnology.[89] And, in the case of Wellesz's monograph – despite the magnitude of his contribution when it was first published – it contains outdated perspectives and several errors.[90]

---

[82] Ibid.   [83] Ibid., 198.   [84] Krueger, *Liturgical Subjects*, 20.

[85] John A. McGuckin, 'Poetry and Hymnography (2): The Greek World', in *The Oxford Handbook of Early Christian Studies*, ed. Susan Ashbrook Harvey and David G. Hunter (Oxford: Oxford University Press, 2008), 641–42.

[86] Wilhelm von Christ and Matthaios Paranikas, *Anthologia graeca carminum christianorum* (Leipzig: Teubner, 1963).

[87] Panagiotes N. Trembelas, Ἐκλογή Ἑλληνικῆς Ὀρθοδόξου Ὑμνογραφίας [*Selection of Orthodox Hymnography*] (Athens: Φοίνικος, 1949).

[88] Egon Wellesz, *A History of Byzantine Music and Hymnography* (Oxford: Clarendon Press, 1961); Dimitri E. Conomos, *Byzantine Hymnography and Byzantine Chant* (Brookline, MA: Hellenic College Press, 1984); Alexander Lingas, 'From Earth to Heaven: The Changing Musical Soundscape of the Byzantine Liturgy', in Nesbitt and Jackson, eds., *Experiencing Byzantium*, 311–58. Our understanding of the musical dimension of Byzantine hymnography prior to the tenth century is imperfect. The surviving liturgical manuscripts that contain musical notation from the last centuries of Byzantium allow for a far greater appreciation of the liturgical music of worship.

[89] Examples include: Dimitri E. Conomos, *Byzantine Trisagia and Cheroubika of the Fourteenth and Fifteenth Centuries: A Study of Late Byzantine Liturgical Chant* (Thessaloniki: Patriarchal Institute for Patristic Studies, 1974); McGuckin, 'Poetry and Hymnography'; Kenneth Levy and Christian Troelsgård, 'Byzantine Chant', in *The New Grove Dictionary of Music and Musicians*, vol. 4, ed. S. Sadie and J. Tyrell (London: Macmillan, 2001), 734–56; Eva C. Topping, *Sacred Songs: Studies in Byzantine Hymnography* (Minneapolis, MN: Light and Life Publications, 1997).

[90] For example, Wellesz mistakenly asserts that the *kontakion*, a form of hymnody performed during vigils, fell into disuse during the seventh century as the *kanon* became the popular genre of

The other path taken by scholarship on hymnology has been to concentrate on specific hymnographers such as Romanos, John of Damascus and Kassia.[91] However, significant gaps remain. For example, there is no edited collection and translation of the hymns of Andrew of Crete. And while Kallistos Ware and Mother Mary have undertaken noteworthy translations of certain liturgical collections of hymns, they are not comprehensive and lack editorial commentary.[92] While I do not wish to diminish past achievements in the study of Byzantine hymnography, significant work awaits scholars:

> The Greek Christian hymns have reached the stage, perhaps, where their topography has now been sufficiently sketched out. They still require, from future generations, a sustained theological and literary analysis, which has not yet been accomplished.[93]

A student of hymnology cannot simply be a historian or a textual scholar. Hymns are characterised by an intricate symbiosis of 'creed, antiphon, poem, prayer, song and sacrament' where 'Byzantine theology, mysticism and liturgical chant' converge.[94] In searching for the emotion of compunction in Byzantine hymns, I join scholars who are grappling with this intricate symbiosis.[95]

The mystical significance of hymnody for Christianity is crucial for understanding the emotion of compunction in Byzantium. The liturgical performance of hymns interwove feeling and mystery, enacting the

hymnography for matins. Wellesz, *A History of Byzantine Music*, 199–204. However, the *kontakion* and *kanon* were in fact intended for different liturgical events and singers continued to perform the former during vigils for many centuries. See Alexander Lingas, 'The Liturgical Place of the Kontakion in Constantinople', in *Liturgy, Architecture and Art of the Byzantine World: Papers of the XVIII International Byzantine Congress (Moscow, 8–15 August 1991) and Other Essays Dedicated to the Memory of Fr John Meyendorff*, ed. C. C. Akentiev (St Petersburg: Vizantinorossika, 1995), 50–57. See also Lingas, 'Medieval Byzantine Chant and the Sound of Orthodoxy', in *Byzantine Orthodoxies: Papers from the Thirty-Sixth Spring Symposium of Byzantine Studies, University of Durham, 23–25 March 2002*, ed. Andrew Louth and Augustine Casiday, Publications of the Society for the Promotion of Byzantine Studies (Aldershot: Ashgate, 2006), 136.

[91] Ephrem Lash, ed. *On the Life of Christ: Chanted Sermons by the Great Sixth-Century Poet and Singer St Romanos*, Sacred Literature Series (Lanham, MD: AltaMira Press, 1998); Andrew Louth, *St John Damascene: Tradition and Originality in Byzantine Theology* (New York, NY: Oxford University Press, 2002); Antonia Tripolitis, *Kassia: The Legend, the Woman and Her Work* (New York, NY: Garland Press, 1992).

[92] *The Festal Menaion* (London: Faber, 1969); *The Lenten Triodion* (Boston, MA: Faber, 1978).

[93] McGuckin, 'Poetry and Hymnography', 653.　　[94] Ibid.

[95] Georgia Frank, 'Sensing Ascension in Early Byzantium', in Nesbitt and Jackson, eds., *Experiencing Byzantium*, 293–309; Krueger, *Liturgical Subjects*; Jaakko Olkinuora, *Byzantine Hymnography for the Feast of the Entrance of the Theotokos: An Intermedial Approach* (Helsinki: Suomen patristinen seura ry, 2015); Thomas Arentzen, *The Virgin in Song: Mary and the Poetry of Romanos the Melodist* (Philadelphia, PA: University of Pennsylvania Press, 2017).

affective encounter between humanity and the Divine. Christ's love for humankind and the nuptial desire of creation for its Creator framed the project of hymnography and its liturgical context:

> καθ' ἣν μακαρίαν καὶ παναγίαν κοίτην τὸ φρικτὸν ἐκεῖνο τῆς ὑπὲρ νοῦν καὶ λόγον ἑνότητος μυστήριον ἐπιτελεῖται, δι' οὗ μία σὰρξ καὶ ἓν πνεῦμα, ὅ τε Θεὸς πρὸς [τὴν Ἐκκλησίαν,] τὴν ψυχήν, καὶ ἡ ψυχὴ πρὸς τὸν Θεὸν γενήσεται· ὦ πῶς σε Χριστέ, θαυμάσω τῆς ἀγαθότητος, οὐ γὰρ ἀμυνῆσαι φάναι τολμήσω, ὁ μήτε πρὸς τὸ θαυμάζειν ἀξίως ἀρκοῦσαν ἔχων τὴν δύναμιν· Ἔσονται γὰρ οἱ δύο εἰς σάρκα μίαν· τὸ δὲ μυστήριον τοῦτο μέγα ἐστίν· ἐγὼ δὲ λέγω εἰς Χριστὸν καὶ τὴν Ἐκκλησίαν.[96]

> It is in this blessed and most holy intercourse that is accomplished this awesome mystery of a union transcending mind and reason by which God becomes one flesh and one spirit with the Church and thus with the soul, and the soul with God. O Christ, how shall I marvel at your goodness? I shall not presume to sing praise because I have not enough strength to marvel in a worthy manner. For, 'they shall be two in one flesh', says the divine Apostle; 'this is a great mystery, I speak of Christ and the Church'.[97]

Maximus argued that knowledge of God divorced from passion could become an intellectual exercise rather than a transformative encounter. The human emotions of the faithful could become divine emotions when such passion was oriented toward God:

> Καὶ διὰ τοῦτο δεῖται τοῦ μακαρίου πάθους τῆς ἁγίας ἀγάπης, τῆς συν-δεσμούσης τὸν νοῦν τοῖς πνευματικοῖς θεωρήμασι καὶ πειθούσης προτιμᾶν τῶν ὑλικῶν τὰ ἄϋλα καὶ τῶν αἰσθητῶν τὰ νοητὰ καὶ θεῖα.[98]

> That is why there is need for the blessed passion of holy love, which binds the intellect to spiritual contemplation and persuades it to prefer what is immaterial to what is material, and what is intelligible and divine to what is apprehended by the senses.[99]

Blessed emotions such as love could escort the faithful beyond a purely intellectual philosophy of God to mystical communion with the Divine. This language of holy passion and union with God in these two texts by Maximus, and in other patristic texts, is suggestive of a Byzantine mode of affective mysticism that will be explored further in the next chapter.

---

[96] Maximus the Confessor, *On Ecclesiastical Mystagogy*, chapter 5, Christian Boudignon, ed. *Maximi Confessoris Mystagogia*, CCSG 69 (Turnhout: Brepols, 2011), 29–30.

[97] My translation is based on George C. Berthold, *Maximus Confessor: Selected Writings* (New York, NY: Paulist Press, 1985), 194.

[98] *Centuries on Love* 3, 67 in Ceresa-Gastaldo, *Capitoli sulla carità*, 176.

[99] The translation is from the second volume of Palmer, Sherrard and Ware, *The Philokalia*, 93.

Although the relationship between religious practices and ritual is not a new field of inquiry, research into the link between ritual and emotion has been recently growing apace.[100] Rituals can manage or regulate emotions as much as they can seek to stir emotion in the participants.[101] However, when the ritual in question is a sacred drama and a complex cultural construct, it should not be reduced to modern conceptions of ritual or confused with dramatic theatre. While Christianity cultivated liturgical practices that invited the faithful to 'ritualize and "perform" their faith as *dramatis personae* in the theatre of the divine economy',[102] it is important to elucidate this notion of theatricality and examine what these rituals signified for the Byzantines. It is not possible to view 'the drama of the Eucharistic liturgy' as akin to a Shakespearean play when its symbolic, cosmic and mystical significance was how the faithful could 'find their own place within the universal, salvific scheme' of the divine economy.[103]

Christian ritual in Byzantium was post-theatrical.[104] Christianity spurned the histrionic arts and decried the theatre, choosing to create a new mode of performance. While it is tempting to portray liturgical practices as theatrical reenactments of the biblical narrative of salvation, the Byzantine rite was not an attempt to elicit the aesthetic appreciation of an audience:

> For all the visual and aural splendour of the Divine Liturgy, Orthodox ritual shows clear signs of an anti-theatrical aesthetic; especially in the wake of Byzantium's iconoclastic crisis in the eighth and ninth centuries, the Church paid special attention to how it realized the visibility of the sacred and achieved a unique aesthetic rooted as much in classical theories of optics as in traditional Orthodox theology.[105]

Liturgical hymns were not simply a remembrance of biblical events or a theatrical display of divine things; they enacted a sacred drama that created a space of participation for the faithful in the mystery of salvation.

---

[100] See, for example, Merridee L. Bailey and Katie Barclay, eds., *Emotion, Ritual and Power in Europe, 1200–1920: Family, State and Church* (Basingstoke: Palgrave, 2017).

[101] Renato Rosaldo, 'Grief and the Headhunter's Rage', in *Text, Play and Story: The Construction and Reconstruction of Self and Society*, ed. Stuart Plattner and Edward Bruner (Washington, DC: American Ethnological Society, 1984), 178–98.

[102] Paul M. Blowers, *Drama of the Divine Economy: Creator and Creation in Early Christian Theology and Piety* (Oxford: Oxford University Press, 2012), 315.

[103] Ibid., 348 and 335 respectively.

[104] Andrew Walker White, *Performing Orthodox Ritual in Byzantium* (Cambridge: Cambridge University Press, 2015), 5.

[105] Ibid., 9. For background on the iconoclastic crisis, see Paul A. Hollingsworth and Anthony Cutler, 'Iconoclasm', in *ODB*, 975–77.

The ritual dynamics of liturgy and its hymns enacted the faith of the Byzantines in a holy milieu. Therefore, when I refer to a hymn dramatising a biblical narrative or enacting the sacred drama of salvation, I do not suggest that this performance should be viewed as a theatrical spectacle. The liturgical world of compunction – its sacred space, mystagogy and affective mysticism – was a theological drama that transcended the mimetic art of theatre and showed forth the reality of Christ's sacrifice.[106] It is this sacred ritual that embodied the emotion of compunction for Byzantine Christianity.

Tracing Compunction as an Emotion in Byzantium

While the first-person life narratives of Byzantium are not necessarily a genuine reflection of personal emotions, the history of emotions provides a methodological framework for approaching how compunction emerged in the performance of hymns.[107] I do not go in search of what the Byzantines were feeling, but employ literature and the feelings embedded therein as my source material. As Sarah McNamer has argued in a different context, literature is the chief archive for the study of emotions.[108] Byzantine hymnography is such an archive and one that has been largely neglected. Hymnography's rich vocabulary of feeling and ritual performativity, existentially grounded in 'theo-drama',[109] saw emotions textualised in hymns become part of liturgical life. That is why I will engage in textual analysis together with a reconstruction of the performance of the text, which offers a richer glimpse into liturgical emotions in the Byzantine world than simply exploring hymnography as poetry.

I argue that compunction for the faithful was an embodied phenomenon that can be reimagined by appreciating the 'literariness' of hymnography and reconsidering how it can serve as a historical source, 'not only as documentary witness reflecting or representing what already exists in a

---

[106] On the Divine Liturgy as a theological rite, see Archimandrite Vasileios, *Hymn of Entry: Liturgy and Life in the Orthodox Church*, trans. Elizabeth Briere (New York, NY: St Vladimir's Seminary Press, 1984), 57–79.

[107] Symeon the New Theologian, Emperor Michael Palaiologos, Nikephoros Blemmydes and John Cantacuzene are examples of people to whom first-person life narratives are attributed. See Michael Angold, 'The Autobiographical Impulse in Byzantium', *DOP* 52 (1998): 52–73; Martin Hinterberger, 'Autobiography and Hagiography in Byzantium', *Symbolae Osloenses: Norwegian Journal of Greek and Latin Studies* 75, no. 1 (2000): 139–64.

[108] McNamer, 'Feeling', 242.

[109] Hans Urs von Balthasar, *Theo-Drama: Theological Dramatic Theory, Vol. 1: Prolegomena*, trans. Graham Harrison (San Francisco, CA: Ignatius Press, 1988).

given culture but as "source" in the generative sense – as font, well-spring'.[110] Byzantine hymns were more than just literary texts; they served as performative scripts for the making of emotion in liturgy.[111] Indeed, emotions are not simply historicised phenomena; they can change the course of history.[112] Determining the social, cultural and religious significance of emotions gained momentum in the 1980s, when Carol Stearns and Peter Stearns coined the term 'emotionology'[113] and historians developed new strategies for overcoming the salient obstacle in researching them – the problematic source material. Although we still face some epistemological limitations in talking about emotions in Byzantium, by differentiating between personal emotional experience and the textualisation of emotions, as well as noting how the experience of emotion in Byzantium was closely linked not only to society and culture but also to theology, we can begin to perceive emotions as the Byzantines did.

This study adopts a hybrid methodology, beginning with an approach that Sarah McNamer has set out:

> First, reconstruct the historical conditions of the performance of a text, through empirical research and informed speculation; next, examine how a text seeks to produce emotion, through careful attention to its affective stylistics; then see how it all adds up, kinetically. This strategy of 'actualizing absence' by bringing external and internal features together has been used to very positive effect in various branches of performance studies.[114]

Although 'the words *are* the feelings', it is essential to combine textual analysis with 'considerations of what is likely to have been seen, heard, touched, even *tasted* at the moment of a text's performance'.[115] These are vital considerations in exploring compunction as an emotion that was performed within the ritual dynamics of liturgical hymns. Emotions were intersubjective phenomena that were embodied within an action and a practice. Compunction unfolded and became meaningful within an 'affective field',[116] where the audience encountered the hymnographer's text and his or her protagonists amidst the experience of liturgical hymns. Hymns

---

[110] McNamer, 'The Literariness of Literature', 1436. While the context of McNamer's article is not Byzantine hymns, her argument is pertinent.

[111] See McNamer, *Affective Meditation*, 1–21.

[112] See, for example, Reddy, *The Navigation of Feeling*, 173–210.

[113] Carol Z. Stearns and Peter N. Stearns, 'Emotionology: Clarifying the History of Emotions and Emotional Standards', *The American Historical Review* 90, no. 4 (1985): 813.

[114] McNamer, 'Feeling', 247.   [115] Ibid., 247–48.

[116] Oliver J. T. Harris and Tim Flohr Sørensen, 'Rethinking Emotion and Material Culture', *Archaeological Dialogues* 17, no. 2 (2010): 150–51.

were performed and experienced within the sacred space and soundscape of liturgy. Although the Byzantine liturgy does not exist in any audiovisual archive, it was contained in liturgical texts, regulated by rubrics, and described by liturgical commentaries and patristic texts, as well as by ekphrastic texts and pilgrims' accounts.[117] That is why my methodology also incorporates elements from the work of other scholars.[118]

Monique Scheer's analysis of Pierre Bourdieu's concept of *habitus* and the notion of emotional practices enriches my methodology for exploring compunction and facilitates a diachronic approach by situating this emotion within the evolving liturgical rituals that mobilised, named, communicated and regulated it:

> Thinking of emotion as a kind of practice can help historians get over the sense that the history of emotions can only be a history of changing emotional norms and expectations but not a record of change in feeling. Emotions change over time not only because norms, expectations, words, and concepts that shape experience are modified, but also because the practices in which they are embodied, and bodies themselves, undergo transformation.[119]

Liturgical practices such as praying, singing and kneeling sought to evoke and embody compunction by inviting the faithful to internalise the emotion these practices performed. They did so in a circular and ontological fashion that went beyond a simplistic linear model of emotional processes and dissolved the dichotomy between passivity and activity.[120] Scheer's comments are pertinent insofar as this is a diachronic study of compunction as a liturgical emotion in Byzantium that begins in the sixth century with Romanos the Melodist, moves to Andrew of Crete in the late seventh and early eighth centuries, and then Kassia in the ninth century. Compunction will be explored as an emotion that emerged in the

---

[117] The main liturgical text that will be examined is the *Triodion*. Although various rubrics will be considered, the chief rubric for the cathedral rite of Constantinople is *The Typikon of the Great Church*: Juan Mateos, *Le Typicon de la Grande Église*, 2 vols. OCA 165, 166 (Rome: Pontificium Institutum Orientalium Studiorum, 1962–63). Liturgical commentaries by Dionysius the Areopagite, Maximus the Confessor, Germanos of Constantinople and Nicholas Cabasilas will be explored in Chapter 2. The array of patristic texts is vast, so the most pertinent references will be invoked. An example of ekphrasis is Paul the Silentiary's poem on Hagia Sophia. For a pilgrim's account see John Wilkinson, trans. *Egeria's Travels* (Warminster: Aris & Phillips, 2002).

[118] Monique Scheer, 'Are Emotions a Kind of Practice (and Is That What Makes Them Have a History)? A Bourdieuian Approach to Understanding Emotion', *History and Theory* 51, no. 2 (2012): 193–220; Bissera V. Pentcheva, 'Performing the Sacred in Byzantium: Image, Breath and Sound', *Performance Research* 19, no. 3 (2014): 120–28; Javier E. Díaz-Vera, 'Exploring the Relationship between Emotions, Language and Space: Construals of Awe in Medieval English Language and Pilgrimage Experience', *Studia Neophilologica* 88 (2016): 165–89.

[119] Scheer, 'Are Emotions a Kind of Practice', 220.   [120] Ibid., 206.

performance of liturgical hymns and as a feeling that could be shaped in subtly different ways by the evolving Byzantine rite and three genres of Byzantine hymnography: the *kontakion* (Romanos' hymns), the *kanon* (Andrew of Crete's *Great Kanon*) and the *sticheron idiomelon* (Kassia's hymn *On the Sinful Woman*).

The liturgical context of hymnody cannot be reconstructed without considering the ritual performativity of the text, especially its musical and spatial contexts. John L. Austin is often cited as elaborating the notion of performative speech as words that engender a new reality by performing an action.[121] John Searle, Jacques Derrida and Judith Butler have since invoked, appropriated and developed Austin's ideas with varying effect.[122] But it was Victor Turner's conception of the human person as *homo performans* ('a self-performing animal') that was a watershed moment for performativity and the theory of ritual.[123] Turner saw ritual performances not merely as the phenomena of a society but as a liminal space, which constructs and mediates culture rather than simply reproducing it.[124] However, as Caroline Walker Bynum has shown, medieval women, constrained as they were by social structures and gendered expectations, are a footnote in Turner's theory of religion.[125] Despite this significant shift in the understanding of ritual performativity, the link between performance and ritual became a popular yet contentious topic. For example, whereas Edward L. Schieffelin sees this relationship as the dramaturgical enactment of symbols and their meanings, Richard Schechner and Willa Appel argue that ritual performance has transformative power.[126]

However, it is difficult to neatly reconcile these modern approaches to performance with those of the medieval era and a Byzantine liturgical context. The performativity of Byzantine hymns should not be presumed as being equivalent to that of the ancient histrionic arts. A 'rupture between theatrical and ritual performance practices' emerged in Byzantium as 'Orthodox ritual established a presence distinct from the theatrical

---

[121] Austin, *How to Do Things with Words* (Oxford: Clarendon Press, 1975).

[122] John R. Searle, *Speech Acts: An Essay in the Philosophy of Language* (London: Cambridge University Press, 1969); Jacques Derrida and Julian Wolfreys, *The Derrida Reader: Writing Performances* (Lincoln, NE: University of Nebraska Press, 1998); Judith Butler, *Gender Trouble: Feminism and the Subversion of Identity* (New York, NY: Routledge, 1990).

[123] Turner, *The Anthropology of Performance* (New York, NY: PAJ Publications, 1986), 81.

[124] Turner, *The Ritual Process: Structure and Antistructure* (Chicago, IL: Aldine, 1969).

[125] Bynum, *Fragmentation and Redemption: Essays on Gender and the Human Body in Medieval Religion* (New York, NY: Zone Books, 1991), 27–52.

[126] Schechner and Appel, *By Means of Performance: Intercultural Studies of Theatre and Ritual* (Cambridge: Cambridge University Press, 1990); Schieffelin, 'Performance and the Cultural Construction of Reality', *American Ethnologist* 12, no. 4 (1985): 707–24.

culture in which it operated'.[127] As we will see in the next chapter, Byzantine hymnody sought to elicit the participation of the faithful in the sacred drama it performed. Therefore, rather than imposing a second-order discourse on Byzantium and its liturgical performances, I investigate the Byzantine notion of performativity. To some extent, the modern understanding of performativity was already apparent in the *lux fiat* of creation and Christ's miraculous speech acts.[128] However, the mystical dimension of worship betokened a symbiosis between materiality and the metaphysical. The performance of the Divine Liturgy was an iconic enactment of divine presence:

> 'performative' engages the spatial and temporal aspects of the liturgical ritual of in-spiriting and recognizes the synergistic role the viewing/participating subject plays in engendering the perceived animation of the inert.[129]

Liturgy animated image, building, sound and light. The sacred space of liturgical action came to life through the interaction of the faithful with art, architecture and song.[130] These are important considerations in mapping compunction within a semantic arrangement and exploring how it was elicited amidst a multisensory liturgical experience.[131] Of course, compunction emerged in a multimodal setting that engendered the movement of various emotions. While I touch on the animation of other emotions during the performance of compunctious hymns, I home in on one.

Byzantine Sacred Music and Emotions

The music of compositions by Romanos the Melodist, Andrew of Crete and Kassia is lost inasmuch as the earliest extant manuscripts of Byzantine

---

[127] White, *Performing Orthodox Ritual*, 9.

[128] Adam G. Cooper, *Holy Eros: A Liturgical Theology of the Body* (Tacoma, WA: Angelico Press, 2014), 32.

[129] Pentcheva, 'Performing the Sacred', 120. See also Pentcheva's more recent monograph, *Hagia Sophia: Sound, Space and Spirit in Byzantium* (Pennsylvania, PA: Pennsylvania State University Press, 2017).

[130] Pentcheva, *The Sensual Icon: Space, Ritual, and the Senses in Byzantium* (Pennsylvania, PA: Pennsylvania State University Press, 2010), 9, 45, 155; *Hagia Sophia*, 18–44. See also the work of Díaz-Vera – albeit in the context of Canterbury Cathedral – who argues that emotion is not only reconstructed by exploring its semantic fields but also by deploying a multimodal perspective that is conscious of visual narratives, architectural data and other modalities. Díaz-Vera, 'Exploring the Relationship between Emotions', 165–89.

[131] On the sensory experience of worship, see Béatrice Caseau, 'The Senses in Religion: Liturgy, Devotion, and Deprivation', in *A Cultural History of the Senses in the Middle Ages, 500–1450*, ed. Richard G. Newhauser (London: Berg Publishers, 2014), 89–110; Caseau, 'Experiencing the Sacred', in Nesbitt and Jackson, eds., *Experiencing Byzantium*, 59–77.

musical notation emerge after the lifetimes of these hymnographers.[132] However, reimagining the general experience of chant and the overall sound of the liturgy – even as early as sixth-century Byzantium – is a matter of informed speculation and empirical research, underpinned by careful investigation of contemporaneous liturgical commentaries, patristic texts and other historical material:

> it is still possible for us to draw meaningful conclusions about the sounds-capes of Byzantine worship from those elements of its acoustic design that may be at least partially recovered ... The sonic outlines of individual services may be traced from the study of liturgical manuscripts by deter-mining the order in which individuals or vocal groups chanted their appointed texts from particular locations in the sacred topography of an ecclesiastical complex or city. In some cases it is possible to enrich the texture of these data with visual depictions of liturgical singers. Further testimony regarding the sonic landscape of Byzantine liturgy may be gleaned from scattered references to chanting in hymns, homilies and hagiography.[133]

Scholars have recently begun exploring these soundscapes and investigat-ing the significance of sacred music for the faithful.[134] This research may also shed light on the performativity of Byzantine hymns and their emotive power. However, one of the difficulties encountered is the absence of an extant treatise devoted entirely to a theory of sacred music in Byzantium.

Although there were certainly treatises on music theory available, such as those written by Aristides Quintilianus in the fourth century, George Pachymeres in the thirteenth century and Manuel Bryennius in the fourteenth century, they did not systematically explore the sacred music of the Byzantine rite.[135] Dionysius the Areopagite apparently

---

[132] And even when it comes to medieval Byzantine neumes, it is still controversial to suggest that these chants found in manuscripts can be transcribed into staff notation and studied through the lens of modern Byzantine musical theory. See Alexander Lingas, 'Performance Practice and the Politics of Transcribing Byzantine Chant', *Acta Musicae Byzantinae* 6 (2003): 56–76.

[133] Lingas, 'From Earth to Heaven', 315.

[134] Pentcheva, 'Performing the Sacred', 125; Carol Harrison, 'Enchanting the Soul: The Music of the Psalms', in *Meditations of the Heart: The Psalms in Early Christian Thought and Practice. Essays in Honour of Andrew Louth*, ed. Andreas Andreopoulos, Augustine Casiday, and Carol Harrison (Turnhout: Brepols, 2011), 205–24; Amy Papalexandrou, 'Perceptions of Sound and Sonic Environment across the Byzantine Acoustic Horizon', in *Knowing Bodies, Passionate Souls: Sense Perceptions in Byzantium*, ed. Susan Ashbrook Harvey and Margaret Mullett (Washington, DC: Dumbarton Oaks Research Library and Collection, 2017), 67–85; Bissera V. Pentcheva, ed. *Aural Architecture in Byzantium: Music, Acoustics, and Ritual* (New York, NY: Routledge, 2017); Icons of Sound project: http://iconsofsound.stanford.edu (retrieved 1 September 2018).

[135] Thomas J. Mathiesen, ed. *Aristides Quintilianus: On Music, in Three Books* (New Haven, CT and London: Yale University Press, 1983); Paul Tannery, ed. *Quadrivium de Georges Pachymère*

wrote such a treatise, *Concerning the Divine Hymns*, but it has not survived.[136] While the sixth book of Augustine's *On Music* suggests that this sacred art is a quest for truth that embodies the beauty of God, the influence of the Bishop of Hippo's writings in Byzantium is uncertain.[137] Nevertheless, Augustine's view of music as being able to stir the emotions of the soul through 'a mysterious inner kinship' between the various modes of chant and feeling reflected Byzantine views on the affective power of sacred song.[138] Byzantium followed Aristotle in believing that melodies affected the listener's soul, as well as being representations of the ordered harmonies underpinning the universe of Plato's *Timaeus*.[139] Indeed, Byzantine music theorists such as Pachymeres believed there was a connection between the musical

(Vatican City: Biblioteca Apostolica Vaticana, 1940); G. H. Jonker, ed. *The Harmonics of Manuel Bryennius* (Gröningen: Wolters-Noordhoff, 1970).

[136] Dionysius alludes to this work in *Celestial Hierarchy* 7.4, Günter Heil and Adolf Martin Ritter, eds., *Corpus Dionysiacum II: Pseudo-Dionysius Areopagita. De coelesti hierarchia, De ecclesiastica hierarchia, De mystica theologia, Epistulae*, Patristische Texte und Studien (Berlin: De Gruyter, 2012), 31. See Andrew Louth, *Denys the Areopagite* (London: Continuum, 1989), 27.

[137] Augustinus, *De musica*, ed. Martin Jacobsson, Corpus Scriptorum Ecclesiasticorum Latinorum 102 (Berlin: De Gruyter, 2017), 193–233; Augustine, *On Music*, trans. Robert Catesby Taliafero in *The Fathers of the Church* 4 (Washington, DC: Catholic University of America Press, 2002), 324–79. See Carol Harrison, 'Augustine and the Art of Music', in *Resonant Witness: Conversations between Music and Theology*, ed. Jeremy S. Begbie and Steven R. Guthrie (Grand Rapids, MI: Eerdmans, 2011), 31. On the possible influence of Augustine in Byzantium, see Aristotle Papanikolaou and George E. Demacopoulos, 'Augustine and the Orthodox: The "West" in the East', in *Orthodox Readings of Augustine*, ed. Aristotle Papanikolaou and George E. Demacopoulos (Crestwood, NY: St Vladimir's Seminary Press, 2008), 11–40.

[138] Augustine expressed this view on sacred chant moving the soul and eliciting devotion in *Confessions* 10.33.49, which is quoted in Harrison, 'Augustine and the Art of Music', 42.

[139] See Johannes Quasten, *Music and Worship in Pagan and Christian Antiquity*, trans. Ramsay Boniface (Washington, DC: National Association of Pastoral Musicians, 1983), 35–39, 137–39; Lukas Richter, 'Antike Überlieferungen in der Byzantinischen Musiktheorie', *Acta Musicologica* 70, no. 2 (1998): 133–208; Alexander Lingas, 'Music', in *Encyclopedia of Ancient Greece*, ed. Nigel Wilson (New York, NY: Routledge, 2010), 485. Aristotle's view of music as an ethical force that embodied emotion in sound and rhythm is reflected in the writings of the Cappadocian Fathers on music. See the relevant catalogue of texts in James McKinnon, ed. *Music in Early Christian Literature* (Cambridge: Cambridge University Press, 1987), 64–74. See also the Platonic resonance in Gregory of Nyssa's *On the Inscriptions of the Psalms* 1.3 in Ronald E. Heine, trans., *Gregory of Nyssa's Treatise on the Inscriptions of the Psalms* (Oxford: Oxford University Press, 1995), 88–92. The question of how this unfolded in a liturgical context will be explored in the next chapter. However, on a theoretical level, Aristides Quintilianus states, 'the ancients saw that we do not turn to singing for a single reason, rather some sing in contentment accompanying pleasure, others in vexation accompanying pain, and still others sing occupied by divine impulse and inspiration accompanying divine suffusion; or even when these are mixed one with another by certain chances and circumstances, or when children, because of their age, or even those advanced in age, because of weakness of nature, are led on by such passions'. Mathiesen, *Aristides Quintilianus: On Music*, 120. Bryennius also explored the relationship between melody and feeling. See Jonker, *The Harmonics of Manuel Bryennius*, 123, 365.

patterns of Antiquity and Orthodoxy, suggesting the East preserved an unbroken cultural link with its past.[140]

Byzantine patristic texts often pondered the effect of music on the emotions in passing. Music and poetry were portrayed as positive forces that could shape emotions and enchant the soul.[141] Gregory the Theologian's poem *On His Own Verses* reflects on how the delight and pleasure of music and poetry could have a role to play in cultivating spirituality:

> Ὥσπερ τι τερπνὸν τοῦτο δοῦναι φάρμακον,
> Πειθοῦς ἀγωγὸν εἰς τὰ χρησιμώτερα,
> Τέχνῃ γλυκάζων τὸ πικρὸν τῶν ἐντολῶν.
> Φιλεῖ δ᾽ ἀνίεσθαί τε καὶ νευρᾶς τόνος·
> Εἴ πως θέλεις καὶ τοῦτο· εἰ μή τι πλέον,
> Ἀντ᾽ ᾀσμάτων σοι ταῦτα καὶ λυρισμάτων.[142]

> My verse could be for [youth] a pleasant potion,
> Leading them towards the Good by mild persuasion,
> Sweetening by art the bitter taste of law.
> Verse helps us to relax the tightened string,
> If we but will, even if it be no more
> Than lyric songs, musical interludes.[143]

Gregory goes on to say that, just as music and poetry were pleasant pedagogical tools for the ancients, Christianity could employ these tools to shape the hearts of young people and lead them to communion with the Divine:

> Ὡς οἱ πάλαι προσῇδον ἐμμελεῖς λόγους,
> Τὸ τερπνὸν, οἶμαι, τοῦ καλοῦ ποιούμενοι
> Ὄχημα, καὶ τυποῦντες ἐκ μελῶν τρόπους.
>
> . . .
>
> Τίς οὖν βλάβη σοι, τοὺς νέους δι᾽ ἡδονῆς
> Σεμνῆς ἄγεσθαι πρὸς Θεοῦ κοινωνίαν;[144]

---

[140] White, *Performing Orthodox Ritual*, 109–13. See also David Bradshaw, *Aristotle East and West: Metaphysics and the Division of Christendom* (Cambridge: Cambridge University Press, 2004), 263–77.

[141] 'Music (and poetry, for that matter; the two were often considered together in this context) was above all a mathematical discipline, analysed in terms of order, rhythm, harmony and measure. And yet it could never simply be a matter for the mind, or for the philosopher: it resonated in time and space; it was heard and felt; it en-chanted the whole of reality, rational and sensible.' Harrison, 'Enchanting the Soul', 206.

[142] PG 37, 1332.

[143] The English translation is from Brian E. Daley, trans., *Gregory of Nazianzus* (London: Routledge, 2006), 164.

[144] *On His Own Verses*, PG 37, 1332.

The ancients sang instruction in their verse
Making delight the vehicle of beauty,
Forming the heart by virtue of song.
...
What harm then, if we lead the young
To share in God by means of holy pleasure?[145]

Although liturgical hymns would have been sparse in Gregory's setting, the use of psalmody in worship was prolific.

Before the hymnography that flourished during the sixth to the ninth centuries, and well before the Byzantine liturgy was consolidated, the singing of the Psalms could engender a kind of affective catoptrics in the faithful. According to Athanasius of Alexandria, for the person singing the Psalms, the words become like a mirror to the emotions of the soul and a source of therapy and correction suited for these emotions.[146] The Psalms presented the faithful with emotions for internalisation through a text and melody that became their own words and their own song through meditation and participation in devotional practices. In hearing the song, they were 'moved by compunction' (κατανύσσεται)[147] and received the words of others in the Psalm as being about their very selves:

Καί μοι δοκεῖ τῷ ψάλλοντι γίνεσθαι τούτους ὥσπερ εἴσοπτρον, εἰς τὸ κατανοεῖν καὶ αὐτὸν ἐν αὐτοῖς καὶ τὰ τῆς ἑαυτοῦ ψυχῆς κινήματα, καὶ οὕτως αἰσθόμενον ἀπαγγέλλειν αὐτούς. Καὶ γὰρ καὶ ὁ ἀκούων τοῦ ἀναγινώσκοντος ὡς περὶ αὐτοῦ λεγομένην τὴν ᾠδὴν καταδέχεται· καὶ ἢ ἐλεγχόμενος ὑπὸ τοῦ συνειδότος κατανυγεὶς μετανοήσει, ἢ περὶ τῆς εἰς Θεὸν ἐλπίδος ἀκούων καὶ τῆς εἰς τοὺς πιστεύοντας γινομένης ἀντιλήψεως, ὡς εἰς αὐτὸν γενομένης τοιαύτης χάριτος ἀγαλλιᾶται, καὶ εὐχαριστεῖν ἄρχεται τῷ Θεῷ.[148]

And it seems to me that these words become like a mirror to the person singing them, so that he might perceive himself and the emotions of his soul, and thus affected, he might recite them. For in fact he who hears the one reading receives the song that is recited as being about him, and either, when he is moved to compunction by his conscience, he will repent, or hearing of the hope that resides in God, and of the succour available to believers – how this kind of grace exists for him – he rejoices greatly and begins to give thanks to God.

---

[145] Daley, *Gregory of Nazianzus*, 165.
[146] *Letter to Marcellinus on the Interpretation of the Psalms* 10 in PG 27, 20D. For an English translation of the Greek text, see Athanasius of Alexandria, *The Life of Antony and the Letter to Marcellinus*, trans. Robert C. Gregg (New York, NY: Paulist Press, 1980), 101–30. The English translations that follow are my own.
[147] *Letter to Marcellinus* 11, PG 27, 21C.   [148] Ibid. 12, PG 27, 24BC.

Similarly, hymnody did not hesitate to draw upon scriptural stories, inviting the faithful to enter into the sacred drama unfolding before them and feel the emotions of biblical characters in a liturgical mimesis.[149]

Outline of Chapters

Chapter 2 explores the liturgical world of compunction – the sacred space of the Byzantine liturgy. It focuses on the cathedral of Hagia Sophia, which was the epicentre of worship in Constantinople, and investigates the liturgical significance of Novella 137, the sixth-century edict of Emperor Justinian that betokened the compunctious character of the Byzantine Eucharist. It also examines the liturgical commentaries of Dionysius the Areopagite, Maximus the Confessor and Germanos of Constantinople for further evidence of experiencing sacred song in Byzantium, before briefly touching upon affective mysticism and its significance for Byzantine hymnody. Chapter 2 also probes the liturgical and hermeneutical framework for compunction in Byzantium – Great Lent and Holy Week.

Chapter 3 examines the compunctious hymns of Romanos the Melodist. It explores the genre of his compositions (*kontakion*) and their liturgical context, reimagining the performance of his hymns during the Lenten period. It does so according to three themes: compunction and repentance; biblical exemplars of compunction; and compunction in the face of eschatological judgment. By framing the approach of this chapter with these three themes, the most relevant elements of compunction in Romanos' oeuvre are examined.

Chapter 4 explores the performance of Andrew of Crete's *Great Kanon*. It examines the genre of this hymn (*kanon*), its liturgical context and its manuscript tradition, investigating how its performance sought to arouse compunction in the faithful. Given there is no critical edition of the *Great Kanon* currently available, three of the earliest manuscripts of the *Triodion* where this hymn appears are cited: Sinai Graecus 734–735, fols. 69r–83v, Vaticanus Graecus 771, fol. 18v, and Grottaferrata Δβ I, fols. 7v–16r.[150]

---

[149] Catherine Brown Tkacz, 'Singing Women's Words as Sacramental Mimesis', *Recherches de théologie et philosophie médiévales* 70, no. 2 (2003): 275; Susan Ashbrook Harvey, '2000 NAPS Presidential Address. Spoken Words, Voiced Silence: Biblical Women in Syriac Tradition', *JECS* 9, no. 1 (2001): 125.

[150] Sinai Graecus 734–735 is available online at the Library of Congress website: https://loc.gov/item/00271075583-ms (retrieved 1 March 2019). Vaticanus Graecus is available online at the Vatican Library website: https://digi.vatlib.it/view/MSS_Vat.gr.771 (retrieved 1 March 2019). I thank Grottaferrata Library and Professor Stefano Parenti for allowing me to study the Grottaferrata Δβ I manuscript.

This approach, together with an examination of rubrics and other relevant sources, assists in reimagining how the *Great Kanon* was performed in Byzantium.

Chapter 5 moves to ninth-century Byzantium and the hymnographer Kassia, who is the only known female author of hymns appearing in the liturgical books of the Byzantine tradition. This chapter explores the liturgical performance of Kassia's hymn *On the Sinful Woman* during Holy Week. As with the previous chapter, the genre of this hymn (*sticheron idiomelon*) and its manuscript tradition are examined. The tears of Kassia's protagonist and how they evoke the mystery of compunction and repentance in Byzantium are investigated. This chapter concludes with a few brief remarks on the sacred music of Kassia's hymn and reflections on the relationship between chant and compunction.

The performance of hymns that sought to portray, arouse and embody compunction were momentous events in the Byzantine experience of this emotion. Compunction became more than a personal feeling of remorse arising from the consciousness of one's own sinfulness and a desire for forgiveness through repentance; it became a liturgical emotion and a collective feeling. Hymnody collapsed the distinctions between singer and scriptural characters, between temporality and the biblical narrative of salvation. Emotions were an embodied experience, enacted through sacred song and liturgical mysticism. Today, we do not conceive of compunction as an emotion intertwined with paradisal nostalgia, a desire for repentance and a wellspring of tears; the Byzantines did.

CHAPTER 2

The Liturgical World of Compunction

The emotion of compunction came to life in the *habitus*[1] and sacred space of the Byzantine liturgy where hymns were performed. Hymns that were sung in cathedrals, monasteries and throughout the city of Constantinople embodied compunction, seeking to arouse this feeling in the faithful who sang or experienced these sacred songs.[2] The liturgical context of these hymns is the hermeneutical prism *sine qua non* for exploring their affective significance and reimagining their performance. While the worship of the Church was invariably shaped by its doctrinal confession, liturgy for the Byzantines was 'both a source and expression of [their] theology'; it was the sacred ritual where the *lex orandi* and *lex credendi* of Byzantine Christianity converged.[3] Liturgy was the 'song of theology' (θεολογίας μελῴδημα),[4] where 'through the unison of divine odes' (τῇ τῶν θείων ᾠδῶν ὁμοφωνίᾳ) the faithful experienced 'the concord of divine things,

---

[1] As discussed in the previous chapter, my methodology draws on the work of Monique Scheer on emotional practices. Although Scheer explores the notion of *habitus* in the work of Pierre Bourdieu, the term itself can be traced to the Aristotelian, Byzantine and Scholastic traditions. The word *habitus* is a translation of Aristotle's ἕξις and, while it denotes a set of mental and physical dispositions and habits acquired primarily through mimetic learning in a certain sociocultural milieu, it marries well with the sacred ritual of liturgy by describing how liturgical practices cultivated a Christian *habitus*. See Scheer, 'Are Emotions a Kind of Practice', 201; Paul M. Blowers, *Maximus the Confessor: Jesus Christ and the Transfiguration of the World* (Oxford: Oxford University Press, 2016), 171–83.

[2] On the stational and processional liturgy of Constantinople, see John F. Baldovin, *The Urban Character of Christian Worship: The Origins, Development and Meaning of Stational Liturgy*, OCA 228 (Rome: Pontificium Institutum Studiorum Orientalium, 1987), 167–226; Vicky Manolopoulou, 'Processing Emotion: Litanies in Byzantine Constantinople', in Nesbitt and Jackson, eds., *Experiencing Byzantium*, 153–71.

[3] Meyendorff, *Byzantine Theology*, 115.

[4] Patriarch Nikephoros of Constantinople, *Treatise on Our Immaculate, Pure and Unmixed Christian Faith and against Those Who Glorify and Worship Idols*, chapter 70, PG 100, 773B. Quoted in Jaroslav Pelikan, *The Christian Tradition. A History of the Development of Doctrine, 2: The Spirit of Eastern Christendom (600–1700)* (Chicago, IL: University of Chicago Press, 1974), 133. Although Pelikan translated θεολογίας μελῴδημα as the 'melody of theology', it is more accurate to translate μελῴδημα as 'song'. See the corresponding entry in Lampe, *Patristic Greek Lexicon*, 842.

their selves and others' (τὴν πρὸς τὰ θεῖα καὶ ἑαυτοὺς καὶ ἀλλήλους ὁμοφροσύνην) as one harmonious choir.[5]

In examining the mystagogy of the Byzantine liturgy, this chapter will focus on how sacred space was portrayed as the *habitus* of compunction. As Dionysius the Areopagite suggested, it was the liturgical world of Byzantium – its symbolic order, sensory splendour and collective practices – which embodied 'the harmonious *habitus* that was ordered toward divine things' (τῆς ἐναρμονίου πρὸς τὰ θεῖα καὶ τεταγμένης ἕξεως) and where heaven and earth converged, not simply in the assembly of a church, but in the hearts of the faithful.[6] Maximus the Confessor developed this proposition further in his own liturgical commentary, *On Ecclesiastical Mystagogy*:

Τὸν γὰρ νοῦν διὰ τῆς σοφίας ἔφασκε κινούμενον, εἰς θεωρίαν ἰέναι· διὰ δὲ τῆς θεωρίας, εἰς γνῶσιν· διὰ δὲ τῆς γνώσεως, εἰς ἄληστον γνῶσιν· διὰ δὲ τῆς ἀλήστου γνώσεως, εἰς τὴν ἀλήθειαν· περὶ ἣν ὁ νοῦς ὅρον τῆς κινήσεως δέχεται, περιγραφομένης αὐτῷ τῆς τε οὐσίας καὶ τῆς δυνάμεως καὶ τῆς ἕξεως καὶ τῆς ἐνεργείας.[7]

The mind, he would say, arrives at contemplation when it is moved by wisdom, by contemplation to knowledge, by knowledge to enduring knowledge, by enduring knowledge to truth. It is here that the mind finds the boundary of its movement, for in it essence, potency, *habitus* and act are circumscribed.[8]

This quotation follows Maximus' earlier comparison of the unity of the church and its members with the mystical unity of the Trinity. According to Maximus, the church is 'an icon of God' that 'realises the same union of the faithful as that in God' (ὡς τὴν αὐτὴν τῷ θεῷ).[9] He portrays liturgical experience as a mystical union between Christ and the faithful, a *habitus* where sacred song and holy ritual guide the faithful to divine things. By exploring the liturgical world of compunction, this chapter will deepen our understanding of this emotion in Byzantium and pave the way to reimagining the performance of the hymns in the next three chapters.

---

[5] Dionysius the Areopagite, *Ecclesiastical Hierarchy* 1.5. The Greek text is from Heil and Ritter, *Corpus Dionysiacum*, 84. The English translation is my own.
[6] *The Celestial Hierarchy* 1.3. Ibid., 9.
[7] *On Ecclesiastical Mystagogy*, chapter 5. Boudignon, *Maximi Confessoris Mystagogia*, 24.
[8] The English translation is my own. The word *habitus* (ἕξις) emerges as a keyword in the thought of Maximus the Confessor. See Michael Bakker, 'Maximus and Modern Psychology', in *The Oxford Handbook of Maximus the Confessor*, ed. Pauline Allen and Bronwen Neil (Oxford: Oxford University Press, 2015), 533–47.
[9] *On Ecclesiastical Mystagogy*, chapter 1. Boudignon, *Maximi Confessoris Mystagogia*, 11.

This chapter will begin by investigating the liturgical significance of Novella 137, the sixth-century edict of Emperor Justinian concerning the eucharistic prayers. It will then explore the sacred space, soundscape and 'lightscape'[10] of Hagia Sophia, which is an important extant (although fragmentary) monument of Byzantium and has become a touchstone for reimagining the Constantinopolitan worship of the medieval past. While Hagia Sophia is a useful case study, Byzantine hymnody was performed in a variety of churches and monasteries across Constantinople and its liturgical hinterland.[11] Nevertheless, as a focal point of liturgical wonder and architectural grandeur, it is impossible to ignore the lasting impression of Hagia Sophia on those who may have frequented other urban or monastic places of worship. This chapter will then examine the liturgical commentaries of Dionysius the Areopagite, Maximus the Confessor and Germanos of Constantinople for further evidence of experiencing sacred song in Byzantium, before briefly touching upon affective mysticism and its significance for Byzantine hymnody. Finally, it will probe the importance of Great Lent and the *Triodion* as a liturgical and hermeneutical framework for compunction.

Compunction and the Divine Liturgy

The value of investigating Justinian's edict regarding the eucharistic prayers is twofold: first, it will show how not only the hymns performed during Great Lent and Holy Week but even the climax of the Byzantine liturgical experience – the Divine Liturgy and the Eucharist – had a compunctious character; second, it will unveil how the art of listening and popular participation in liturgical events shaped the emotions of the faithful.[12] Although the majority of worshippers would have been unable to read, sounds and images were the religious literature of the illiterate.[13] In 399, the emotional contagion, fellow-feeling and tears streaming down

---

[10] See Claire Nesbitt, 'Shaping the Sacred: Light and the Experience of Worship in Middle Byzantine Churches', *Byzantine and Modern Greek Studies* 36, no. 2 (2012): 139–60; Claire Nesbitt and Mark Jackson, 'Experiencing Byzantium', in *Experiencing Byzantium*, 4.

[11] For a reconstruction of the early Byzantine basilicas and Justinianic churches, see Thomas F. Mathews, *The Early Churches of Constantinople: Architecture and Liturgy* (University Park, PA: Pennsylvania State University Press, 1971), 11–102.

[12] On the art of listening and popular participation of the liturgy, see Carol Harrison, *The Art of Listening in the Early Church* (Oxford: Oxford University Press, 2013), 183–269; Taft, *Through Their Own Eyes*, 29–132.

[13] Mary B. Cunningham, 'Byzantine Views of God and the Universe', in James, ed., *A Companion to Byzantium*, 159.

the faces of the faithful that John Chrysostom's sermon *On Eutropius* aroused were accomplished with the rhetoric of a homily during a liturgy in the Great Church of Constantinople:

> Have I softened your passion and cast out your anger? Have I quenched your inhumanity? Have I drawn you into sympathy? I very much think so—the faces indicate it and the fountains of tears.[14]

Homilies, hymnody and sacred space staged the liturgical narrative of salvation for the Byzantines and were the 'scripts for the performance of feeling' enacted by the faithful, turning listeners into spectators and eliciting an affective response.[15]

The significance of the eucharistic prayers as a 'speech act effecting the production of ritualized subjects' and as a shared discourse that transformed the faithful into an emotional community is underscored by a law Emperor Justinian published in 565.[16] Novella 137 ordered the clergy to do the following:

> Πρὸς τούτοις κελεύομεν πάντας ἐπισκόπους τε καὶ πρεσβυτέρους μὴ κατὰ τὸ σεσιωπημένον, ἀλλὰ μετὰ φωνῆς τῷ πιστοτάτῳ λαῷ ἐξακουομένης τὴν θείαν προσκομιδὴν καὶ τὴν ἐπὶ τῷ ἁγίῳ βαπτίσματι προσευχὴν ποιεῖσθαι, πρὸς τὸ κἀντεῦθεν τὰς τῶν ἀκουόντων ψυχὰς εἰς πλείονα κατάνυξιν καὶ τὴν πρὸς τὸν δεσπότην θεὸν διανίστασθαι δοξολογίαν.[17]

> Moreover, we order all bishops and priests to say the prayers used in the divine oblation and holy baptism not silently, but with a voice that can be heard by the faithful people, so that the souls of those who hear may be moved to greater compunction and raise up glorification to God.[18]

Although the ultimate purpose of the eucharistic prayers was the transformation of the bread and wine into the body of blood of Christ, they also

---

[14] The translation of the text is from Wendy Mayer and Pauline Allen, eds., *John Chrysostom* (New York, NY: Routledge, 2000), 137. For the Greek text, see PG 52, 395. For an analysis of the emotive power of this homily, see Andrew Mellas, 'Tears of Compunction in John Chrysostom's *On Eutropius*', *Studia Patristica* 83 (2017): 159–72.

[15] McNamer, *Affective Meditation*, 12. See also Ruth Webb, 'Imagination and the Arousal of the Emotions in Greco-Roman Rhetoric', in *The Passions in Roman Thought and Literature*, ed. Susanna Morton Braund and Christopher Gill (Cambridge: Cambridge University Press, 1997), 112–27. On emotional scripts and the prehistory of compunction, see Robert Kaster, *Emotion, Restraint and Community in Ancient Rome* (Oxford: Oxford University Press, 2005), 3–12, 66–83.

[16] Krueger, *Liturgical Subjects*, 108; Rosenwein, *Emotional Communities*, 24–26.

[17] Justinian, *Corpus iuris civilis, 3. Novellae*, ed. Rudolf Schöll and Wilhelm Kroll (Berlin: Apud Weidmannos, 1954), 699.

[18] The English translation is based on the one in Robert F. Taft, 'Was the Eucharistic Anaphora Recited Secretly or Aloud? The Ancient Tradition and What Became of It', in *Worship Traditions in Armenia and the Neighboring Christian East*, ed. Roberta R. Ervine (Crestwood, NY: St Vladimir's Seminary Press, 2006), 38.

recounted the history of salvation from creation to the Second Coming, arousing compunction and glorification.[19] One version of the eucharistic prayers, which appears in the eighth-century manuscript known as Barberini Graecus 336 – the earliest extant Byzantine euchologion (collection of prayers) – is worth quoting extensively:

Ἄξιον καὶ δίκαιον σὲ ὑμνεῖν, σοὶ εὐχαριστεῖν, σὲ προσκυνεῖν ἐν παντὶ τόπῳ τῆς δεσποτείας σου· σὺ γὰρ εἶ Θεὸς ἀνέκφραστος, ἀπερινόητος, ἀόρατος, ἀκατάληπτος, ἀεὶ ὤν, ὡσαύτως ὤν· σὺ καὶ ὁ μονογενής σου Υἱὸς καὶ τὸ Πνεῦμά σου τὸ ἅγιον. Σὺ ἐκ τοῦ μὴ ὄντος εἰς τὸ εἶναι ἡμᾶς παρήγαγες καὶ παραπεσόντας ἀνέστησας πάλιν, καὶ οὐκ ἀπέστης πάντα ποιῶν, ἔως ἡμᾶς εἰς τὸν οὐρανὸν ἀνήγαγες καὶ τὴν βασιλείαν σου ἐχαρίσω τὴν μέλλουσαν ... Μεμνημένοι τοίνυν τῆς σωτηρίου ταύτης ἐντολῆς καὶ πάντων τῶν ὑπὲρ ἡμῶν γεγενημένων· τοῦ σταυροῦ, τοῦ τάφου, τῆς τριημέρου ἀναστάσεως, τῆς εἰς οὐρανοὺς ἀναβάσεως, τῆς ἐκ δεξιῶν καθέδρας, τῆς δευτέρας καὶ ἐνδόξου πάλιν παρουσίας ... Τὰ σὰ ἐκ τῶν σῶν σοὶ προσφέροντες κατὰ πάντα καὶ διὰ πάντα.[20]

It is right and fitting to hymn you, to give you thanks, to worship you in every place of your dominion; for you are God, ineffable, incomprehensible, invisible, inconceivable, ever existing, eternally the same; you and your only-begotten Son and your Holy Spirit. You brought us out of non-existence into being, and when we had fallen you raised us up again, and left nothing undone until you had brought us up to heaven and had granted us your Kingdom that is to come ... Remembering therefore this our Saviour's command [to eat his body and drink his blood] and all that has been done for us: the Cross, the Tomb, the Resurrection on the third day, the Ascension into heaven, the Sitting at the right hand, the Second and glorious Coming again ... We offer you your own from your own, in everything and for everything.[21]

The text portrays the Second Coming as an event the clergy and laity remember and therefore an event that has already occurred in liturgical time, which offers an inaugurated eschaton. Although this is different from the historical eschaton, the eschatological character of the Eucharist was, according to the Byzantine liturgical commentaries we shall examine, equally profound and has implications for the hymns that will be explored in the subsequent chapters. This aspect of the Eucharist will be considered

---

[19] It is important to note that several versions of the eucharistic prayers would have been in use in sixth-century Byzantium. See the exploration of which eucharistic prayers Justinian may have had in mind in Krueger, *Liturgical Subjects*, 111–26.

[20] Stefano Parenti and Elena Velkovska, eds., *L'Eucologio Barberini Gr. 336* (Rome: Edizioni Liturgiche, 1995), 32, 34.

[21] The English translation is based on the edition prepared by the Greek Orthodox Archdiocese of Thyateira and Great Britain, *The Divine Liturgy of Our Father among the Saints, John Chrysostom* (Oxford: Oxford University Press, 1995), 31, 33.

more closely against the backdrop of Hagia Sophia as 'the eschatological anticipation of the new creation'[22] and in the context of liturgical commentaries. Here it is important to examine how the eucharistic prayers portrayed the liturgy as a shared action and how they sought to arouse compunction in the faithful by placing them at the centre of the divine drama of salvation. However, I acknowledge that the purpose of Justinian's edict was twofold. It also provoked glorification during the Eucharist. Indeed, compunction formed part of a constellation of liturgical emotions that emerged during the performance of the Eucharist. While the next three chapters will examine the emotion of compunction in the ferial hymnography of Great Lent and Holy Week, and in the hymns of evensong or matins before a liturgy, it is important to emphasise that even the liturgical celebration of the Eucharist was characterised by an atmosphere of compunction, despite its generally festive character.[23]

Before, during and after the eucharistic prayers, the performance of the liturgy was 'a corporate work' that demanded 'the dynamic involvement of the people', since it was impossible for the clergy to enact the Eucharist without the congregation.[24] As John Chrysostom and other patristic sources attest:

Τὰ τῆς εὐχαριστίας πάλιν κοινά· οὐδὲ γὰρ ἐκεῖνος εὐχαριστεῖ μόνος, ἀλλὰ καὶ ὁ λαὸς ἅπας. Πρότερον γὰρ αὐτῶν λαβὼν φωνήν, εἶτα συντιθεμένων ὅτι ἀξίως καὶ δικαίως τοῦτο γίνεται, τότε ἄρχεται τῆς εὐχαριστίας. Καὶ τί θαυμάζεις, εἴ που μετὰ τοῦ ἱερέως ὁ λαὸς φθέγγεται, ὅπου γε καὶ μετ' αὐτῶν τῶν Χερουβὶμ καὶ τῶν ἄνω δυνάμεων, κοινῇ τοὺς ἱεροὺς ἐκείνους ὕμνους ἀναπέμπει;[25]

---

[22] Meyendorff, *Byzantine Theology*, 208.

[23] During Great Lent in Constantinople, the Divine Liturgy of St John Chrysostom was 'not celebrated on weekdays, but only on Saturdays and on the day of Annunciation, while the Liturgy of St Basil was celebrated on Sundays'. On Wednesdays and Fridays, 'the Liturgy of the Presanctified is celebrated'. Getcha, *The Typikon Decoded*, 162. On the Liturgy of the Presanctified see ibid., 169–73. Although the eucharistic prayers in the Liturgy of St Basil are different from those of Chrysostom, they echo the theme of how Christ's incarnation, crucifixion and resurrection opened the gates of paradise and accomplished the salvation of creation. See *L'Eucologio Barberini Gr. 336*, edited by Stefano Parenti and Elena Velkovska (Rome: Edizioni Liturgiche, 1995), 12–18. See also the English translation in Walter D. Ray, *Tasting Heaven on Earth: Worship in Sixth-Century Constantinople* (Grand Rapids, MI: Eerdmans, 2012), 93–99. Although Barberini Graecus 336 is the earliest surviving witness of the Byzantine liturgy of Basil and dates from the eighth century, the text is incomplete and must be cross-referenced with Grottaferrata Γβ VII of the late tenth century. The critical edition of this manuscript is Gaetano Passarelli, *L'Eucologio Cryptense Γβ VII* (Thessaloniki: Patriarchal Institute for Patristic Studies, 1982).

[24] Kallistos Ware, 'The Meaning of the Divine Liturgy for the Byzantine Worshipper', in *Church and People in Byzantium*, ed. Rosemary Morris (Birmingham: Centre for Byzantine, Ottoman and Modern Greek Studies, University of Birmingham, 1990), 22.

[25] *On the Second Epistle to the Corinthians*, homily 18. PG 61, 527.

> Everything in the eucharistic thanksgiving is shared in common; for the priest does not offer thanksgiving alone, but the whole people give thanks with him. For after he has replied to their greeting, they then give their consent that 'it is just and right', and only then does he commence the eucharistic thanksgiving. Why are you astonished that the people speak together with the priest, when they send up in common those sacred hymns, even with the very Cherubim and the heavenly powers?[26]

Therefore, considering the excerpt from one of the eucharistic prayers quoted earlier, the decree of Emperor Justinian that these prayers be heard and the patristic evidence that the liturgy was a shared action, I agree with scholars such as Kallistos Ware and Robert Taft who have argued that, in the performance of the Byzantine liturgy, the faithful were not merely spectators in the sacred drama unfolding before them, but active participants.[27]

The eucharistic prayers place the faithful at the centre of the sacred drama that the liturgy performed, enkindling feelings of nostalgia, compunction and joy. It is on their behalf that God becomes human, is crucified and is buried. And it is on their behalf that the resurrection and the Second Coming are accomplished. The eucharistic prayers began with the divine act of creation ('you brought us out of non-existence into being'), continued with the exile from Eden ('when we had fallen you raised us up') and ended with salvific action and eschatological promise ('and left nothing undone until you had brought us up to heaven'). The laity gave thanks together with the clergy for these works of God, which opened the way to paradisal bliss. The text portrayed the compunction that Emperor Justinian wished to instil in their hearts as a desire to partake in this salvific mystery and a thanksgiving for Christ's incarnation, crucifixion, resurrection and ascension. Paradoxically, the only thing that the faithful could offer in thanksgiving for God's benefactions was the very sacrifice of Christ ('we offer you your own from your own, in everything and for everything'). It is not simply through hearing the eucharistic prayers, but 'through becoming an offering of thanksgiving' that the 'faithful partake in the Divine Liturgy' and feel compunction.[28]

Christians recited liturgical prayers, such as the eucharistic anaphora, aloud in Late Antiquity and Byzantium.[29] Even if 'that usage—the true ancient tradition—began to fall into disuse', it was 'condemned as an

---

[26] I have based my translation on the following two works that cite this passage: Taft, *Through Their Own Eyes*, 29; Ware, 'The Meaning of the Divine Liturgy', 21.

[27] See also Vassa Larin, '"Active Participation" of the Faithful in Byzantine Liturgy', *St Vladimir's Theological Quarterly* 57, no. 1 (2013): 67–88.

[28] Archimandrite Vasileios, *Hymn of Entry*, 59, 76.   [29] Taft, 'Eucharistic Anaphora', 45.

abusive innovation and forbidden' by Emperor Justinian.[30] Nevertheless, irrespective of when and where the communal recitation of the eucharistic prayers may have fallen into disuse, this was not the only aspect of Byzantium's sacred rituals that sought to evoke the feeling of compunction. The sixth-century hymns of Romanos the Melodist and the hymnography of other poets such as Andrew of Crete and Kassia in later centuries, as well as homilies and sacred art, 'converged to construct Christians within a single imaginary' that perpetuated the biblical narrative of salvation.[31] As we will see in the next three chapters, the hymns of the *Triodion* and their liturgical performance also staged the sacred drama of salvation and sought to arouse tears of compunction.

In monastic settings, communal participation in sacred song was commonly observed.[32] This de rigueur monastic practice was so vital that, early in the ninth century, Theodore, the abbot of the Stoudios monastery in Constantinople, castigated his monks for their lacklustre singing:

> Ἐπειδὴ δὲ χθὲς ὠργίσθην ὑμῖν διὰ τὴν ψαλμῳδίαν, παρακαλῶ καὶ δέομαι τεταγμένως καὶ κεκανονισμένως ψάλλειν· ἀλλὰ μὴ ἁπλῶς καὶ ὡς ἔτυχε συγκεχυμένως· καὶ τοῦτο λυπεῖν οὐκ ἐμὲ τὸν ἁμαρτωλόν, ἀλλὰ τὸ Πνεῦμα τὸ ἅγιον. Αὐτὸ γάρ ἐστι τὸ κελεῦον· «Ψάλατε συνετῶς».[33]

> Ever since yesterday I have been angry with you on account of the psalmody; I ask and beseech you to chant in an orderly manner and according to the rules, and not simply haphazardly or confusedly. For this grieves not me, the sinner, but the Holy Spirit. It is the Spirit that exhorts: 'Sing psalms intelligently.'[34]

In the liturgical life of the Stoudios monastery, the singing of psalms and hymns constructed the monk as an instrument of liturgy and embodied

---

[30] Ibid.   [31] Krueger, *Liturgical Subjects*, 67.

[32] See the survey of the evidence for musical life preserved in Byzantine monastic foundation documents in Rosemary Dubowchik, 'Singing with the Angels: Foundation Documents as Evidence for Musical Life in Monasteries of the Byzantine Empire', *DOP* 56 (2002): 277–96. See also the examination of Theodore the Stoudite's ninth-century views on common participation in liturgical song in Daniel Galadza, '"Open your Mouth and Attract the Spirit": St Theodore Stoudite and Participation in the Icon of Worship', in *Church Music and Icons: Proceedings of the Fifth International Conference on Orthodox Church Music, University of Eastern Finland, Joensuu, Finland, 3–9 June 2013*, ed. Ivan Moody and Maria Takala-Roszczenko (Joensuu: International Society of Orthodox Church Music, 2015), 441–55.

[33] *Small Catechesis* 99 in *Sancti patris nostri et confessoris Theodori Studitis praepositi Parva catechesis*, edited by Emmanuel Auvray (Paris: Apud Victorem Lecoffre, 1891) 341.

[34] The English translation is based on that in Roman Cholij, *Theodore the Stoudite: The Ordering of Holiness* (Oxford: Oxford University Press, 2002), 85. The text that Theodore quotes in his catechetical sermon is Psalm 46:8, which is suggestive of how the mind played an intrinsic role in the liturgical performance of emotions.

the virtuous life of holiness that ascetics desired.[35] However, popular participation in the singing of hymns also occurred in urban settings.[36] When John Chrysostom observed that the people 'send up in common those sacred hymns', he was writing from the viewpoint of a bishop who experienced metropolitan worship.[37] Indeed, the sacred songs of cathedrals and urban churches were 'designed for the popular participation of the ordinary laity' and 'their active participation' was assured through 'easily remembered responses or refrains' that echoed a soloist or that encouraged choral execution.[38] A refrain was able to 'decentralize the first person singular of the song' and 'create a self in which the singer and the congregation share'.[39] According to Basil the Great, psalmody was not only a vehicle for 'joining people together into a harmonious union of one choir',[40] it impressed upon each soul a personal compunction amidst unity: 'all in common as if from one mouth and one heart offer the psalm of confession to the Lord, while each fashions his personal words of repentance'.[41]

The fourth-century deacon and hymnographer Ephrem the Syrian, who influenced the work of Romanos the Melodist, drew connections between sacred song, feeling compunction and experiencing the divine: 'Wherever there is psalmody with compunction, there also is God with the Angels' ("Οπου ψαλμὸς μετὰ κατανύξεως, ἐκεῖ καὶ ὁ Θεὸς μετὰ τῶν Ἀγγέλων).[42] Similarly, John Chrysostom believed that the 'songs of David cause great

---

[35] I owe this insight to Derek Krueger's conference paper, 'Liturgical Instruction and Theories of Singing in Middle Byzantine Monasticism: From Constantinople to Athos', *Spatialities of Byzantine Culture*, Uppsala University, 18–21 May 2017.

[36] See the fourth-century *Itinerarium Egeriae* in which Egeria travels to Constantinople and Jerusalem and observes how the faithful participate in sacred song: sections 24.3–24.10, translated in Wilkinson, *Egeria's Travels*, 143–45. Further evidence is available in the excerpts from *Homily on Psalm 1* and *Letters* by Basil the Great, which are cited and translated in McKinnon, *Music in Early Christian Literature*, 65–69.

[37] *On the Second Epistle to the Corinthians*, homily 18. PG 61, 527.

[38] Taft, *Through Their Own Eyes*, 60.

[39] Thomas Arentzen, 'Voices Interwoven: Refrains and Vocal Participation in the Kontakia', *JÖB* 66 (2017): 10.

[40] *Homily on Psalm 1*, Basil the Great, *Exegetical Homilies*, trans. Sister Agnes Clare Way (Washington, DC: Catholic University of America Press, 1963), 152.

[41] Letter 208, cited in McKinnon, *Music in Early Christian Literature*, 69.

[42] K. G. Phrantzoles, ed. Ὁσίου Ἐφραίμ τοῦ Σύρου ἔργα [*The Works of St Ephrem the Syrian*], vol. 5 (Thessalonike: To Perivoli tes Panagias, 1994), 244. The English translation is my own. For the influence of Ephrem on Romanos, see William L. Petersen, *The Diatessaron and Ephrem Syrus as Sources of Romanos the Melodist*, CSCO 475 (Leuven: Peeters, 1985), 169–200. I note this passage is from the corpus of works attributed to Ephrem Graecus. On this issue, see Démocratie Hemmerdinger-Iliadou, 'Éphrem Grec', in *Dictionnaire de Spiritualité* (Paris: Beauchesne, 1960), 800–15.

fountains of tears' in the singer.[43] Thus, it is not surprising that the epicentre of Christian worship in sixth-century Constantinople was also a place of psalmody and compunction, notwithstanding the sheer wonder its majestic architecture could inspire. A poem that was composed for the inauguration of Hagia Sophia on 24 December 562 situates compunction within the liturgical world of this sacred space:

Νοητῶς αἱ θυσίαι ἐνταῦθα ἐν τῷ πνεύματι καὶ ἀληθείᾳ,   οὐκ ἐν κνίσσαις καπνῶν καὶ αἱμάτων ῥοαῖς
ἀνενδότως θεῷ   εἰς ὀσμὴν εὐωδίας προσάγονται·
προσευχῶν δάκρυα   μετ' εὐλαβείας
καὶ ψαλμῶν ᾄσματα   πρὸς κατάνυξιν
ἐν ὀργάνοις τοῦ πνεύματος   μελῳδούμενα, [καὶ] κοιμίζοντα
τὰς ἐκ τῶν παθῶν δαιμονίους ὁρμάς,   ἡδονὴν σώφρονα   [ἐμ]ποιοῦντα εἰς σωτηρίαν,
ἥν δωρεῖται τοῖς ἀνθρώποις ὁ Χριστός,
   | : ἡ πάντων ζωὴ καὶ ἀνάστασις. : |[44]

Here, noetically, sacrifices in spirit and truth, not in odours of burnt offerings and streams of blood, are ceaselessly offered to God as a sweet-smelling fragrance. The tears of prayers with piety and the songs of psalmody for compunction are sung with instruments of spirit, putting to sleep the demonic impulses of the passions, creating prudent pleasure for salvation, which Christ gives to people,
   the life and resurrection of all.[45]

Compunction is presented as intertwined with prayer and psalmody and their somatic and melodic manifestations – tears and song. Far from eschewing feeling, the liturgical rites of Hagia Sophia counteracted tainted passions with the remedial power of blessed emotions, such as compunction.

Hagia Sophia: The Church of the Holy Wisdom

Several scholars have recently sought to reimagine the rich, affective and multisensory experience that the architecture, acoustics and lightscape of Hagia Sophia engendered during liturgical performances.[46] The awe that

[43] *Homilies on 1 Timothy*, 14, cited in McKinnon, *Music in Early Christian Literature*, 87–88.
[44] *On the Consecration of Hagia Sophia* (24 December 562), strophe 16, in Constantine A. Trypanis, *Fourteen Early Byzantine Cantica* (Vienna: Böhlau in Kommission, 1968), 146.
[45] The English translation is my own.
[46] See Pentcheva, *Hagia Sophia*; Nadine Schibille, *Hagia Sophia and the Byzantine Aesthetic Experience* (Farnham: Ashgate, 2014); Lingas, 'From Earth to Heaven', 311–58; Ray, *Tasting Heaven on Earth*, 19–82; Neil Moran, 'The Choir of Hagia Sophia', *Oriens Christianus* 89 (2005): 1–7; Nesbitt, 'Shaping the Sacred', 139–60.

the liturgy at Hagia Sophia could inspire is encapsulated in the legendary account of the conversion of Russia, in which the imperial envoys return after their visit to Constantinople and tell Prince Vladimir about their liturgical experience:

> we knew not whether we were in heaven or on earth. For on earth there is no such splendour or such beauty and we are at a loss how to describe it. We only know that God dwells there among men, and their service is fairer than the ceremonies of other nations. For we cannot forget that beauty.[47]

While Hagia Sophia was a majestic embodiment of Byzantine aesthetics, according to the sixth-century descriptions of the building by Prokopios and Paul the Silentiary, its architectural fabric reflected spiritual realities.[48] Paul's *Ekphrasis of Hagia Sophia* also suggests that images of Christ, the prophets, the apostles and the Theotokos adorned the interior.[49] However, the interior of Justinian's Hagia Sophia was largely 'aniconic, eschewing the human figure'.[50] The holy ritual performed within this sacred space

---

[47] Samuel Hazard Cross and Olgerd P. Sherbowitz-Wetzor, eds. and trans., *The Russian Primary Chronicle: Laurentian Text* (Cambridge, MA: Harvard University Press, 1973), 111.

[48] For the Greek text (with German translation) of Prokopios' *Buildings* and Paul the Silentiary's *Ekphrasis of Hagia Sophia* and *Ekphrasis of the Ambo*, see Otto Veh, ed. *Prokop: Werke*, vol. 5 (Munich: Heimeran, 1977), 16–375. There is an English translation of the two texts by Paul the Silentiary in Cyril Mango, *The Art of the Byzantine Empire, 312–1453: Sources and Documents* (Toronto: University of Toronto Press, 1986), 91–102. See also Mary Whitby, 'The Occasion of Paul the Silentiary's Ekphrasis of S. Sophia', *The Classical Quarterly* 35, no. 1 (1985): 215–28.

[49] 'Not only upon the walls which separate the priest from the choir of singers has [Emperor Justinian] set plates of naked silver, but the columns, too, six sets of twain in number, he has completely covered with the silver metal, and they send forth their rays far and wide. Upon them the tool wielded by a skilled hand has artfully hollowed out discs more pointed than a circle, within which it has engraved the figure of the immaculate God who, without seed, clothed himself in human form. Elsewhere it has carved the host of winged angels ... Elsewhere the sharp steel has fashioned those former heralds of God by whose words, before God had taken on flesh, the divine tidings of Christ's coming spread abroad. Nor has the artist forgotten the images of those who abandoned the mean labours of their life—the fishing basket and the net—and those evil cares in order to follow the command of the heavenly King, fishing even for men and, instead of casting for fish, spread out the nets of eternal life. And elsewhere art has depicted the Mother of Christ, the vessel of eternal life, whose holy womb did nourish its own Maker' (ἄλλοθι δὲ Χριστοῖο κατέγραφε μητέρα τέχνη, φέγγεος ἀενάοιο δοχήϊον, ἧς ποτε γαστὴρ γαστέρος ἐργατίνην ἁγίοις ἐθρέψατο κόλποις). *Ekphrasis of Hagia Sophia*, verses 686–711 in Veh, *Prokop: Werke*, 340, 342; Mango, *The Art of the Byzantine Empire*, 87. Paul the Silentiary also mentions a woven cloth of gold and silver adorned with the figures of Christ, Peter and Paul. See Veh, *Prokop: Werke*, 342, 344; Mango, *The Art of the Byzantine Empire*, 88–89.

[50] Pentcheva, *Hagia Sophia*, 165. Indeed, the sixth-century images described by Paul the Silentiary in his *Ekphrasis of Hagia Sophia* may have been imperceptible in the enormous interior of the cathedral. I acknowledge that the question of icons before Iconoclasm is a contested issue. However, after the end of Iconoclasm, images became a prominent feature of worship, and figural programs emerged in iconography. See Leslie Brubaker, 'Icons before Iconoclasm?' *Settimane di Studio del Centro Italiano di Studi sull'Alto Medioevo* 45, no. 2 (1998): 1215–54; Jaś Elsner, 'Iconoclasm as Discourse: From Antiquity to Byzantium', *The Art Bulletin* 94, no. 3 (2012): 368–94.

enacted divine transcendence through 'the visual effects of vibrant and glittering materiality, reverberant acoustics, and thick and redolent incense', which sought to transport the faithful to 'a space between heaven and earth'.[51] Hagia Sophia was conceived as a cosmological image, a microcosm of the universe that bridged the earthly and heavenly realms by uniting them in the sacred space of the building and transfiguring the congregation's experience of beauty into a quest for divine reality.[52]

As the 'material manifestation of beauty that stirs the emotions and occasions the experience of love', the aesthetics of Hagia Sophia could arouse a desire for divine beauty.[53] As Gregory of Nyssa suggested in his homilies on the Song of Songs – albeit before Justinian's Hagia Sophia was built – it is astonishing how the incitement of fleshly desire can wield salvific power and lead the soul to a nobler desiring of divine things. Gregory exhorted his audience:

> ἐπειδὴ τοίνυν σοφία ἐστὶν ἡ λαλοῦσα, ἀγάπησον ὅσον δύνασαι ἐξ ὅλης καρδίας τε καὶ δυνάμεως, ἐπιθύμησον ὅσον χωρεῖς. προστίθημι δὲ θαρρῶν τοῖς ῥήμασι τούτοις καὶ τὸ ἐράσθητι· ἀνέγκλητον γὰρ τοῦτο καὶ ἀπαθὲς ἐπὶ τῶν ἀσωμάτων τὸ πάθος, καθώς φησιν ἡ σοφία ἐν ταῖς Παροιμίαις τοῦ θείου κάλλους νομοθετοῦσα τὸν ἔρωτα.[54]

> Therefore, since it is Wisdom who speaks, *love* her as much as you are able, with your whole heart and strength; *desire* her as much as you can. To these words I am bold to add, *Be in love*, for this passion, when directed to things incorporeal, is blameless and impassible, as Wisdom says in Proverbs when she bids us to be in love with the divine Beauty.[55]

Two centuries later, in the hymn *On the Consecration of Hagia Sophia*, the Old Testament Wisdom[56] manifests herself as the Logos of John 1:14 – the Logos who became flesh, who was the 'power of God

---

[51] Pentcheva, *Hagia Sophia*, 3. On the use of incense (and other fragrances) to evoke a paradisal atmosphere in Hagia Sophia (and other sacred spaces in Byzantium), see Béatrice Caseau, 'Euodia: The Use and Meaning of Fragrances in the Ancient World and Their Christianization (100–900 AD)' (PhD dissertation, Princeton University, 1994), 289–92; Susan Ashbrook Harvey, *Scenting Salvation: Ancient Christianity and the Olfactory Imagination* (Berkeley, CA: California University Press, 2006), 65–98; Caseau, 'The Senses in Religion', 93–95.

[52] Robert F. Taft, 'The Liturgy of the Great Church: An Initial Synthesis of Structure and Interpretation on the Eve of Iconoclasm', *DOP* 34/35 (1980/81): 47–48; Meyendorff, *Byzantine Theology*, 208; Helen G. Saradi, 'Space in Byzantine Thought', in *Architecture as Icon: Perception and Representation of Architecture in Byzantine Art*, ed. Slobodan Ćurčić and Evangelia Hadjitryphonos (New Haven, CT: Yale University Press, 2010), 103.

[53] Schibille, *Hagia Sophia and the Byzantine Aesthetic Experience*, 191.

[54] Homily 1 in St Gregory of Nyssa, *Homilies on the Song of Songs*, trans. Richard A. Norris, Jr (Atlanta, GA: Society of Biblical Literature, 2012), 24.

[55] Ibid., 25.   [56] 'Wisdom built herself a house and supported it with seven pillars.' Proverbs 9:1.

and wisdom of God'[57] and whose 'sojourn in the body' the inauguration of Hagia Sophia celebrated.[58]

Beyond the Incarnation of the Logos through the Theotokos, Hagia Sophia was portrayed as a sanctuary in which Christ could dwell:

Ἐν σαρκὶ ἐνοικήσας ὁ Λόγος   κατοικεῖν ἐν ναοῖς χειροτεύκτοις   εὐδοκεῖ
ἐνεργείᾳ τοῦ πνεύματος
μυστικαῖς τελεταῖς   τὴν αὐτοῦ παρουσίαν πιστούμενος,
καὶ βροτοῖς χάριτι   συνδιαιτᾶται
ὁ τοῖς πᾶσι ἀχώρητος   καὶ ἀπρόσιτος·
καὶ οὐ μόνον ὁμόστεγος   τοῖς ἐν γῇ ἐστιν οὐράνιος,
ἀλλὰ δείκνυσι καὶ τραπέζης κοινοὺς   καὶ τῆς σαρκὸς αὐτοῦ   δεξιοῦται τῇ εὐωχίᾳ,
ἣν προτίθησι τοῖς πιστοῖς ὁ Χριστός,
   | : ἡ πάντων ζωὴ καὶ ἀνάστασις. : |[59]

Having resided in the flesh, the Logos is well pleased, through the activity of the Spirit, to dwell in temples built by hand, assuring his presence by mystical rites; and he who cannot be contained by the universe and who is unapproachable, lives by grace among mortals.

And not only does he who is heavenly share a roof with those on earth, but he offers them a common table and welcomes them to the banquet of his flesh, which is set before the faithful by Christ,

the life and resurrection of all.[60]

Through liturgical performance, the church building of Hagia Sophia became a mediator between materiality and divine reality. The architectural space of Hagia Sophia had symbolic significance for the Byzantines, revealing the beauty of creation and inviting the faithful to become a 'performative image' of God in the sacred space animated by the ritual of liturgy.[61]

Before we explore this performative dimension more closely, it is important to note that the cosmic beauty Hagia Sophia embodied was an eschatological one. The liturgy celebrated in Hagia Sophia was an image of 'the new creation' and a 'transfigured cosmos' that manifested 'the fullness of the Kingdom' of God.[62] The eucharistic image that the hymn *On the Consecration of Hagia Sophia* evoked is characterised by paradisal hues, which betoken the eschaton. Within the church building itself, the

---

[57] 1 Corinthians 1:24.   [58] Strophe 1. Trypanis, *Fourteen Early Byzantine Cantica*, 141–42.

[59] Strophe 4.   [60] The English translation is my own.

[61] Pentcheva, 'Performing the Sacred', 122. See also Pentcheva, 'Hagia Sophia and Multisensory Aesthetics', *Gesta: International Centre for Medieval Art* 50, no. 2 (2011): 93–111.

[62] Meyendorff, *Byzantine Theology*, 208–9.

'jewelled crosses found throughout the mosaic decoration of Hagia Sophia' symbolised the divine light of the eschaton.[63] In scriptural and patristic tradition, the cross also symbolised the triumph of Christ during the Second Coming. Moreover, Hagia Sophia's cruciform design, which was crowned with a circular dome – an ancient symbol of eternity – reflected the eschatological universe of Christianity that the Eucharist enacted.

This cosmological interpretation of eschatology, which was consummated liturgically, has its antecedents in two of the Cappadocian Fathers: Basil the Great and Gregory of Nyssa.[64] According to Basil, when the faithful stood to partake in the Sunday liturgy, it represented an image of the age to come:

Διὸ καὶ ἀρχὴ οὖσα ἡμερῶν, οὐχὶ πρώτη παρὰ Μωϋσέως, ἀλλὰ μία ὠνόμασται. «Ἐγένετο γάρ, φησίν, ἑσπέρα, καὶ ἐγένετο πρωΐ, ἡμέρα μία»· ὡς τῆς αὐτῆς ἀνακυκλουμένης πολλάκις. Καὶ μία τοίνυν ἡ αὐτὴ καὶ ὀγδόη τὴν μίαν ὄντως ἐκείνην καὶ ἀληθινὴν ὀγδόην, ἧς καὶ ὁ ψαλμῳδὸς ἔν τισιν ἐπιγραφαῖς τῶν ψαλμῶν ἐπεμνήσθη, δι' ἑαυτῆς ἐμφανίζουσα, τὴν μετὰ τὸν χρόνον τοῦτον κατάστασιν, τὴν ἄπαυστον ἡμέραν, τὴν ἀνέσπερον, τὴν ἀδιάδοχον, τὸν ἄληκτον ἐκεῖνον καὶ ἀγήρω αἰῶνα.[65]

On account of this, although it is the beginning of days, Moses names it not 'first' but 'one'. For it is written, 'There was evening, and there was morning, one day' (Gen 1.5), as if the same one often repeated. Now, 'One' and 'Eighth' are the same, which indicates of itself that the really 'one' and true 'eighth'—which the Psalmist mentions in some titles of psalms—are the state after this time, the unceasing, unending, perpetual day, that never-ending and ever-young age.[66]

Basil's words, which were written well before Justinian's Hagia Sophia was constructed, show how the relationship between liturgy and the eschaton was not necessarily founded on the wonder and grandeur of a cathedral. However, Hagia Sophia amplified this eschatological experience by linking its mosaic decoration with its symbolic lightscape of worship, which 'provided an ethereal guide to the worshipper'.[67] The solar light of daybreak and the flickering candlelight of evensong interacted with the

---

[63] Schibille, *Hagia Sophia and the Byzantine Aesthetic Experience*, 131.

[64] See John A. McGuckin, 'Eschatological Horizons in the Cappadocian Fathers', in *Apocalyptic Thought in Early Christianity*, ed. Robert J. Daley (Grand Rapids, MI: Baker Academic, 2009), 193–210; Mario Baghos, 'St Basil's Eschatological Vision: Aspects of the Recapitulation of History and the Eighth Day', *Phronema* 25 (2010): 85–103.

[65] *On the Holy Spirit*, chapter 27, section 66. PG 32, 192AB.

[66] St Basil the Great, *On the Holy Spirit*, trans. Stephen M. Hildebrand (Crestwood, NY: St Vladimir's Seminary Press, 2011), 106.

[67] Nesbitt, 'Shaping the Sacred', 159.

'opulent decoration' of Hagia Sophia, arousing the emotional, spiritual and sensory faculties of the faithful.[68] The lightscape of worship transformed the jewelled crosses, concave surfaces of the domes and mosaics into coruscating images of divine light, which 'symbolised the luminous cross of the Parousia' and the 'eschatological light of the New Jerusalem'.[69] Prokopios alluded to this lightscape when describing Hagia Sophia as possessing a radiance that 'comes into being within it' and 'an abundance of light' that bathes the interior.[70]

Although it is uncertain what iconographical images may have appeared in sixth-century Hagia Sophia, the homily that Photios, Patriarch of Constantinople, delivered on Holy Saturday in 867 before the Emperors Michael III and Basil I, during the unveiling of the restored icon of the Virgin holding the child Jesus, shows the affective and performative significance of this image for the faithful. Photios portrays the image as a 'beautiful spectacle' that draws the soul through the eyes of the body towards the divine:

> Καὶ γὰρ οἱονεὶ τῇ μὲν στοργῇ τῶν σπλάγχνων τὴν ὄψιν πρὸς τὸ τεχθὲν συμπαθῶς ἐπιστρέφουσα, οἷα δὲ τῷ ἀπαθεῖ καὶ ὑπερφυεῖ τοῦ τόκου εἰς ἄσχετον ἅμα καὶ ἀτάραχον ἁρμοζομένη κατάστημα διαθέσεως παραπλη-σίως φέρει τὸ ὄμμα σχηματιζόμενον. Εἴποις ἂν αὐτὴν (μηδ' εἴ τις ἐπερω-τῷη, πῶς δὲ παρθενεύεις καὶ τέτοκας;) μηδ' ἂν τὸ φθέγξασθαι παραιτήσασθαι. Οὕτω διεσαρκώθη τὰ χείλη τοῖς χρώμασιν. <ὥστε> καὶ συνεπτύχθαι μόνον καὶ ἠρεμεῖν ὡς ἐν μυστηρίοις, ἀλλ' οὐκ ἔχειν δι' ὅλου τὴν ἡσυχίαν ἀκίνητον, οὐδὲ μιμήσει τὴν μορφὴν ἐνωραΐζεσθαι, ἀλλ' αὐτόχρημα τυγχάνειν ἀρχέτυπον.[71]

> For, as it were, she fondly turns her eyes on her begotten child in the affection of her heart, yet assumes the expression of a detached and imperturbable mood at the passionless and wondrous nature of her off-spring, and composes her gaze accordingly. You might think her not incapable of speaking, even if one were to ask her, 'How did you give birth and remain a virgin?' To such an extent have the lips been made flesh by the colours that they merely appear pressed together and stilled as in the mysteries, yet their silence is not at all inert, nor does she resemble the fairness of her form; she truly is the archetype.[72]

---

[68] Schibille, *Hagia Sophia and the Byzantine Aesthetic Experience*, 142.

[69] Ibid., 132, 150. See also Pentcheva, *The Sensual Icon*, 5.

[70] *Buildings*, 10.1, 30–31. Quoted in Nesbitt, 'Shaping the Sacred', 141.

[71] Homily 17.2 in Vasileios Laourdas, ed. Φωτίου Ομιλίαι [*The Homilies of Photios*] (Thessalonike: Centre for Macedonian Studies, 1959), 167.

[72] The translation is based on that in Cyril Mango, ed. *The Homilies of Photius Patriarch of Constantinople* (Cambridge, MA: Harvard University Press, 1958), 290.

In Byzantine visuality, these religious images were rendered lifelike in the space between an icon and the faithful's gaze.[73] The interaction between viewer and image also had emotional significance. Indeed, according to the fourteenth-century assessment of Manuel Philes, an achievement of Byzantine art was to 'represent in material form the emotions of the spirit'.[74] Therefore, the 'beautiful spectacle' of the Virgin in Hagia Sophia that Photios described was an icon that sought to transform the faithful from spectators into participants during the sacred performance unfolding before them, inviting human emotions to become liturgical emotions.[75]

The faithful themselves were portrayed as icons in this performance by a central hymn of the Divine Liturgy. The *Cheroubikon*, which accompanied the processional entry with the Holy Gifts in sixth-century Byzantium, begins thus:

Οἱ τὰ Χερουβεὶμ μυστικῶς εἰκονίζοντες, καὶ τῇ ζωοποιῷ Τριάδι τὸν τρισάγιον ὕμνον προσᾴδοντες . . .[76]

We who in a mystery represent the Cherubim and sing the thrice-holy hymn to the life-giving Trinity . . .[77]

However, the translation could also be: 'We who in this mystery are icons of the Cherubim', which has profound implications:

An icon, as already noted, is much more than a bare copy or exterior imitation; it implies participation, and so if the earthly worshippers are 'icons of the cherubim', this means that they share directly in what the cherubim are doing in heaven.[78]

It is important to continue here the discussion that began in the previous chapter on the Byzantine notion of performativity, since it is in this

---

[73] Robert S. Nelson, 'To Say and to See: Ekphrasis and Vision in Byzantium', in *Visuality before and beyond the Renaissance: Seeing as Others Saw*, ed. Robert S. Nelson (Cambridge: Cambridge University Press, 2000), 144.

[74] *Manuelis Philae Carmina*, quoted in Henry Maguire, *Art and Eloquence in Byzantium* (Princeton, NJ: Princeton University Press, 1981), 91.

[75] On the Byzantine notion of visuality and bridging the gap between iconography and the divine, see Roland Betancourt, 'Tempted to Touch: Tactility, Ritual, and Mediation in Byzantine Visuality', *Speculum* 91, no. 3 (2016): 660–89.

[76] *The Divine Liturgy*, 22. On the history and performance of the *Cheroubikon* in Hagia Sophia, see Robert F. Taft, *The Great Entrance: A History of the Transfer of Gifts and Other Preanaphoral Rites of the Liturgy of St John Chrysostom*, OCA 200 (Rome: Pontificium Institutum Orientalium Studiorum, 1978), 53–89; Moran, 'The Choir of Hagia Sophia', 3–6. The twelfth-century historian George Kedrenos suggests Justin II introduced the singing of the *Cheroubikon* during the Great Entrance in 573/4. See I. Bekker, ed. *Georgius Cedrenus, Ioannis Scylitzae Ope* (Bonn: Weber, 1838), 685 (lines 3–4).

[77] *The Divine Liturgy*, 21.   [78] Ware, 'The Meaning of the Divine Liturgy', 11.

liturgical context that the performative dimension of hymns emerges as a phenomenon connected to the sacred rite of the Eucharist. The sacramental meaning of τελείωσις, which usually means perfection or sanctification, is also associated with the eucharistic mystery: the 'consecration of elements [bread and wine]' or the Eucharist as the 'consummation of other sacraments'.[79] The verbal form of this word – τελειόω – means to 'perform'.[80] Thus, the performance of sacred hymns in Byzantium was not simply a theatrical event, but an initiation into divine things and the enactment of 'the final mystery'.[81] And it was not simply the clergy but also the faithful that played an intrinsic role in the performance of this mystery.

The faithful were not only icons in this mystery but also participants in the sonic environment of worship. Emperor Justinian fastidiously regulated the order of Hagia Sophia. He fixed the number of people that officiated there at '60 presbyters, 100 deacons, 40 deaconesses, 90 subdeacons, 110 lectors, and 25 cantors'.[82] The singers were 'an elite vocal ensemble' including 'soloists, some of whom were high-voiced eunuchs'.[83] During the performance of simpler choral chants in Hagia Sophia and in other churches of Constantinople, the faithful were able to participate in sacred hymns through refrains, which transformed listeners into singers.[84] Although 'the surviving manuscripts containing texts sung in the rite of Hagia Sophia postdate the traumas of Iconoclasm', codices from the last centuries of Byzantium 'faithfully preserve archaic patterns of call and response' that emerged 'a millennium ago to facilitate congregational participation in Late Antiquity'.[85] These patterns demand the participation of the clergy, choirs, soloists and readers, who would lead the congregation or sing on their behalf.[86] However, the sonic architecture of Hagia Sophia could also invite the faithful to experience divine presence through the amazing reverberation engendered by the spherical dome and the ambo in the centre of the church, which the cantors would climb upon to perform sacred songs. The building of Hagia Sophia 'acts like a musical instrument' that combines choral song and sonic architecture to create 'an

---

[79] Lampe, *Patristic Greek Lexicon*, 1383–84. On icons and τελείωσις, see Pentcheva, *The Sensual Icon*, 2–3, 40, 64–65, 128, 189–91.

[80] Lampe, *Patristic Greek Lexicon*, 1382.

[81] The fourteenth-century *Life in Christ* by Nicholas Cabasilas described the Divine Liturgy as 'the final mystery' since beyond this mystery 'it is not possible to go, nor can anything be added to it'. PG 150, 548B. Quoted in Ware, 'The Meaning of the Divine Liturgy', 7.

[82] Novella 6, cited in Taft, *Through Their Own Eyes*, 57.   [83] Lingas, 'From Earth to Heaven', 320.

[84] Arentzen, *The Virgin in Song*, 13.   [85] Lingas, 'From Earth to Heaven', 321–22.

[86] Ibid., 322.

enveloping and immersive sound field' of reverberation and harmonics, which culminates in an 'acoustic waterfall' for the faithful.[87] Of course, this raises the question of whether the words of hymns were rendered unintelligible:

> Singing there, on the ambo, would likely have allowed the voices to spread out with some additional amplification from the reverberation in the church, with the drawback of excessive reverberation time: the intelligibility of the words (especially in music) would suffer were an utterance to collide with previous echoes still bouncing around the space.[88]

Although this sonic phenomenon that combined 'human chant' with 'cosmic sound' would have created an awe-inspiring experience that engendered divine presence,[89] the cavern beneath the ambo of Hagia Sophia was often used by the cantors to 'minimize the effects of reverberation' so that it was 'easier for the congregation to hear the singers' and understand the songs.[90] However, the superabundance and significance of Hagia Sophia was difficult to diminish. As Prokopios' description of Hagia Sophia attests, the dome of the church that Justinian's builder-scientists – Isidoros of Miletos and Anthemios of Tralles – constructed does not 'rest upon solid masonry' but covers the interior space 'with its golden chain suspended from Heaven' (τῇ σειρᾷ τῇ χρυσῇ ἀπὸ τοῦ οὐρανοῦ), uniting not only the earthly with the heavenly but the Homeric, Neoplatonic and Christian 'chain of being that connected all levels of reality'.[91]

Byzantine Christianity understood well the ontology of music and its emotive power. While it may be possible to reimagine part of the emotive universe of Byzantium and its sacred soundscapes, how music shaped feeling, 'the question of *why* music arouses emotions', ultimately remains as much a mystery in the modern world as it would have in the Byzantine world, which followed classical Greek philosophy in viewing sacred music as mediating the divine mystery of cosmic harmony.[92] Even today, if we were to conduct a listening experiment which manipulated a piece of music to activate mechanisms such as brain stem reflex, emotional contagion, episodic memory and musical expectancy, we would only acquire a physiological or neurological understanding of how music

---

[87] Pentcheva, 'Performing the Sacred', 125.   [88] Papalexandrou, 'Perceptions of Sound', 72.

[89] Pentcheva, 'Performing the Sacred', 126–27.   [90] Papalexandrou, 'Perceptions of Sound', 73.

[91] Anthony Kaldellis, 'The Making of Hagia Sophia and the Last Pagans of New Rome', *Journal of Late Antiquity* 6, no. 2 (2013): 364–65. The passage by Prokopios quoted in Kaldellis' article is from *Buildings* 1.1.46.

[92] Patrik N. Juslin, László Harmat and Tuomas Eerol, 'What Makes Music Emotionally Significant? Exploring the Underlying Mechanisms', *Psychology of Music* 42, no. 4 (2014): 600.

influences feelings.[93] After all, sacred music was portrayed as a sonic phenomenon that engendered the sacred and, together with the materiality and lightscape of Hagia Sophia, as well as the smell of incense and the taste of the Eucharist, enacted the Incarnation of the Logos.

Liturgical Commentaries

Although the subject of Byzantine liturgical commentaries is an abundant field of study that this chapter cannot adequately explore, these commentaries are a rich source of information on how Christianity experienced sacred song and how the liturgy shaped emotions in Byzantium.[94] They also illustrate the eschatological character of liturgical events, which is a catalyst for compunction in the hymnography this book examines. Therefore, the late fifth-, early sixth-century *Ecclesiastical Hierarchy* of Dionysius the Areopagite (and relevant sections of the *Celestial Hierarchy*), the seventh-century *On Ecclesiastical Mystagogy* of Maximus the Confessor and the eighth-century *Ecclesiastical History and Mystical Contemplation* of Germanos of Constantinople will be briefly explored with these specific purposes in mind. While these are not the only commentaries that were written in Byzantium, they are the most relevant ones for the liturgical performance of the hymns by Romanos the Melodist, Andrew of Crete and Kassia during the Middle Byzantine period (sixth to eleventh centuries). These liturgical commentaries are coextensive in time with these three hymnographers. Moreover, Germanos' commentary was an influential and popular work in Byzantium for many centuries.[95]

Dionysius the Areopagite's *Ecclesiastical Hierarchy* is an early commentary on the liturgical rites of Christianity and its sacramental theology.[96] However, it is often divorced from Dionysius' *Celestial Hierarchy*, which is

---

[93] Ibid., 601. See also Nicolas Lossky, *Essai sur une théologie de la musique liturgique* (Paris: Éditions du Cerf, 2003), 49–68; Harrison, 'Enchanting the Soul', 205–24; Dimitri E. Conomos, 'C. S. Lewis and Church Music', in *Rightly Dividing the Word of Truth: Studies in Honour of Metropolitan Kallistos of Diokleia*, ed. Andreas Andreopoulos and Graham Speake (Oxford: Peter Lang, 2016), 213–34.

[94] For a systematic exploration of these liturgical commentaries, see René Bornert, *Les commentaires byzantins de la Divine Liturgie du VIIᵉ au XVᵉ siècle* (Paris: Institut Français d'Études Byzantines, 1966).

[95] Over sixty manuscripts preserve Germanos' liturgical commentary – more than any other Byzantine commentary on the liturgy. Indeed, 'the *Historia* represents the most prevalent and widespread understanding of a church building in Byzantium'. See Vasileios Marinis, 'The *Historia Ekklesiastike kai Mystike Theoria*: A Symbolic Understanding of the Byzantine Church Building', *BZ* 108, no. 2 (2015): 754.

[96] The critical edition of the Greek text is in Heil and Ritter, *Corpus Dionysiacum*, 61–132. For an introduction to the mystagogy of Dionysius the Areopagite, as well as the ecclesial and scholarly

usually assigned to the 'Christian Neoplatonism' section of scholarly bibliographies. Nevertheless, Dionysius does not suggest that these two hierarchies – earthly and heavenly – are divorced from each other; the author presents them as two aspects of the same hierarchy.[97] This hierarchy is none other than the creation of God and, according to Dionysius, extends beyond the visible world into the celestial world but remains a single community bound by divine providence. And it is here that the eschatological dimension in the Areopagite's thought emerges. The hierarchy of Dionysius 'is the gift of the Incarnation and the anticipation of the eschaton' – it is 'the present reality of the world which is', but it is also an icon of the world that is to come.[98]

Amidst the various details of the rites of initiation, the sacraments and the eucharistic gathering that Dionysius provides in the *Ecclesiastical Hierarchy*, there is an important passage on sacred song, which suggests that the sensual appearance of holy ritual invites the faithful to 'gaze into its more divine beauty' (εἰς τὸ θειότερον αὐτῆς ἀποβλέψωμεν κάλλος).[99] Indeed, 'psalmody and reading of Scripture' are not simply a recitation of biblical texts:

τοὺς δὲ πρὸς τὸ εἶναι παναγνοὺς ἐνδεεῖς τελέως ἀποκαθαίρουσιν, τοὺς δὲ ἱεροὺς ἄγουσιν ἐπὶ τὰς θείας εἰκόνας καὶ ἐποψίας αὐτῶν καὶ κοινωνίας, ἑστιῶσι δὲ τοὺς πανιέρους ἐν μακαρίοις καὶ νοητοῖς θεάμασιν ἀποπληροῦσαι τὸ ἑνοειδὲς αὐτῶν τοῦ ἑνὸς καὶ ἑνοποιοῦσαι.[100]

they perfectly purify those in need to be completely pure, lead those who are sacred to the divine images and their vision and communion, and establish those who are altogether holy, filling them and unifying their likeness to the One with blessed and intelligible spectacles.[101]

According to Dionysius, the performativity of the liturgical word of Christianity does not simply reflect the heavenly liturgy; it unites these

reception of the *Corpus Areopagiticum*, see Alexander Golitzin, *Mystagogy: A Monastic Reading of Dionysius Areopagita*, ed. Bogdan G. Bucur (Collegeville, MN: Liturgical Press, 2013), xix–xxxviii, 1–58; Louth, *Denys the Areopagite*, 17–32; Jaroslav Pelikan, 'The Odyssey of Dionysian Spirituality', in *Pseudo-Dionysius: The Complete Works*, ed. Colm Luibhéid and Paul Rorem (New York, NY: Paulist Press, 1987), 11–24.

[97] Andreas Andreopoulos, 'Mystical and Apophatic, Beyond Philosophical: A Defence of the Liturgical Reading of the Corpus Areopagiticum', paper presented at the *Seventeenth International Conference on Patristic Studies* (Oxford, 2015).

[98] Golitzin, *Mystagogy*, 220.

[99] *Ecclesiastical Hierarchy* 4.3.2 in Heil and Ritter, *Corpus Dionysiacum*, 97; Luibhéid and Rorem, *Pseudo-Dionysius*, 226.

[100] *Ecclesiastical Hierarchy* 4.3.3 in Heil and Ritter, *Corpus Dionysiacum*, 97–98.

[101] The English translation is based on the one in Luibhéid and Rorem, *Pseudo-Dionysius*, 227–28.

two realms. This is particularly apparent in the link between earthly and
angelic chant:

Διὸ καὶ ὕμνους αὐτῆς ἡ θεολογία τοῖς ἐπὶ γῆς παραδέδωκεν ἐν οἷς ἱερῶς
ἀναφαίνεται τὸ τῆς ὑπερτάτης αὐτῆς ἐλλάμψεως ὑπερέχον.[102]

Wherefore theology has transmitted to those on earth the hymns sung by
the first rank of angels whose gloriously transcendent enlightenment is
thereby made manifest.[103]

Dionysius is referring to the mystical dimension of music employed in
worship. As we saw earlier in this chapter, the sonic environment of Hagia
Sophia could enrich and amplify liturgical song in such a way that it
echoed the hymns of the angels. Dionysius likens these divine hymns to
the 'sound of many waters' proclaiming the glory of God but, unfortu-
nately, his treatise *Concerning the Divine Hymns*, which explicates 'the
supreme hymns sung by those angels that dwell beyond heaven' (τὰς
ὑπερτάτας τῶν ὑπερουρανίων νοῶν ὑμνολογίας), is not one of his extant
works.[104]

Liturgical song is not the only link between earthly and heavenly
worship. According to Dionysius, the liturgical world of Byzantium
was a multisensory mystagogy that activated the sensorium, aroused
emotions and invited the mind to experience divine realities through
phenomena:

ἐπεὶ μηδὲ δυνατόν ἐστι τῷ καθ' ἡμᾶς νοῖ πρὸς τὴν ἄϋλον ἐκείνην ἀνα-
ταθῆναι τῶν οὐρανίων ἱεραρχιῶν μίμησίν τε καὶ θεωρίαν, εἰ μὴ τῇ κατ'
αὐτὸν ὑλαίᾳ χειραγωγίᾳ χρήσαιτο τὰ μὲν φαινόμενα κάλλη τῆς ἀφανοῦς
εὐπρεπείας ἀπεικονίσματα λογιζόμενος καὶ τὰς αἰσθητὰς εὐωδίας ἐκτυπώ-
ματα τῆς νοητῆς διαδόσεως καὶ τῆς ἀΰλου φωτοδοσίας εἰκόνα τὰ ὑλικὰ
φῶτα καὶ τῆς κατὰ νοῦν θεωρητικῆς ἀποπληρώσεως τὰς διεξοδικὰς ἱερὰς
μαθητείας καὶ τῆς ἐναρμονίου πρὸς τὰ θεῖα καὶ τεταγμένης ἕξεως τὰς τῶν
ἐνθάδε διακοσμήσεων τάξεις καὶ τῆς Ἰησοῦ μετουσίας τὴν τῆς θειοτάτης
εὐχαριστίας μετάληψιν, καὶ ὅσα ἄλλα ταῖς οὐρανίαις μὲν οὐσίαις ὑπερκοσ-
μίως, ἡμῖν δὲ συμβολικῶς παραδέδοται.[105]

---

[102] *Celestial Hierarchy* 7.4 in Heil and Ritter, *Corpus Dionysiacum*, 31. Chapter 7 is where Dionysius
writes about the first rank of angels: the seraphim, cherubim and thrones.

[103] The English translation is based on Luibhéid and Rorem, *Pseudo-Dionysius*, 165. Although the
Greek text does not explicitly mention the first rank of angels, this is the context of Dionysius'
exposition.

[104] Ibid. While the treatise *Concerning the Divine Hymns* is lost, Dionysius briefly alludes to this text in
his *Celestial Hierarchy* when he talks about the divine hymns of the angels.

[105] *Celestial Hierarchy* 1.3 in Heil and Ritter, *Corpus Dionysiacum*, 8–9.

since it is not even possible for our mind to be lifted up towards that immaterial imitation and contemplation of the heavenly hierarchies, unless it were to use the corporeal guidance that our nature requires, reckoning the beautiful phenomena as representations of the invisible comeliness, the sensible fragrances as patterns of the intelligible distribution, the material lights as an image of the immaterial illumination, the sacred and diffuse discipleship as the mind's contemplative plenitude, the arrangements of orders here below as the harmonious *habitus* that is ordered toward divine things, the participation of the most divine Eucharist as the participation in Jesus. And so it goes for all the spiritual essences, which are symbolically imparted to us in a heavenly manner.[106]

Dionysius' description of this Christian *habitus* presents the liturgical world of Byzantium as the nexus of the earthly and heavenly realms. It is a sacred space of symbols – probably icons, incense and candles – that enact divine presence.[107] According to Dionysius, it is during the liturgical events that take place in this sacred *habitus* that the materiality of earthly worship and the heavenly world of the angelic liturgy are united in the hearts of the faithful.

Dionysius' thinking on the liturgical world of Byzantium has implications for the emotions.[108] According to Dionysius' logic and his vision of a unified ecclesiastical and celestial hierarchy, the mystagogy of the liturgy grafts human emotion upon a transcendent realm of feeling. Dionysius' view of emotions reflects the more positive of the 'two currents in Christian ascetic literature' during his time.[109] While human freedom from the power of emotions was the goal of Christian asceticism, the Evagrian tradition saw this struggle as a suppression of emotion and did not regard asceticism as a transformation of emotions. Within Dionysius' liturgical framework, human emotions could become liturgical emotions by participating in the grace of the celestial hierarchy: 'for if such feelings have meaning in the transcendent realm, that sublimation is presumably the goal for our ascetic endeavour here below'.[110]

---

[106] My English translation is based on Luibhéid and Rorem, *Pseudo-Dionysius*, 146.

[107] Although it is uncertain whether the liturgical use of icons, incense and candles was prevalent in Dionysius' time (late fifth to early sixth century), the above passage from his *Celestial Hierarchy* is suggestive of such objects being used in churches. On icons, see the discussion of how domestic spaces were the loci in which icons were first adopted for Christian use in Thomas F. Mathews, *The Clash of Gods: A Reinterpretation of Early Christian Art* (Princeton, NJ: Princeton University Press, 1999), 177–90.

[108] Louth, *Denys the Areopagite*, 46.

[109] Ibid. See also Ware, 'The Meaning of "Pathos"', 315–22; Blowers, 'Hope for the Passible Self', 216–29.

[110] Louth, *Denys the Areopagite*, 46.

The overarching narrative of Dionysius' liturgical framework is the biblical story of salvation. The liturgy enacts the sacred works of God throughout salvation history:[111]

Καὶ τὰς ἱερὰς θεουργίας ὁ ἱεράρχης ὑμνήσας ἱερουργεῖ τὰ θειότατα καὶ ὑπ' ὄψιν ἄγει τὰ ὑμνημένα διὰ τῶν ἱερῶς προκειμένων συμβόλων, καὶ τὰς δωρεὰς τῶν θεουργιῶν ὑποδείξας εἰς κοινωνίαν αὐτῶν ἱερὰν αὐτός τε ἔρχεται καὶ τοὺς ἄλλους προτρέπεται.[112]

And the hierarch, having hymned the sacred divine acts, celebrates the most divine acts and brings to view the things praised through the symbols sacredly displayed. And having shown the gifts of the divine acts, he himself comes into sacred communion with them, and exhorts [the faithful] to follow him.[113]

These 'divine acts' celebrated in the liturgy that Dionysius speaks of are 'the acts of God in creation and redemption culminating in the Incarnation', which are recounted in the earliest eucharistic prayers of Byzantium.[114] And it is these divine acts of God in human history that are performed in the liturgy and which have a transformative effect on the faithful, including their emotions.

In many ways, Maximus the Confessor's seventh-century liturgical commentary, *On Ecclesiastical Mystagogy*, echoed the mystagogy of Dionysius. Maximus suggested that the 'entrance of the holy mysteries' (τῆς εἰσόδου τῶν ἁγίων μυστηρίων) during the liturgy leads the faithful 'to the vision of spiritual things' (πρὸς τὴν τῶν νοητῶν ἐποψίαν).[115] Mystagogy was not simply the acquisition of supernatural knowledge but a participation in a mystery that transformed the faithful. Through the 'spiritual delight of the divine songs' (πνευματικὴν τῶν θείων ἀσμάτων

---

[111] Although I acknowledge that 'salvation history' is not a phrase that appears in Byzantine hymnography or in the Greek patristic sources, I employ this term to signify how liturgy and hymnody enacted the biblical story of salvation. See Meyendorff, *Byzantine Theology*, 123; Robert F. Taft, *The Byzantine Rite: A Short History* (Collegeville, MN: The Liturgical Press, 1992), 46; Krueger, *Liturgical Subjects*, 107. However, I note that Byzantine Christianity followed Apostle Paul and the early church fathers in conceiving of the history of salvation not in a linear sense but as intrinsically linked to the notion of divine economy and the mystery of Christ's salvific act on the cross. See John Behr, *The Mystery of Christ: Life in Death* (Crestwood, NY: St Vladimir's Seminary Press, 2006); *Irenaeus of Lyons: Identifying Christianity* (Oxford: Oxford University Press, 2013), 185–203.

[112] *Ecclesiastical Hierarchy* 3.2 in Heil and Ritter, *Corpus Dionysiacum*, 81.

[113] The translation is based on Luibhéid and Rorem, *Pseudo-Dionysius*, 211.

[114] Andrew Louth, 'Pagan Theurgy and Christian Sacramentalism in Denys the Areopagite', *Journal of Theological Studies* 37, no. 2 (1986): 435.

[115] *On Ecclesiastical Mystagogy*, chapter 13. For the Greek text, see Boudignon, *Maximi Confessoris Mystagogia*, 42. For the English translation, see Berthold, *Maximus Confessor*, 200.

τερπνότητα), the faithful became part of this mystagogy and were 'moved toward the unfading and blessed love of God' (πρὸς μὲν τὸν ἀκήρατον τοῦ Θεοῦ καὶ μακάριον ἀνακινοῦσαν ἔρωτα).[116] Although Maximus continued Dionysius' redemptive view of human passion, presenting the liturgy as a sacred space that transformed emotions, there is a strong eschatological scheme in Maximus' commentary.[117]

Indeed, eschatology for Maximus was not simply a future occurrence but a present reality commemorated in the Eucharist and experienced in the polytemporal vision of the liturgy.[118] The performance of the liturgy enacted the eschaton, collapsing past, present and future into liturgical time.[119] While the beginning of the liturgy signified the birth of Christ and the Little Entrance his crucifixion, resurrection and ascension, the proclamation of the Gospel marked the end of history and all that followed took place in the age to come.[120] To underscore this eschatological view of liturgical life, Maximus compared the unity of the liturgical community of the faithful with the mystical unity of the Holy Trinity. According to Maximus, the church reflects the mystery of the Trinity and the liturgical unity of the faithful is an icon of the ineffable unity of God.[121] This unity was not restricted to the earthly – it extended to the heavenly:

Ὅλος γὰρ ὁ νοητὸς κόσμος ὅλῳ τῷ αἰσθητῷ μυστικῶς τοῖς συμβολικοῖς εἴδεσι τυπούμενος φαίνεταιντοῖς ὁρᾶν δυναμένοις· καὶ ὅλος ὅλῳ τῷ νοητῷ ὁ αἰσθητὸς γνωστικῶς κατὰ νοῦν τοῖς λόγοις ἁπλούμενος ἐνυπάρχων ἐστίν.[122]

For the whole of the spiritual world appears mystically imprinted on the whole sensible world in symbolic forms, for those who are capable of seeing this, and conversely the whole sensible world is spiritually explained in the mind in the principles which it contains.[123]

---

[116] On Ecclesiastical Mystagogy, chapter 11, Boudignon, Maximi Confessoris Mystagogia, 40; Berthold, Maximus Confessor, 199.

[117] On Ecclesiastical Mystagogy, chapter 24, Boudignon, Maximi Confessoris Mystagogia, 55–71; Berthold, Maximus Confessor, 206–13.

[118] Meyendorff, Byzantine Theology, 218–20; Taft, Through Their Own Eyes, 156–58.

[119] See Andrew Louth, 'The Ecclesiology of Saint Maximus the Confessor', International Journal for the Study of the Christian Church 4, no. 2 (2004): 109–20; Derek Krueger, 'Liturgical Time and Holy Land Reliquaries in Early Byzantium', in Saints and Sacred Matter: The Cult of Relics in Byzantium and Beyond, ed. Cynthia Hahn and Holger A. Klein (Washington, DC: Dumbarton Oaks Research Library and Collection, 2015), 118–24.

[120] Ware, 'The Meaning of the Divine Liturgy', 20; Louth, 'The Ecclesiology of Saint Maximus', 114.

[121] On Ecclesiastical Mystagogy, chapter 1. Boudignon, Maximi Confessoris Mystagogia, 11; Berthold, Maximus Confessor, 177–78.

[122] On Ecclesiastical Mystagogy, chapter 2. Maximi Confessoris Mystagogia, 16.

[123] Berthold, Maximus Confessor, 189.

The Byzantine liturgical world was conceived as a sacred space of symbols that revealed divine realities and through which the intellect could apprehend the spiritual significance embedded in the sensible world. According to Maximus, body and mind played an intrinsic role in this liturgical event. The human person was presented as 'a mystical church' in which the nave was the body and the soul was the sanctuary:

> ὡς δι' ἱερατείου δὲ τῆς ψυχῆς τοὺς κατ' αἴσθησιν λόγους καθαρῶς ἐν πνεύματι τῆς ὕλης περιτμηθέντας κατὰ τὴν φυσικὴν θεωρίαν διὰ λόγου τῷ Θεῷ προσκομίζοντα, καὶ ὡς διὰ θυσιαστηρίου τοῦ νοός, τὴν ἐν ἀδύτοις πολυύμνητον τῆς ἀφανοῦς καὶ ἀγνώστου μεγαλοφωνίας σιγὴν τῆς θεότητος δι' ἄλλης λάλου τε καὶ πολυφθόγγου σιγῆς προσκαλούμενον, καὶ ὡς ἐφικτὸν ἀνθρώπῳ κατὰ μυστικὴν θεολογίαν αὐτῇ συγγινόμενον, καὶ τοιοῦτον γινόμενον οἷον εἰκὸς εἶναι δεῖ τὸν ἐπιδημίας ἀξιωθέντα Θεοῦ, καὶ ταῖς αὐτοῦ παμφαέσιν αἴγλαις ἐνσημανθέντα.[124]

> Through the sanctuary of his soul he conveys to God the principles of sense perception, purely in spirit, cut off from matter, according to natural contemplation through reason. Finally, through the altar of the mind he summons the silence abounding in song in the innermost recesses of the unseen and unknown utterance of divinity by another silence rich in speech and tone. And as far as is possible for the human person, he dwells familiarly within mystical theology and becomes theology as is fitting for one made worthy of his indwelling and he is marked with his dazzling splendour.[125]

For Maximus, the personal and liturgical dimensions of worship intersect in the performance of the eucharistic mystery, which can transform the human person into theology itself. As part of this transformation, liturgical song sought to arouse blessed emotions that could awaken the mind and move the soul toward divine passion.[126]

The relationship between cognition and emotion portrayed here can be a bewildering one for the modern world. Although the Byzantines inherited ancient Greek concepts of the mind or intellect (νοῦς), viewing it as the highest function of the soul (ψυχή) – in contrast to the Stoic idea of emotions as an irrational movement of the soul – it was unclear whether the mind was distinct from the soul.[127] According to the Byzantine

---

[124] *On Ecclesiastical Mystagogy*, chapter 4. Boudignon, *Maximi Confessoris Mystagogia*, 19.

[125] The English translation is based on Berthold, *Maximus Confessor*, 190.

[126] See especially chapter 11. Boudignon, *Maximi Confessoris Mystagogia*, 40; Berthold, *Maximus Confessor*, 199.

[127] On the abiding influence of Stoicism on early Christianity, see Sorabji, *Emotion and Peace of Mind*, 343–400.

spiritual literature that was assembled in the eighteenth-century anthology known as the *Philokalia*, the intellect dwells in the depths of the soul and is the eye of the heart.[128] The heart was not merely a physical organ but the nexus of mind, body and soul.[129] It was 'the first rational organ of the body' where 'the mind and all the thoughts of the soul are to be found'.[130] This understanding of the heart also emerged in a liturgical context, where sacred drama was not simply intellectual worship but entreated the faithful to 'bend the knee of the heart'.[131]

As the next three chapters will show, Byzantine hymns portrayed blessed passions as a movement of the soul that embraced the body and escorted the mind. Here it is important to underscore that, for Maximus, the transformation of human emotion into liturgical emotion occurs not simply through asceticism but 'within a sacramental framework'.[132] And, as was noted earlier, the overarching narrative of this liturgical framework is biblical. However, this detail is sometimes lost in the rich eschatology of Maximus' commentary. It is only with the liturgical commentary of Germanos of Constantinople that a synthesis of the allegorical and the historical methods of interpreting the Divine Liturgy was accomplished.[133] Germanos saw 'multiple layers of meaning' in each element of the liturgy, holding 'historical and allegorical meanings in complex tension' and 'refusing to allow one to eclipse the other'.[134]

For Germanos the church is not only heaven on earth but the sacred space where the crucifixion and resurrection of Christ are enacted. The opening chapter of his *Ecclesiastical History and Mystical Contemplation* engages a complex array of ecclesiastical symbols and scriptural allusions:

---

[128] Palmer, Sherrard and Ware, trans. *The Philokalia: The Complete Text.*

[129] See Meyendorff, *Byzantine Theology*, 69–72; Bradshaw, 'The Mind and the Heart', 576–98.

[130] Gregory Palamas, *Triads in Defence of the Holy Hesychasts* I, 2.3 in John Meyendorff, trans. *Gregory Palamas: The Triads* (New York, NY: Paulist Press, 1983), 43.

[131] From the seventh ode of the *kanon* that accompanies the *Akathist Hymn* in the *Triodion*. Ware and Mother Mary, *The Lenten Triodion*, 440. For the Greek text of the *kanon*, see PG 105, 1020–28.

[132] Demetrios Bathrellos, 'Passions, Ascesis and the Virtues', in *The Oxford Handbook of Maximus the Confessor*, 304.

[133] Taft, 'Commentaries', in *ODB*, 488–89. I acknowledge there is still some debate over the authorship of the *Ecclesiastical History and Mystical Contemplation*. See Alexander P. Kazhdan, 'Germanos I', in *ODB*, 846. See also Andrew Louth, 'Mystagogy in Saint Maximus', in *Seeing Through the Eyes of Faith: New Approaches to the Mystagogy of the Church Fathers*, ed. Paul Van Geest (Leuven: Peeters, 2016), 376; Kallistos Ware, 'Symbolism in the Liturgical Commentary of St Germanos of Constantinople', in ibid., 424–25.

[134] Georgia Frank, 'Romanos and the Night Vigil in the Sixth Century', in *Byzantine Christianity: A People's History of Christianity*, ed. Derek Krueger (Minneapolis, MN: Fortress Press, 2006), 77.

Ἐκκλησία ἐστὶ ναὸς Θεοῦ, τέμενος ἅγιον, οἶκος προσευχῆς, συνάθροισις λαοῦ, σῶμα Χριστοῦ· ὄνομα αὐτῆς νύμφη Χριστοῦ· τῷ ὕδατι τοῦ βαπτίσματος αὐτοῦ καθαρθεῖσα, καὶ τῷ αἵματι ραντισθεῖσα τῷ αὐτοῦ καὶ νυμφικῶς ἐστολισμένη, καὶ τῷ τοῦ ἁγίου Πνεύματος μύρῳ σφραγιζομένη κατὰ τὸν προφητικὸν λόγον· «μύρον ἐκκενωθὲν ὄνομά σοι» καὶ «εἰς ὀσμὴν μύρου σου δραμοῦμεν», ὅτι «ὡς μύρον ἐπὶ κεφαλῆς τὸ καταβαῖνον ἐπὶ πώγωνα, τὸν Ἀαρών».

Ἐκκλησία ἐστὶν ἐπίγειος οὐρανός, ἐν ᾧ ὁ ἐπουράνιος Θεὸς ἐνοικεῖ καὶ ἐμπεριπατεῖ, ἀντιτυποῦσα τὴν σταύρωσιν καὶ τὴν ταφὴν καὶ τὴν ἀνάστασιν Χριστοῦ· δεδοξασμένη ὑπὲρ τὴν σκηνὴν τοῦ μαρτυρίου Μωσέως, ἐν ᾗ τὸ ἱλαστήριον καὶ τὰ Ἅγια τῶν Ἁγίων.[135]

The church is the temple of God, a holy place, a house of prayer, a gathering of people, the body of Christ. It is called the bride of Christ. It is cleansed by the water of his baptism, sprinkled with his blood, adorned like a bride, and sealed with sweet oil of the Holy Spirit according to the prophetic saying: 'Your name is perfume poured out' [Song of Songs 1:3] and 'we run after the fragrance of your myrrh' [Song 1:4], which is 'like the sweet oil, running down the beard, the beard of Aaron' [Psalm 132:2].

The church is an earthly heaven, where the heavenly God dwells and walks about. It represents symbolically the crucifixion, burial and resurrection of Christ. It is glorified more than Moses' tabernacle of witness, in which were the mercy seat and the Holy of Holies.[136]

Although Germanos does not preclude the Dionysian and Maximian proposition of the earthly liturgy embodying heavenly worship, he sees embedded in the church building the Passion of Christ, viewing the Eucharist as typifying Christ's earthly life. Moreover, Germanos identifies the church with the faithful, presenting the congregation as the bride of Christ and the Eucharist as the consummation of this mystical marriage. Drawing on the exegetical tradition of the Song of Songs, Germanos suggests the figures of the bride and bridegroom have personal, ecclesiastical, and even cosmological significance.

More than Dionysius the Areopagite and Maximus the Confessor, Germanos of Constantinople saw the liturgy as the realisation of salvation history. The image of Christ 'walk[ing] about' throughout the church building cited above, as well as subsequent allusions to the apse as 'the cave in Bethlehem where Christ was born'[137] and the holy table as 'the spot in the tomb where Christ was placed',[138] remedy the tendency of

---

[135] Paul Meyendorff, ed., *St Germanus of Constantinople on the Divine Liturgy* (Crestwood, NY: St Vladimir's Seminary Press, 1984), 56.
[136] The English translation is based on Meyendorff, ibid., 57.   [137] Chapter 3, ibid., 59.
[138] Chapter 4, ibid.

Dionysius and Maximus to marginalise to some extent the earthly ministry of Christ in favour of an eschatological theme that betokens a mystical ascent to heaven. For Germanos, when the choir and the faithful sang the Trisagion, it was an enactment of the angels singing 'Glory to God in the highest' during Christ's birth.[139] For Maximus, any aspect of salvation history that the Trisagion might represent is elided in favour of its mystical and eschatological significance.[140] The Trisagion invites the faithful to blend their voices with the heavenly choir of angels and manifests human nature's future state of bliss, where it will be taught to sing 'through harmony with the unchangeable ceaseless movement around God' (διὰ ταυτότητα τῆς ἀτρέπτου περὶ Θεὸν ἀεικινησίας).[141] In Germanos' commentary, the historical scheme of the liturgy is more prevalent than the eschatological scheme, so that through the 'remembrance of the history of Christ' in sacred ritual and the singing of 'the hymn of the angels', the faithful were able to feel their salvation unfold in the sacred space of the church.[142] However, this was not a remembrance that merely retold biblical stories as past events, it rendered them 'a present reality within the life of the Church' and invited the faithful to participate in what Byzantine liturgical commentators portrayed as a 're-presentation or re-actualization' of the salvific acts of Christ.[143]

In this regard, Germanos foreshadows one of the last liturgical commentators of Byzantium. While Nicholas Cabasilas' fourteenth-century *Commentary on the Divine Liturgy* was written several centuries later, the following excerpt from this commentary underscores the emotive power of sacred ritual and echoes the historical scheme in Germanos' own commentary:

Διὰ τοῦτο ἐχρῆν τὴν ταῦτα ἡμῖν ἐνθεῖναι δυναμένην θεωρίαν ἐν τῇ συντάξει τῆς ἱερουργίας σημαίνεσθαι, ἵνα μὴ τῷ νῷ λογιζώμεθα μόνον, ἀλλὰ καὶ βλέπωμεν τοῖς ὀφθαλμοῖς τρόπον δή τινα τὴν πολλὴν τοῦ πλουσίου πενίαν, τὴν ἐπιδημίαν τοῦ πάντα τόπον κατέχοντος, τὰ ὀνείδη τοῦ εὐλογημένου, τὰ πάθη τοῦ ἀπαθοῦς, ὅσον μισηθείς, ὅσον ἠγάπησεν· ἡλίκος ὢν, ὅσον ἐταπείνωσεν ἑαυτόν· καὶ τί παθὼν καὶ τί δράσας, ταύτην ἡτοίμασεν ἐνώπιον ἡμῶν τὴν τράπεζαν· καὶ οὕτω θαυμάσαντες τὴν καινότητα τῆς σωτηρίας, ἐκπλαγέντες τὸ πλῆθος τῶν οἰκτιρμῶν, αἰδεσθῶμεν

---

[139] Chapter 25, ibid., 75.   [140] See chapters 13 and 19 of *On Ecclesiastical Mystagogy*.
[141] Chapter 19 of *On Ecclesiastical Mystagogy* in Boudignon, *Maximi Confessoris Mystagogia*, 47. The English translation is my own.
[142] Pelikan, *The Spirit of Eastern Christendom*, 136.
[143] John Breck, *The Power of the Word: In the Worshiping Church* (Crestwood, NY: St Vladimir's Seminary Press, 1986), 123.

τὸν οὕτως ἐλεήσαντα, τὸν οὕτω σώσαντα καὶ πιστεύσωμεν αὐτῷ τὰς ψυχάς, καὶ παραθώμεθα τὴν ζωήν, καὶ φλέξωμεν τὰς καρδίας τῷ πυρὶ τῆς ἀγάπης αὐτοῦ· καὶ τοιοῦτοι γενόμενοι, τῷ πυρὶ τῶν μυστηρίων ὁμιλήσω-μεν ἀσφαλῶς καὶ οἰκείως.[144]

That is why it was necessary that holy works of this sort, capable of inspiring such feelings in us, should find a place in the ordering of the liturgy. It was necessary, not only that we should think about, but also that to some extent we should see the utter poverty of him who possesses all, the coming on earth of him who dwells everywhere, the shame of the blessed one, the passion of the impassible; that we should see how much he was hated and how much he loved; how great he was and how he humbled himself; what torments he endured, what he accomplished in order to prepare for us this table. Thus, in beholding the newness of salvation, amazed by the abundance of mercy, we are brought to venerate him who had such compassion for us, who saved us at so great a price: to entrust our souls to him, to dedicate our lives to him, to enkindle in our hearts the flame of his love.[145]

Cabasilas and Germanos did not portray liturgy as a spectacle or a *mysterium tremendum*; it was a shared action that sought to arouse a personal response to the divine drama of salvation from the faithful. However, as 'a symbolic drama, re-enacting in visible form the different stages of Christ's earthly life', this 'incarnational' interpretation of the liturgy did not preclude the 'eschatological scheme', which Maximus' *On Ecclesiastical Mystagogy* exemplified.[146] For the Byzantines, the liturgical enactment of salvation history rendered the eschaton 'proleptically present' as 'a transcendent reality' that passed through the boundaries of history to engender the transfiguration of the world.[147] As we will see in the next three chapters, the emotive power of the biblical narrative of salvation and the compunction that the eschaton could arouse were harnessed by hymnographers such as Romanos the Melodist, Andrew of Crete and Kassia.

Before turning to the notion of affective mysticism, it is worth noting the wide applicability of the liturgical commentaries by Dionysius, Maximus and Germanos. Although Germanos is probably describing the cathedral liturgy of Hagia Sophia and Maximus is likely commenting on the liturgy of Constantinople in a general way, the symbolic and mystical frameworks their commentaries establish do not collapse if they are applied

[144] Chapter 1, section 12 in René Bornert et al., eds., *Nicolas Cabasilas: Explication de la Divine Liturgie*, SC 4 (Paris: Éditions du Cerf, 1967), 66–68.

[145] My English translation is based on the one in Nicholas Cabasilas, *A Commentary on the Divine Liturgy*, trans. J. M. Hussey and P. A. McNulty (London: SPCK, 1977), 29.

[146] Ware, 'The Meaning of the Divine Liturgy', 20.   [147] Breck, *The Power of the Word*, 129.

to the performance of the Byzantine liturgy in other urban or monastic settings.[148] Germanos' commentary is 'part of a long exegetical tradition on the liturgy that disregards the functional aspects of church buildings' and relies on 'the adaptability of Byzantine liturgical rites'.[149] The somewhat vague descriptions of church buildings in these commentaries suggest that while cathedrals as magnificent as Hagia Sophia may have greatly enhanced the symbolism and mysticism of sacred ritual, the liturgy could be as effectively celebrated in a humble church as in a majestic cathedral. Therefore, while the hymns I will explore may have been performed in a variety of ecclesiastical settings throughout Constantinople and beyond, their liturgical significance was coloured by the commentaries of Dionysius, Maximus and Germanos.

Affective Mysticism

Although the mystical dimension of Christian worship is apparent from its very beginnings, the language of 'mystery' was often reserved for such things as the unknowability of God, the hidden mysteries of Scripture and theology itself.[150] Nevertheless, the Byzantine liturgical experience was also conceived as a mystery that escorted the faithful beyond an intellectual philosophy of God to a transformative encounter and mysterious communion between the human and the divine. This vision of the liturgy is apparent as early as the fifth-century *Ecclesiastical Hierarchy* of Dionysius the Areopagite, but it emerged even earlier in the writings of Gregory of Nyssa, who envisaged liturgical worship as a mystery replete with divine action – psalmody, memory and drama – and even in the last chapter of Clement the Alexandrian's *Exhortation to the Greeks*, which employed the terminology of mystery in relation to the process of Christian initiation.[151]

Modern scholars have employed the term 'affective mysticism' to describe the 'overtly emotional religiousness' that emerged in Western

---

[148] On Maximus' commentary, see Robert F. Taft, 'Is the Liturgy Described in the Mystagogia of Maximus Confessor Byzantine, Palestinian, or Neither?' *Bollettino della Badia Greca di Grottaferrata* 8 (2011): 223–70. On Germanos' commentary, see Taft's 'The Liturgy of the Great Church', 45–75.

[149] Marinis, 'The *Historia Ekklesiastike kai Mystike Theoria*', 753–70.

[150] See the definitions for μυστήριον in Lampe, *Patristic Greek Lexicon*, 891–93.

[151] Clement of Alexandria, *The Exhortation to the Greeks, the Rich Man's Salvation, and the Fragment of an Address Entitled to the Newly Baptised*, ed. and trans. G. W. Butterworth. Loeb Classical Library 92 (Cambridge, MA: Harvard University Press, 1960), 250–63. See also Jean Daniélou, 'Le mystère du culte dans les sermons de Saint Grégoire de Nysse', in *Vom Christlichen Mysterium*, ed. Anton Mayer and Johannes Quasten (Dusseldorf: Patmos-Verlag, 1951), 76.

Christianity in the twelfth century in relation to the Song of Songs.[152] Similarly, the literary genre of affective meditation on the Passion asked readers to place themselves in the midst of Jesus' suffering and feel compassion for the crucified Christ by internalising this divine drama. However, it is only half the story to suggest that such emotionalism was 'alien' to Orthodox Christianity.[153] The mysticism of Eastern Christianity should not be 'confused with the later western interest in subjective religious experience or in detailed itineraries for the spiritual journey'.[154] Emotions formed part of the desire for and experience of the divine mystery in Byzantium. However, they were transformed together with the whole of human nature in this mystical experience, which entailed repentance before the face of God.[155] Affective mysticism emerged as a 'metamorphosis of the passions' in commentaries on the Song of Songs by Origen in the third century and Gregory of Nyssa in the fourth century.[156] In this exegetical tradition, the Song was an allegory that exemplified the affective mysticism of the encounter between the human and the divine. In the New Testament, John the Evangelist and Paul the Apostle interpreted the ostensible eroticism in the nuptial imagery of the Song of Songs as the love of Christ (the bridegroom) for the Church (the bride).[157] However, Origen and Gregory of Nyssa went further than this interpretation. The passion of the lovers in the Song of Songs was not only the love between Christ and the Church; it was the love of Christ for the human person made in his image.[158]

Germanos' commentary on the performance of the liturgy followed this interpretation, portraying the church as the faithful in this nuptial metaphor. According to Germanos, it was the faithful who were Christ's beloved and it was the liturgy that sealed them with the sweet oil of the Holy Spirit,

---

[152] Herbert Moller, 'Affective Mysticism in Western Civilization', *Psychoanalytic Review* 52, no. 2 (1965): 116.

[153] Ibid.

[154] Philip Sheldrake, 'Mysticism: Critical Theological Perspectives', in *Blackwell Companion to Christian Mysticism*, ed. Julia Lamm (Oxford: Wiley-Blackwell, 2012), 535. See also Patricia Dailey, 'The Body and Its Senses', in *The Cambridge Companion to Christian Mysticism*, ed. Amy Hollywood and Patricia Z. Beckman (Cambridge: Cambridge University Press, 2012), 264–76.

[155] Vladimir Lossky, *Essai sur la théologie mystique de l'Église d'Orient* (Aubier: Éditions Montaigne, 1944), 237.

[156] Niklaus Largier, 'Medieval Mysticism', in *The Oxford Handbook of Religion and Emotion*, ed. John Corrigan (Oxford: Oxford University Press, 2008), 366.

[157] John 3:29; Ephesians 5:23–27.

[158] Origen, *The Song of Songs: Commentary and Homilies*, trans. R. P. Lawson (New York, NY: The Newman Press, 1957), 21; Gregory of Nyssa, *Homilies on the Song of Songs*, 399–411.

which the perfume poured out at the beginning of the Song of Songs prefigured. Not unlike how the sensuality of holy ritual invited the faithful to gaze into divine beauty, the performance of hymns sought to lead the faithful to what Gregory of Nyssa described as 'the divine and sober drunkenness', where there is no difference between the impassioned words of the Song of Songs and the 'mystagogic instruction given to [Christ's] disciples'.[159] Not unlike Gregory's interpretation of the Song of Songs, which moved from the sensual and corporeal to the spiritual and mystical, highlighting the affective interplay between human and divine, the performance of hymns wove together human and divine passion. In liturgical performance, the true realm of emotions was in the soul's ever-intensifying desire for Christ the bridegroom and such emotions could be felt when the yearning soul was 'surrounded by the divine night' and experienced the 'mystical kiss' of holy passion.[160] Through the ritual of liturgy, the faithful could 'inhabit the mythic space' of hymnography and 'play out the roles of the mythic drama'.[161] It was in this affective mysticism that human emotion could be transformed into divine emotion.

The affective mysticism of Byzantine hymns represented the potential for human feelings to become liturgical emotions in the mystagogy of the liturgy. In this sense, affective mystagogy is a more apt expression than affective mysticism. The mystical significance of the liturgy that Byzantine liturgical commentators explored is an important element of this experience. While these sophisticated liturgical commentaries may not have necessarily represented the popular understanding of the liturgical experience and its mystagogy, hymnody emerged as the performance of salvation that invited the Byzantine faithful to experience this mystery and transform their passions. Hymns created a space of participation for the faithful, 'an inner space of "experience", "exploration" and "amplification" of the emotional as well as sensory life of the soul'.[162] While hymns were not devoid of Christian dogma, they primarily dramatised the human encounter with the divine.

As we will see in the following chapters, Byzantine hymns presented the congregation with the words and song of those that had gone before them, so that with 'courage like Jacob', with the 'tears of the harlot', 'like the woman with the issue of blood', the faithful could cry: 'stretch out your

---

[159] Ibid., 325–27.   [160] Ibid., 193, 341.   [161] Arentzen, *The Virgin in Song*, 32.
[162] Niklaus Largier, 'Inner Senses–Outer Senses: The Practice of Emotions in Medieval Mysticism', in *Codierungen von Emotionen im Mittelalter/Emotions and Sensibilities in the Middle Ages*, ed. C. Stephen Jaeger and Ingrid Kasten (Berlin: De Gruyter, 2003), 5.

hand to me as once you did to Peter'.[163] In doing so, they invited the faithful to feel liturgically. One precondition for this to occur is the nature of the ecclesial community the liturgy was portrayed as engendering:

καθ' ἣν οὐδεὶς τὸ παράπαν οὐδὲν ἑαυτῷ τοῦ κοινοῦ διωρισμένος ἐστί, πάντων συμπεφυκότων ἀλλήλοις καὶ συνημμένων κατὰ τὴν μίαν ἁπλῆν τε καὶ ἀδιαίρετον τῆς πίστεως χάριν καὶ δύναμιν.[164]

absolutely no one at all is in himself separated from the community since everyone converges with all the rest and joins together with them by the one, simple and indivisible grace and power of faith.[165]

According to John Chrysostom, this 'body of the faithful is one' and 'is divided by neither time nor place'.[166] The other precondition for this to occur was the Incarnation, which 'taught [the flesh] to feel things beyond its nature' (τὰ ὑπὲρ φύσιν ἰδίαν διδασκομένη φρονεῖν) by uniting it to the divine in the person of Christ.[167] After all, patristic tradition attributed Christ's emotions not simply to his human nature but ascribed them to the one incarnate Logos, who 'suffered in the flesh, and was crucified in the flesh, and experienced death in the flesh'.[168] And, according to this tradition, what the Logos assumed, he also healed and transformed. It was in liturgical worship that this mystery could be felt and grasped.[169]

Great Lent and the *Triodion* as the Liturgical Framework for Compunction

While the origins of Great Lent as a period of fasting and prayer that mark the journey to Pascha have a history dating back to first centuries of Christianity, it was the liturgical reforms of the Monastery of Saint John the Forerunner at Stoudios in Constantinople in the early ninth century that were a watershed in the historical development of the *Triodion*, the

---

[163] These quotations are taken from various strophes of the *Great Kanon* in Ware and Mother Mary, *The Lenten Triodion*, 391, 381, 408, 391.

[164] *On Ecclesiastical Mystagogy*, chapter 1. Boudignon, *Maximi Confessoris Mystagogia*, 13.

[165] Berthold, *Maximus Confessor*, 187.

[166] *Homily on the Apostolic Saying that States: But Know This, that in the Last Days Perilous Times Will Come*, chapter 6, PG 56, 277. Quoted in Panayiotis Nellas, *Deification in Christ: The Nature of the Human Person*, trans. Norman Russell (New York, NY: St Vladimir's Seminary Press, 1997), 145.

[167] Cyril of Alexandria, *Commentary on the Gospel of John* 7 (on John 11:33). PG 74, 53A. The English translation is my own.

[168] Cyril of Alexandria, *The Twelve Chapters*, Anathema 12, translated in Russell, *Cyril of Alexandria*, 188.

[169] Pelikan, *The Spirit of Eastern Christendom*, 135.

liturgical book of Lenten hymns in Byzantium.[170] Theodore the Stoudite (759–826), his brother Joseph the Stoudite (762–832) and their successors collected, composed and edited hymns written by various hymnographers since the fifth century, from Jerusalem, Constantinople and other parts of the Byzantine Empire. Although the evolution of the *Triodion* continued until the fifteenth century, the earliest extant manuscript of this Stoudite hymnal – Sinai Graecus 734–735 in the tenth century[171] – shows that the performance of Andrew of Crete's *Great Kanon* and Kassia's hymn *On the Sinful Woman* had been enshrined in the sacred rituals of Great Lent as early as the ninth century. These liturgical hymns were not performed exclusively in monastic communities, spreading to the cathedrals and churches of urban communities.[172]

There is not currently any scholarly consensus on the history of the *Triodion* and its evolution in Byzantium. A critical history of this hymnal and its extensive manuscript tradition is beyond the scope of this book. Nevertheless, the *Triodion* and Great Lent are the liturgical and hermeneutical framework for the compunctious hymns of Romanos the Melodist, Andrew of Crete and Kassia. The performance of these hymns and the emotions they sought to elicit cannot be properly considered apart from this context. Therefore, it is essential to consider the main elements of this context that can be retrieved from history with some confidence and how they framed the liturgical performance of the hymns I explore. Three elements are noteworthy: the Lenten fast, the scriptural narratives of Lent and the thematic structure of the Sundays of Lent.

Christianity developed the practice of fasting during the forty days of Great Lent in the fourth century. Before this development, Christians only

---

[170] See Ware and Mother Mary, *The Lenten Triodion*, 28–43; Thomas Pott, *Byzantine Liturgical Reform: A Study of Liturgical Change in the Byzantine Tradition*, trans. Paul Meyendorff (Crestwood, NY: St Vladimir's Seminary Press, 2010), 115–51; Getcha, *The Typikon Decoded*, 35–38. The historical development of the *Triodion* is explored in Карабиновъ, И., Постная Тріодь. Историческій обзоръ ея плана, состава, редакцій и славянскихъ переводовъ (С.-Петербургъ: Типографія В. Д. Смирнова, 1910). However, this monograph is only available in Russian. There is a similar study in Greek by Εὐάγγελος Θεοδώρου that relies on Karabinov's work – Evangelos Theodorou, Η Μορφωτική Αξία τοῦ Ἰσχύοντος Τριωδίου [*The Formative Value of the Prevailing Triodion*] (Athens: University of Athens, 1958), which I have consulted. Byzantine *Triodia* could also include hymns for the paschal season, however, the hymnal for the period beginning with Pascha and ending with the Sundays of Pentecost and All Saints, is more commonly known as the *Pentekostarion*.

[171] See Andrew John Quinlan, *Sin. Gr. 734–735. Triodion. Excerpta ex Dissertatione ad Doctorum* (Newberry Springs, CA: Pontificium Institutum Orientalium, 2004).

[172] Krueger, *Liturgical Subjects*, 165.

fasted during Holy Week in anticipation of Pascha.[173] Although it ostensibly signified abstinence from foods such as meat and animal products, according to John Chrysostom, true fasting was also abstinence from sinful passions and other forms of injustice:

Μὴ γὰρ δὴ στόμα νηστευέτω μόνον, ἀλλὰ καὶ ὀφθαλμὸς, καὶ ἀκοή, καὶ πόδες, καὶ χεῖρες, καὶ πάντα τὰ τοῦ σώματος ἡμῶν μέλη·[174]

The fast should be kept not by the mouth alone but also by the eye, the ear, the feet, the hands and all the members of our body.[175]

Through the measure of agony, tiredness and weakness that could arise from fasting, the faithful became conscious of their dependence on God and his mercy.[176] The inward brokenness this could occasion is perhaps most strikingly apparent – and indeed absent – in the parable of the Publican and the Pharisee of Luke 18:10–13. Although the Pharisee fasted, he lacked the repentance of the Publican and was condemned for his hollow virtue and self-righteousness. In the Lenten hymns we will examine, fasting is often presented as an abstinence from depraved passions and is embodied by the prayers and tears of various biblical exemplars of compunction, such as the Publican.

Narratives from the Old Testament were afforded prominence in the lectionary that was heard by the faithful during Great Lent. Indeed, it was through the liturgical services of Lent that church-goers were able to hear and experience the scriptural stories of Genesis, Exodus and other books of the Old Testament, alongside the singing of hymns, which would often engage in a 'dialectical relationship with the biblical lection' to enkindle the emotions of the congregation.[177] Byzantine hymnody challenged the faithful's familiarity with Scripture by 'musing over' biblical stories, weaving multifarious scriptural images together and inviting 'a continuous and imaginative reading of the Bible'.[178] In the seventh century, these Old Testament liturgical texts were assembled in the book known as the *Prophetologion*.[179] A critical edition of the *Prophetologion* that analysed seventy-one manuscripts from the ninth until the fourteenth centuries

[173] Paul F. Bradshaw and Maxwell E. Johnson, *The Origins of Feasts, Fasts and Seasons in Early Christianity* (Collegeville, MN: Liturgical Press, 2011), 92–108; Ware, 'The Historical Development of the Great Fast', in Ware and Mother Mary, *The Lenten Triodion*, 28–34.
[174] *Homilies on the Statues*, 3.4. PG 49, 53.
[175] The translation is based on Ware's quotation in *The Lenten Triodion*, 17.   [176] Ibid., 16.
[177] Krueger, *Liturgical Subjects*, 36.   [178] Pentiuc, *The Old Testament*, 212.   [179] Ibid., 209.

was published in the twentieth century.[180] Together with the *Typikon of the Great Church*, which was a tenth-century *synaxarion* that included rubrics for the cathedral rite of Constantinople, as well as the *Praxapostolos*,[181] we have the earliest manuscript witnesses to the lectionary system of Constantinople.[182] From time to time, this can cast some uncertainty on what lectionary Romanos the Melodist or Andrew of Crete may have been following a few centuries earlier.[183] However, these witnesses often reflect practices that developed as early as the sixth century in Constantinople, as is evidenced by sermons or hymns composed centuries before the tenth-century rubrics and the *Prophetologion*.[184]

Perhaps the most important Old Testament texts heard throughout Great Lent and Holy Week were Genesis, Exodus and Psalms. Indeed, the Psalter was chanted in its entirety twice each week during Lent and the faithful would have sung the Old Testament biblical canticles during the weekdays of Lent.[185] As we saw in the previous chapter, according to Athanasius of Alexandria, the faithful could enter the narratives of the Psalter and feel the emotions embodied in psalmody, as if they were their own feelings. And as we will see in Chapter 4 on Andrew of Crete, the canticles were the songs of thanksgiving that righteous biblical figures such as Moses sang during the story of salvation and which often underpinned the genre of hymnography

---

[180] Carsten Høeg, Günther Zuntz and Gundrun Engberg, eds., *Prophetologium*, MMB Série Lectionaria 1 (Copenhagen: Ejnar Munksgaard, 1939–81). The earliest witness to the *Prophetologion* is the manuscript Sinai Graecus 7, which has been dated to the ninth century.

[181] The Constantinopolitan *Praxapostolos* was a liturgical text that contained New Testament readings from Acts, Pauline Epistles and other Epistles. For further background, see Galadza, *Liturgy and Byzantinization*, 62–63; Georgios Andreou, 'Il *Praxapostolos* bizantino dell'XI secolo: Vladimir 21/ Savva 4 del Museo Storico di Mosca: edizione e commento' (PhD dissertation, Pontifical Oriental Institute, 2008).

[182] For the period of Great Lent and Holy Week, see Juan Mateos, *Le Typicon de la Grande Église: Tome II, Le cycle des fêtes mobiles*. OCA 166 (Rome: Pontificium Institutum Orientalium Studiorum, 1963), 2–90. For background on the *Typikon of the Great Church* itself, see *Le Typicon de la Grande Église: Tome I, Le cycle des douze mois* (Rome: Pontificium Institutum Orientalium Studiorum, 1962), x–xix; Baldovin, *The Urban Character of Christian Worship*, 190–97. Note that the earliest manuscript that preserves the *Typikon* in its entirety – Patmos 266 – is dated to the beginning of the tenth century but reflects liturgical practices of the ninth century and prior centuries. See Anton Baumstark, 'Das Typikon der Patmos-Handschrift 266 und die Altkonstantinopolitanische Gottesdienstordnung', *Jahrbuch für Liturgiewissenschaft* 6 (1926): 98–111; Gabriel Bertonière, *The Sundays of Lent in the Triodion: The Sundays without a Commemoration*, OCA 253 (Rome: Pontificio Istituto Orientale, 1997), 33; Andrea Luzzi, 'Synaxaria and the Synaxarion of Constantinople', in *The Ashgate Research Companion to Byzantine Hagiography. Volume 2: Genres and Contexts*, ed. Stephanos Efthymiadis (Farnham: Ashgate, 2014), 201.

[183] In the case of the *Great Kanon*, it is not clear whether Andrew composed it during his time in Constantinople.

[184] Krueger, *Liturgical Subjects*, 25; Bertonière, *The Sundays of Lent*, 29–42.

[185] Ware and Mother Mary, *The Lenten Triodion*, 38.

known as the *kanon*. Genesis narrated the fall and exile from Paradise, which framed the Lenten journey of compunction, repentance and salvation. And the passage from death to life that the crossing of the Red Sea betokens in Exodus prefigured the new Passover that the forty-day journey to Pascha enacted. Indeed, the Lenten journey recalled 'the forty years in which the Chosen People journeyed through the wilderness' and evoked the 'liberation from the bondage of Egypt' that intimated the faithful's emancipation from 'domination by sinful passions'.[186]

Similarly, the dramatic succession of Sundays in the *Triodion* sought to guide the faithful along the path to feeling compunction. The *Triodion* contained liturgical hymns for Great Lent and Holy Week but also the preparatory Sundays and feasts that preceded Great Lent. A brief outline of the Sundays of Great Lent, its preparatory Sundays and Holy Week is provided below.[187] Although in the post-Byzantine period Orthodox churches observe another preparatory Sunday for Lent – the Sunday of the Publican and the Pharisee – this was added as late as the twelfth century in Byzantium to the beginning of the *Triodion* cycle (before the Sunday of the Prodigal Son) to inaugurate the Lenten theme of repentance through the parable in the Lukan Gospel and the hymnography that expanded this narrative.[188]

(1) *Sunday of the Prodigal Son.* According to the *Typikon of the Great Church*, this Sunday marks the beginning of the Lenten cycle and has as its protagonist the prodigal son, who is an icon of repentance. The Gospel passage for that day (Luke 15:11–32) and the hymns in the *Triodion* portray sin as exile from one's homeland and enslavement to depraved passion. This is juxtaposed with the journey home and restoration that begin with compunction.

(2) *Sunday of the Last Judgment* (Carnival Sunday). The theme of this Sunday, which formed part of the liturgical calendar as early as the ninth century, is taken from the Gospel passage assigned for that day (Matthew 25:31–46). By remembering the eschaton as an event that was already taking place liturgically in the hearts of the faithful, the eschatological mood this evoked invited an internalisation of the Last Judgment and sought to arouse compunction.

---

[186] Ibid., 48.

[187] The brief overview that follows relies on the detailed analysis in Getcha, *The Typikon Decoded*, 141–232; Ware and Mother Mary, *The Lenten Triodion*, 44–64.

[188] However, there is a hymn *On the Pharisee and the Publican*, which was possibly composed in the sixth century. See Trypanis, *Fourteen Early Byzantine Cantica*, 41–50.

(3)   *Sunday of the Exile from Paradise* (Cheese-Fare Sunday). The origin
      of this Sunday is ancient. It was probably already an established part
      of the liturgical cycle in the lifetime of Romanos the Melodist. In the
      hymns of the *Triodion*, the tears that Adam and Eve weep before the
      closed gates of Eden are connected with the forty-day fast of Christ in
      the desert, juxtaposing the estrangement from paradise with the hope
      of redemption. The *Typikon of the Great Church* assigns Matthew
      6:14–21 for that Sunday to alleviate the sombre mood with the
      forgiveness that is afforded to the faithful by God if they too forgive
      their neighbour.

(4)   *First Sunday of Lent.* After the two preceding Sundays, which reca-
      pitulate the beginning (creation and fall) and end (the Last Judg-
      ment) of salvation history, the faithful arrived at the first Sunday of
      Great Lent. Although this day eventually became the 'Sunday of
      Orthodoxy', celebrating the ninth-century victory over Iconoclasm,
      this was an addition to the more ancient commemoration of the
      prophets, which heralded the journey towards the crucifixion and
      resurrection of Christ.

(5)   *Second Sunday of Lent.* Although in late Byzantium this became the
      Sunday that commemorated the fourteenth-century defender of
      Hesychasm, Gregory Palamas, according to the *Typikon of the Great
      Church*, it originally celebrated the feast of the second-century martyr
      known as Polycarp of Smyrna, who was an exemplar of the ascetic
      struggle. The hymns for this day also revisit the theme of the prodigal
      son and his repentance.

(6)   *Third Sunday of Lent.* This Sunday is dedicated to the veneration of the
      Cross and foreshadows the crucifixion of Christ during Holy Week.
      During this stage of the Lenten journey, the faithful could adore the
      Cross in Hagia Sophia.[189] The proposition of the faithful crucifying
      and transforming their passions emerges in the hymns for this day.

---

[189] Although scholars suggest that the true cross was transferred to Constantinople in the seventh
century under Emperor Heraclius, a relic of the cross is thought to have arrived there earlier.
However, it is unclear whether this occurred in the fourth century, when Helena is portrayed as
discovering the true cross, or in the sixth century, when a relic is thought to have been transferred
from Apamea in Syria to Constantinople. See Cyril Mango and Roger Scott, trans., *The Chronicle
of Theophanes the Confessor: Byzantine and Near East History AD 284–813* (Oxford: Clarendon
Press, 1997), 455–68; Michael Whitby and Mary Whitby, trans., *Chronicon Paschale 284–628 AD*
(Liverpool: Liverpool University Press, 1989), 156; Robin M. Jensen, *The Cross: History, Art, and
Controversy* (Cambridge, MA: Harvard University Press, 2017), 56–61, 116–22. On the relic from
Apamea, see Anna Kartsonis, 'The Responding Icon', in *Heaven on Earth: Art and the Church in
Byzantium*, ed. Linda Saffran (University Park, PA: Pennsylvania State University Press, 1998), 64.

(7) *Fourth Sunday of Lent.* Although not specified in the *Typikon of the Great Church*, this Sunday of Lent eventually marked the feast of John Klimakos, who was the late sixth-, early seventh-century author of the *Ladder of Divine Ascent*. This most likely occurred in late Byzantium but reflected the much earlier significance of the *Ladder* as a treatise that embodied the ideal pattern of Lenten asceticism for the faithful. Indeed, the *Ladder* was read during the Hours of Great Lent (a service that was incorporated during matins).

(8) *Fifth Sunday of Lent.* This Sunday commemorates Mary of Egypt, a fifth-century saint who exemplified repentance in the Byzantine tradition, though her feast was probably transferred from its fixed commemoration of April 1 to this moveable Sunday after the tenth century.[190] Before she left Jerusalem to dedicate herself to asceticism in the desert beyond the Jordan, Mary was a notorious harlot. As we will see in Chapter 4, as early as the eleventh century, her vita was read during the performance of Andrew of Crete's *Great Kanon*.

(9) *Palm Sunday.* After the celebration of Christ's raising of Lazarus on the previous day, this Sunday invites the faithful to follow Jesus into Jerusalem and experience his Passion. Both these feasts emerged in the early Christian era in Jerusalem. The hymnody for these days invokes liturgical time by portraying these events as occurring 'today' rather than in the distant past, bidding the faithful to be part of this sacred story.

(10) *Holy Week.* The first three days of Holy Week commemorate a number of events: the sufferings of Joseph in Genesis as a prefiguration of Christ's Passion; the barren fig tree as a symbol of judgment; the parables of the talents and the ten virgins; and the woman who repented at the feet of Christ with tears of compunction, anointing him with myrrh. Holy Thursday marks Jesus washing the disciples' feet, the institution of the Eucharist and the betrayal of Christ. Holy Friday is the crucifixion and death of Christ. And Holy Saturday is the burial of Christ and his descent into Hades, as well as an anticipation of his resurrection.

---

[190] Mary of Egypt's historical identity remains rather shadowy inasmuch as the seventh-century *Life of Mary of Egypt*, which is thought to have been written by Sophronios of Jerusalem, belongs to an earlier and wider Byzantine tradition of repentant harlots. See Derek Krueger, 'Scripture and Liturgy in the *Life of Mary of Egypt*', in *Education and Religion in Late Antique Christianity: Reflections, Social Contexts and Genres*, ed. Peter Gemeinhardt, Lieve Van Hoof and Peter Van Nuffelen (New York, NY: Routledge, 2016), 131–41.

Although the summary above is a concise overview of the richness of the *Triodion*, it outlines the predominant themes of the liturgical cycle of Lent and Holy Week and links them to the subject of this book. In the next three chapters, the significance of these links will become more apparent.

The 'humaneness of Byzantine hymnography' that emerged in the *Triodion* presented the faithful with an anthropological paradigm, portraying a person as only truly a person and only truly free when she or he is 'in communion with God'.[191] However, this system was based on a liturgical exegesis of the biblical narrative of salvation. Unlike the discursive thought of patristic texts and exegetical treatises, the performativity of hymns dramatised the adventure of salvation as a personalising narrative in the sacred space of liturgy, which was the *habitus* of compunction. It invited the Byzantine faithful to become part of the Lenten journey of exile, compunction and repentance. Indeed, the hymns of the *Triodion* would have been rendered all the more poignant when the faithful finally arrived at the summit of this journey, the 'day without evening' (ἐν τῇ ἀνεσπέρῳ ἡμέρᾳ), the 'day of Resurrection' (Ἀναστάσεως ἡμέρᾳ) and sang the words of the first *kanon* in the *Pentekostarion*: 'Let us be radiant, O people! Pascha, the Lord's Pascha' (λαμπρυνθῶμεν λαοί, Πάσχα, Κυρίου Πάσχα).[192]

---

[191] Meyendorff, *Byzantine Theology*, 124.
[192] John of Damascus, *Kanon for the Sunday of Pascha*, ninth ode, third strophe and first ode, first strophe. PG 96, 844B and 840BC.

CHAPTER 3

Romanos the Melodist

Romanos the Melodist lived in Constantinople during the reign of Emperor Justinian. Despite the posthumous fame that Romanos enjoyed in Byzantium and beyond, we know precious little about his life. While there are some historical references in the sixth-century hymns he composed, the short narrative of his life emerges later in manuscripts such as the tenth-century *Typikon of the Great Church* and the *Menologion of Basil II*, which was made around the year 1000 for the emperor. I do not propose to rehearse José Grosdidier de Matons' analysis of the biographical sources available on Romanos.[1] However, some brief remarks about Romanos' life and times will contextualise my exploration of his hymns.

The *Typikon of the Great Church* assigns the celebration of the feast of saint Romanos to the first day of October:

Τῇ αὐτῇ ἡμέρᾳ [Μηνὶ ὀκτωβρίῳ α'], τοῦ ὁσίου Ῥωμανοῦ τοῦ ποιητοῦ καὶ μελῳδοῦ τῶν κοντακίων ... Τελεῖται δὲ ἡ αὐτοῦ μνήμη ἐν τῷ αὐτῷ τῆς ἁγίας ἀειπαρθένου Θεοτόκου ναῷ ἐν τοῖς Κύρου.[2]

On the same day [1 October] commemoration of the venerable Romanos, the poet and melodist of the *kontakia* ... His memory is celebrated in his own church of the holy and ever-virgin Theotokos in *ta Kyrou*.[3]

This text only provides a few details about the life of Romanos: he composed liturgical hymns known as *kontakia*;[4] he resided in the *ta Kyrou* district of Constantinople; and he died on October 1.[5] The early tenth-century Patmos 266, fol. 17v, has a few more biographical details than Holy Cross Jerusalem 40, on which Mateos based his edition of the text.

---

[1] See José Grosdidier de Matons, *Romanos le Mélode et les origines de la poésie religieuse à Byzance* (Paris: Beauchesne, 1977), 159–98.

[2] *Le Typicon de la Grande Église: Tome II*, 56.   [3] The English translation is my own.

[4] See Elizabeth M. Jeffreys, 'Kontakion', in *ODB*, 1148.

[5] In the Byzantine liturgical cycle, the feast of a saint is celebrated on the day of his/her death.

It refers to Romanos' coming to Constantinople during the reign of
Anastasios and receiving the gift of composing hymns from the Theotokos.

   Further detail emerges in the brief hagiographical account of Romanos
that appears in the *Menologion of Basil II*, an illustrated version of the
synaxarion of Constantinople:

> The venerable Romanos was from Syria and became a deacon of the holy
> church of Berytos. Arriving in Constantinople in the reign of the emperor
> Anastasios, he went and settled in the church of the most holy Theotokos in
> the *ta Kyrou* district, where he received the gift of the *kontakia*. In piety he
> would celebrate and pass the night, praying during the vigil at Blachernae,
> before returning to *ta Kyrou*. On one of these nights, the most holy
> Theotokos appeared to him while he was asleep and gave him a paper scroll
> and said, 'Take this paper and eat it'. It seems that the saint opened his
> mouth and swallowed the paper. Now it was the festival of Christ's
> Nativity. And immediately awakening from his sleep he was astonished
> and glorified God. Thereupon he mounted the ambo and began to chant,
> 'Today the Virgin gives birth to him who is above all being'. He also
> composed nearly one thousand *kontakia* for other festivals before departing
> for the Lord.[6]

Although the *synaxarion* suggests Romanos wrote one thousand hymns,
only eighty-nine are attributed to him in extant manuscripts, of which
almost sixty are considered genuine.[7] Most notable is the account of
Romanos' miraculous birth as a hymnographer, which sees the Theotokos act as a kind of Byzantine Muse who inspires the composition and
performance of his most famous *kontakion*.[8] Romanos' encounter with
the Mother of God in a dream is relevant for the performance of liturgical
hymns and their portrayal as divine songs. As noted in Chapter 2, the
Byzantines conceived the singing of hymns as an imitation of the angelic
choir, a notion that also appears in Romanos' hymn *On the Three
Children*:

---

[6] For the Greek text, see José Grosdidier de Matons, *Romanos le Mélode*, 161–62. My translation into
English is based on those by Krueger and Lash. See Derek Krueger, *Writing and Holiness: The
Practice of Authorship in the Early Christian East* (Philadelphia, PA: University of Pennsylvania Press,
2004), 189; Lash, *On the Life of Christ*, xxvii.

[7] Romanos the Melodist, *Sancti Romani Melodi Cantica: Cantica Genuina*, ed. Paul Maas and C. A.
Trypanis (Oxford: Clarendon Press, 1963). Grosdidier de Matons argues that a few of the *kontakia*
Maas and Trypanis deem dubious are genuine. See Romanos le Mélode, *Hymnes*, ed. José Grosdidier
de Matons, 5 vols. (Paris: Éditions du Cerf, 1964–81).

[8] Romanos' ingestion of the scroll echoes the biblical accounts of the prophet Ezekiel (Ezekiel 3:1–3)
and John the Evangelist (Revelation 10:8–9). On Byzantine notions of divine inspiration and
authorship, see Aglae Pizzone, ed. *The Author in Middle Byzantine Literature* (Berlin: De Gruyter,
2014); Krueger, *Writing and Holiness*.

Στήσαντες οὖν οἱ παῖδες   χορὸν ἐν μέσῳ καμίνου,
   οὐράνιον ἐκκλησίαν   ἀπειργάσαντο τὴν κάμινον,
ψάλλοντες μετ' ἀγγέλου   τῷ ποιητῇ τῶν ἀγγέλων
καὶ πᾶσαν τὴν λειτουργίαν   τῶν ἀσάρκων ἐκμιμούμενοι·[9]

Standing then as a choir in the midst of the furnace,
the three children made the furnace a heavenly church,
chanting with the angel to the creator of angels
and imitating the entire liturgy of the bodiless powers.[10]

Not unlike the liturgy, which was portrayed as a fusion of the earthly and heavenly realms, the Byzantine conception of hymnody was a sacred symphony that blended human and divine elements.

The *Menologion of Basil II* also confirms that Romanos' literary output took place in Constantinople during the time of Emperor Justinian, which is evident from Romanos' own hymns. One of Romanos' *kontakia*, *On Earthquakes and Fires*, sings the praises of Justinian and alludes to the reconstruction of Hagia Sophia.[11] Justinian's reign was an age of political and cultural transformation:

> It was the chief catalyst in forging the Byzantine alloy, a world in which Christian, Roman, Greek, and many local elements fused to create a new medieval civilization within imperial borders.[12]

Alongside the military, legal and architectural accomplishments during the age of Justinian, a prolific literary culture began to flourish.[13]

Although some writers, such as the historian Prokopios of Caesarea, followed classical models and imitated traditional styles of authorship, Romanos straddled the worlds of antiquity and Byzantium. His *kontakia* represent a unique fusion of rhetoric inherited from the ancient Greek world, the fourth-century Syriac poetry of Ephrem and the Christian

---

[9] Romanos le Mélode, *Hymnes. Tome I: Ancien Testament*, ed. José Grosdidier de Matons. SC 99 (Paris: Éditions du Cerf, 1964), 396.

[10] The English translation is my own.

[11] Romanos le Mélode, *Hymnes. Tome V: Nouveau Testament et Hymnes de Circonstance*, ed. Grosdidier de Matons. SC 283 (Paris: Éditions du Cerf, 1981), 470–99. See also Eva C. Topping, 'On Earthquakes and Fires: Romanos' Encomium to Justinian', *BZ* 71, no. 1 (1978): 22–35.

[12] Michael Maas, 'Roman Questions, Byzantine Answers: Contours of the Age of Justinian', in *The Cambridge Companion to the Age of Justinian*, ed. Michael Maas (Cambridge: Cambridge University Press, 2005), 3–27.

[13] See Andrew Louth, 'Justinian and His Legacy', in *The Cambridge History of the Byzantine Empire c. 500–1492*, ed. Jonathan Shepard (Cambridge: Cambridge University Press, 2008), 99–129; Claudia Rapp, 'Literary Culture under Justinian', in Maas, ed., *The Cambridge Companion to the Age of Justinian*, 376–400.

discourse of the Cappadocian Fathers.[14] Romanos' hymns amplified the stories of Scripture, endowing them with liturgical and musical dimensions. His use of dramatic dialogue marked the 'emergence of biblical epic in the context of Christian worship'[15] and framed the human–divine encounter in dialogic terms, intensifying 'moments of desire and distance, familiarity and alienation', which unfolded in the vivid experience of the scriptural event the hymn evoked.[16]

Byzantine Hymnography and the *Kontakion*

The history of Byzantine hymnography has occasionally been portrayed as a tale of two genres: *kontakion* and *kanon*.[17] Despite mistaken perceptions that the '*kanon* replaced the *kontakion* toward the end of the seventh century',[18] the story is not so simple. J. B. Pitra and Egon Wellesz posited that the *kontakion* was neglected as a liturgical hymn after Romanos' lifetime, before it eventually fell into obscurity and was no longer composed.[19] However, the *kontakion* continued to flourish after the seventh century.[20] Far from 'falling into disuse from the eighth century onwards', the *kontakion* 'continued to flourish until the twelfth century'.[21] Rather than the *kanon* supplanting the *kontakion* in the office of matins, the liturgical place of the *kontakion* was elsewhere. The 'parallel existence [of] two major liturgical traditions in Byzantium' – the Constantinopolitan and Jerusalemite traditions – adds to the complexity of the tale.[22] We will

[14] Wellesz, *A History of Byzantine Music*, 184; Averil Cameron, 'Disputations, Polemical Literature and the Formation of Opinion in the Early Byzantine Period', in *Dispute Poems and Dialogues in the Ancient and Mediaeval Near East: Forms and Types of Literary Debates in Semitic and Related Literatures*, ed. G. J. Reinink and H. L. J. Vanstiphout (Leuven: Departement Oriëntalistiek, 1991), 91–108.

[15] Frank, 'Romanos and the Night Vigil', 76.   [16] Largier, 'Inner Senses–Outer Senses', 10.

[17] Wellesz, *A History of Byzantine Music*, 179–239.

[18] Leena Mari Peltomaa, 'Hymnography, Byzantine', in *The Encyclopedia of Ancient History*, ed. Roger S. Bagnall, et al. (Malden: Wiley-Blackwell 2013), 3363.

[19] J. B. Pitra, *Analecta sacra Spicilegio Solesmeni parata*, Vol. 1 (Paris: Jouby et Roger, 1876), xxxvii; Wellesz, *A History of Byzantine Music*, 157.

[20] José Grosdidier de Matons, 'Liturgie et hymnographie: kontakion et canon', *DOP* 34/35 (1980–81): 31–43.

[21] Andrew Louth, 'Christian Hymnography from Romanos the Melodist to John Damascene', *JECS* 57 (2005): 199. See also Mary B. Cunningham, 'The Reception of Romanos in Middle Byzantine Homiletics and Hymnography', *DOP* 62 (2008): 251–60.

[22] Alexander Lingas, 'How Musical was the "Sung Office"? Some Observations on the Ethos of the Byzantine Cathedral Rite', in *The Traditions of Orthodox Music: Proceedings of the First International Conference on Orthodox Church Music, University of Joensuu, Finland, 13–19 June 2005*, ed. Ivan Moody and Maria Takala-Roszczenko (Joensuu: International Society for Orthodox Church Music, 2007), 219. On the history of Jerusalem's liturgy, see Daniel Galadza, *Liturgy and Byzantinization in Jerusalem* (Oxford: Oxford University Press, 2017).

return to this complexity in the next chapter. Here it suffices to say that the *kontakion* and the *kanon* signify hymnic genres that can be characterised as *Byzantine* and liturgical.[23]

The elements of a *kontakion* included at least one proem or prelude introducing the polystrophic poem, a series of metrically identical strophes developing the narrative and a refrain acting as a unifying thread for all the stanzas.[24] Romanos also weaves an acrostic as a kind of poetic signature – 'by the humble Romanos' – through the proem and strophes, which is evidence that he wrote the hymns, though it is not discernible during the performance of a *kontakion*.[25] Rhythmically, the *kontakion* is based on stress accent, eschewing the quantitative metres of classical Greek that Gregory the Theologian's poetry favoured.[26] Although Romanos' *kontakia* display these formal elements, their exploration of scriptural characters' personal thoughts and sensory perceptions, as well as their use of dramatic dialogue to engage the faithful, set them apart.[27] An important function of dramatic dialogue is creating 'a sense of timelessness' by momentarily dehistoricising the scriptural narrative and calling on the faithful to 'participate and experience for themselves the events being described'.[28]

The notion of hymnography as 'rewritten Bible' is apparent in Romanos' *kontakia*.[29] The mystagogic character of hymnody initiates the

---

[23] While hymns certainly existed before the likes of Romanos the Melodist, 'it is difficult to discern the boundaries between Christian hymnography, psalmody, scripture and homiletics prior to the 4th century'. See Alexander Lingas, 'Hymnography', in *The Encyclopedia of Greece and the Hellenic Tradition*, ed. G. Speake (Chicago, IL: Fitzroy-Dearborn, 2000), 786–87.

[24] Grosdidier de Matons, *Romanos le Mélode*, 37–48.

[25] Interestingly, Romanos did not refer to his hymns as *kontakia*. *Kontakion* is a ninth-century word that refers to the shaft that scrolls were rolled around. Some of the words Romanos' acrostics use to describe his compositions include 'hymn (ὕμνος)', 'poem (ποίημα)' and 'prayer (προσευχή)'. See Krueger, *Writing and Holiness*, 169–88; *Liturgical Subjects*, 31–41.

[26] For Gregory's poetry, see Caroline White, trans. *Gregory of Nazianzus: Autobiographical Poems* (Cambridge: Cambridge University Press, 1996).

[27] Georgia Frank, 'Dialogue and Deliberation: The Sensory Self in the Hymns of Romanos the Melodist', in *Religion and the Self in Antiquity*, ed. David Brakke, M. L. Satlow and S. Wetzman (Indianapolis, IN: Bloomington, 2005), 163–79; Derek Krueger, 'Romanos the Melodist and the Early Christian Self', in *Proceedings of the 21st International Congress of Byzantine Studies: London, 21–26 August 2006*, ed. Elizabeth Jeffreys (Aldershot: Ashgate, 2006), 255–74.

[28] Mary B. Cunningham, 'Dramatic Device or Didactic Tool? The Function of Dialogue in Byzantine Preaching', in *Rhetoric in Byzantium: Papers from the Thirty-Fifth Spring Symposium of Byzantine Studies, Exeter College, University of Oxford, March 2001*, ed. Elizabeth Jeffreys (Aldershot: Ashgate, 2001), 106. For more on this theme, see Jan Krans and Joseph Verheyden, eds., *Patristic and Text-Critical Studies: The Collected Essays of William L. Petersen* (Leiden: Brill, 2012), 50, 153.

[29] The term 'rewritten Bible' was coined by Géza Vermès in 1961 in *Scripture and Tradition in Judaism: Haggadic Studies* (Leiden: Brill, 1961), 67.

congregation into Christian dogma by guiding them through a biblical theophany.[30] Similar to the idea and practice of hymnography as rewritten Bible, the poetry of Romanos can be viewed through the lens of narratology. Although Romanos ostensibly sings a biblical story to his audience, he does so in a way that creates a narrative world, which mediates the faithful's encounter with God. The Melodist's use of dramatic dialogue fused 'the world of the biblical characters and the world of the congregation', asking the faithful to act out the performance of his hymns on 'the stage of the mind'.[31] The emotive significance of the way he conflates these two worlds is intriguing. As we will see, the immediacy of the story world engenders an intersubjective space where the emotions of biblical characters and the feelings of the faithful could entwine.

Romanos' deployment of rhetorical techniques such as ethopoeia and ekphrasis[32] turned an audience of listeners into spectators and participants.[33] This is particularly relevant insofar as there is a link between rhetoric and emotion in Romanos' poetry.[34] Indeed, many of Byzantium's greatest hymnographers were not only great rhetoricians – they were masters of pathopoeia. The essence of rhetoric was performance and presentation.[35] As we will see, Romanos knew well the power of rhetoric to enkindle and quell the passions of the faithful. After all, it was not ancient Greek treatises on psychology that discussed the emotions but

---

[30] Bogdan G. Bucur, 'Exegesis of Biblical Theophanies in Byzantine Hymnography: Rewritten Bible?', *Theological Studies* 68, no. 1 (2007): 92–112. Although this is not the place to canvass whether 'rewritten Bible' is a genre or textual strategy, it illuminates how hymnographers rewrote scriptural narratives to accentuate their emotive dimension.

[31] Uffe Holmsgaard Eriksen, 'Drama in the Kontakia of Romanos the Melodist: A Narratological Analysis of Four Kontakia' (PhD dissertation, Aarhus University, 2013), 248.

[32] Ekphrasis is generally defined as a descriptive speech that sought to render an absent person, place, feast or work of art visible. See Alexander Kazhdan and Elizabeth Jeffreys, 'Ekphrasis', in *ODB*, 683. On ekphrasis shaping the emotions of the audience, see Ruth Webb, *Ekphrasis, Imagination and Persuasion in Ancient Rhetorical Theory and Practice* (Aldershot: Ashgate, 2009), 72–74.

[33] Sarah Gador-Whyte, 'Rhetoric and Ideas in the Kontakia of Romanos the Melodist' (PhD dissertation, University of Melbourne, 2011), 180–236; Arentzen, *The Virgin in Song*, 14–32. Of course, this notion this can be contextualised more broadly insofar as liturgical space was the setting for Romanos' hymns. Although seeing and hearing were pivotal in liturgical experience, touch, taste and smell could also initiate the faithful into divine mysteries. More recently, Gador-Whyte has published a monograph that examines the theology of Romanos' poetry and the performative nature of his rhetoric – *Theology and Poetry in Early Byzantium: The Kontakia of Romanos the Melodist* (Cambridge: Cambridge University Press, 2017).

[34] Gador-Whyte, 'Rhetoric and Ideas', 209–23. For how Romanos' hymns inspired an affective relationship between the Theotokos and the faithful in Constantinople, see Arentzen, *The Virgin in Song*, 46–86.

[35] Mary Whitby, 'Rhetorical Questions', in James, ed., *A Companion to Byzantium*, 241.

essays on oratory, such as Aristotle's *Rhetoric*.[36] The dramatic dialogue of Romanos' hymnography echoes 'the intensely dialogic environment of the classical city-state' to which the emergence of emotion as a concept in antiquity 'responded, at least in part'.[37] Aristotle's definition of emotions as 'things on account of which people change and differ in regard to their judgments, and upon which attend pain and pleasure'[38] illuminates the liturgical atmosphere of the *kontakion* as much as it did the Assembly or the Agora in antiquity.

Another dramatic and musical element of the *kontakion* that had the potential to engage the congregation was the refrain. Although the ostensible purpose of the refrain was to highlight a certain theme, it often became a dramatic device that not only echoed throughout the narrative but also served as a cry, prayer or question that was taken up by the characters in the hymn and the congregation. *On the Victory of the Cross* sees the refrain – 'again to Paradise'[39] – become a point of contention between its two main characters, Hades and Satan, before becoming the prayer of the faithful in the final strophe:

> ἡμῖν τὸ ξύλον σου   ἀποδίδωσι
> καθ᾽ ἡμέραν καὶ καιρὸν   πλοῦτον ἀτίμητον·
> τοὺς γὰρ πάντας εἰσάγει   πάλιν εἰς τὸν παράδεισον.[40]

> To us your Tree gives back,
> every day, every moment, wealth beyond price,
> for it brings us all
> > *again to Paradise.*[41]

Scholars of Byzantine chant have generally agreed with Wellesz's proposition that during the performance of *kontakia*, although a soloist would sing the proem and strophes, the choir and faithful would chant the refrain.[42] The congregation's participation in the singing of the refrain is also

---

[36] See David Konstan, 'Rhetoric and Emotion', in *A Companion to Greek Rhetoric*, ed. Ian Worthington (Oxford: Blackwell Publishing, 2007), 411–25.

[37] Ibid., 423.   [38] Aristotle, *Rhetoric*, book 2, chapter 1 (quoted ibid., 414).

[39] Lash, *On the Life of Christ*, 155.

[40] Romanos le Mélode, *Hymnes. Tome IV: Nouveau Testament*, ed. Grosdidier de Matons. SC 283 (Paris: Éditions du Cerf, 1967), 310.

[41] Lash, *On the Life of Christ*, 163.

[42] Wellesz argued that the omission of the refrains in the *Psaltikon*, which was the soloist's book of melodies in Byzantium, suggests that the refrain was sung by the choir or by the faithful. See *A History of Byzantine Music*, 143–44. For further arguments in support of this proposition, see Johannes Koder, 'Imperial Propaganda in the Kontakia of Romanos the Melode', *DOP* 62 (2008): 286–90.

suggested by the seventh-century *Miracles of St Artemios*.[43] For the purposes of this study, I accept the proposition that the faithful sang the refrain.[44]

Manuscripts, Editions and Translations

Kontakia are found in two manuscript traditions that emerged between the tenth and thirteenth centuries in Byzantium – the *Kontakarion* and the *Psaltikon*. The former generally preserved the text of the hymns for the liturgical calendar.[45] The latter contained musical notation for liturgical use by the soloist and originated in the cathedral rite of Constantinople.[46] The modern critical editions of Romanos' *kontakia* by the Oxford editors, Maas and Trypanis, and by the French scholar, Grosdidier de Matons, rely on these manuscript traditions.[47] It is not my purpose to revisit and reconsider these traditions. Therefore, I have based my research on the modern critical editions of Romanos' works, preferring Grosdidier de Matons' more recent edition, which was published between 1964 and 1981 as part of the Sources Chrétiennes collection.

There is still some uncertainty over which of Romanos' *kontakia* are genuine and which are dubious. Of the eighty-nine *kontakia* extant in manuscripts in the name of Romanos (in the acrostic) or attributed to Romanos, Maas and Trypanis believe all the hagiographical ones are dubious, arguing that fifty-nine are genuine. However, Grosdidier de Matons finds five of these hagiographical *kontakia* to be authentic.[48] Rather than investigate which scholar is correct, I have refrained from citing the *kontakia* considered dubious by Maas and Trypanis.

---

[43] Miracle 18 is examined below in the discussion on the liturgical context of the *kontakion*. See Virgil S. Crisafulli and John W. Nesbitt, eds., *The Miracles of St Artemios: A Collection of Miracle Stories by an Anonymous Author of Seventh-Century Byzantium* (Leiden: Brill, 1997), 114–15.

[44] See Krueger, *Liturgical Subjects*, 30; Arentzen, 'Voices Interwoven', 1–10.

[45] Grosdidier de Matons, *Romanos le Mélode*, 67–118. However, there are some *Kontakaria* that also contain musical notation.

[46] Christian Troelsgård, *Byzantine Neumes: A New Introduction to the Middle Byzantine Notation* (Copenhagen: Museum Tusculanum Press, 2011), 85. However, some *Psaltika* are referred to as *Kontakaria*. See, for example, the Florentine *Psaltikon* copied at the monastery of Grottaferrata during the thirteenth century in Carsten Høeg, *Contacarium Ashburnhamense: Codex Bibl. Laurentianae Ashburnhamensis 64 phototypice depictus*, MMB Série Principale 4 (Copenhagen: Ejnar Munksgaard, 1956).

[47] I follow the numbering and quote the Greek text of the *kontakia* edited in the more recent edition, Romanos le Mélode, *Hymnes*. However, I have also consulted the Oxford edition (*Sancti Romani melodi cantica*) and adopted the English titles (which do not appear in the manuscript tradition) given to Romanos' *kontakia* therein.

[48] For the dubious *kontakia* edited by Trypanis and Maas, see *Sancti Romani melodi cantica: cantica dubia* (Berlin: De Gruyter, 1970).

An English translation of all the *kontakia* attributed to Romanos –
genuine and dubious – is yet to be released. Although I have noted the
English translations by Marjorie Carpenter and Robert Schork, I prefer to
use the translations by the late Archimandrite Ephrem Lash.[49] Where a
kontakion has not been translated by Lash, the translations from the Greek
text are my own.

The Liturgical Context of the *Kontakion*

The *kontakion* was an integral part of the cathedral rite in Constantinople
until the Fourth Crusade in 1204.[50] It formed part of the ritual of
nocturnal worship known as the night vigil (παννυχίς), which was celebrated towards the beginning of the major feasts in the liturgical calendar.[51] Evidence supporting this view can be found in Romanos' very own
kontakia. The first strophe of his hymn *On the Man Possessed with Devils*
briefly describes the liturgical setting and the faithful present, before
turning to the scriptural narrative in question:

> Ὁ λαὸς ὁ πιστὸς   ἐν ἀγάπῃ Χριστοῦ
>   συνελθὼν ἀγρυπνεῖ ἐν ψαλμοῖς καὶ ᾠδαῖς·
>   ἀκορέστως δὲ ἔχει τοὺς ὕμνους Θεῷ·
>   ἐπειδὴ οὖν Δαυὶδ ἐμελώδησε,
>   καὶ ἀναγνώσει εὐτάκτῳ γραφῶν ἐπευφράνθημεν·
>   αὖθις Χριστὸν ἀνυμνήσωμεν   καὶ τοὺς ἐχθροὺς στηλιτεύσωμεν·[52]

> The people of Christ, faithful in their love,
> have gathered to keep vigil with psalms and odes;
> unceasingly they sing hymns to God.
> Now that the Psalms of David have been sung,
> and we were gladdened by the well-ordered reading of Scripture,
> let us again raise a hymn to Christ and denounce the enemies.

As well as referring to the night vigil, these lines evoke a vivid image of how
the Byzantines experienced this liturgical gathering and the performance of

---

[49] Lash, *On the Life of Christ*; Romanos the Melodist, *Sacred Song from the Byzantine Pulpit: Romanos the Melodist*, trans. R. J. Schork (Gainesville, FL: University Press of Florida, 1995); Marjorie Carpenter, trans., *Kontakia of Romanos, Byzantine Melodist*, 2 vols. (Columbia, MO: University of Missouri Press, 1970–73).

[50] 'The Liturgical Place of the Kontakion', 53. The Latin conquest ushered in a period of decline, ending Byzantium's reign as a political superpower. See Steven Runciman, *The Last Byzantine Renaissance* (Cambridge: Cambridge University Press, 1970), 1–23.

[51] Frank, 'Romanos and the Night Vigil', 63.

[52] Romanos le Mélode, *Hymnes. Tome III: Nouveau Testament*, ed. Grosdidier de Matons. SC 114 (Paris: Éditions du Cerf, 1965), 54, 56.

Romanos' hymns. Scriptural recitation was combined with psalmody and hymnody. The text also alludes to the faithful partaking in the singing of hymns, explicitly inviting them to do so through the use of verbs in the hortative voice – 'let us raise a hymn' (ἀνυμνήσωμεν) and 'let us denounce' (στηλιτεύσωμεν).

Moreover, this text intimates the homiletic nature of the *kontakion*. As is evident from Romanos' vita, the theme of his hymns was suited to the liturgical festival at hand. Romanos' *kontakia* imaginatively retold the stories of Scripture, unveiling the emotions of scriptural characters and inviting worshippers to enter the sacred drama unfolding before them. They followed liturgical cycles and lectionary readings, encouraging contemplation of biblical celebrations.[53] Indeed, some *kontakia* suggest that a scriptural event is taking place as a present reality and entreat the congregation to cry out and sing a hymn as it transpires:

> Χορὸς ἀγγελικὸς   ἐκπληττέσθω τὸ θαῦμα,
> βροτοὶ δὲ ταῖς φωναῖς   ἀνακράξωμεν ὕμνον,
> ὁρῶντες τὴν ἄφατον   τοῦ Θεοῦ συγκατάβασιν
> ὂν γὰρ τρέμουσι   τῶν οὐρανῶν αἱ δυνάμεις,
> νῦν γηράλαιαι   ἐναγκαλίζονται χεῖρες
>   τὸν μόνον φιλάνθρωπον.[54]

> Let the angelic choir be amazed at the wonder,
> and let us mortals shout our hymn of praise,
> as we see the ineffable condescension of God;
> for aged hands now cradle the One before whom
> the powers of heaven tremble,
>   *the only Lover of humankind.*[55]

Not only does the hymn encourage the faithful to sing to 'the One before whom the powers of heaven tremble' and ponder the paradox of him cradled as a helpless baby, it also invites them to consider their place in this sacred narrative.

Further evidence for the performance of Romanos' *kontakia* during the night vigil and their enduring significance in Constantinople can be found in the *Miracles of St Artemios*. According to this text, Romanos' *kontakia* were sung a century after his death as part of the night vigil at the church of St John the Baptist in the Constantinopolitan quarter of Oxeia, where the relic of St Artemios was kept. Miracle 33 suggests that 'the holy night vigil

---

[53] Krueger, *Liturgical Subjects*, 75.
[54] Proem 1, *On the Presentation in the Temple*. Romanos le Mélode, *Hymnes. Tome II: Nouveau Testament*, ed. Grosdidier de Matons. SC 110 (Paris: Éditions du Cerf, 1965), 174.
[55] Lash, *On the Life of Christ*, 27.

was being celebrated' (τῆς πνευματικῆς παννυχίδος ἐπιτελουμένης) on 'the eve of the Lord's day' and that it included the singing of 'three evening antiphons' (τρία ἀντίφωνα τὰ ἑσπερινά).[56] Miracle 18, which recounts a burglary, is insightful:

> There was a certain man who from a tender age used to attend the all-night vigil of the Forerunner and who sang the hymns of humble Romanos among the saints right up to the present day. In the time of the reign of Emperor Herakleios, this man was burglarized as the birthday of the holy Forerunner was dawning.[57]

According to the narrative, St Artemios reveals 'Theodosios the *psaltes*' (Θεοδόσιος ὁ ψάλτης)[58] as the culprit. But what is more remarkable in the account of this miracle is that a member of a lay congregation who was not the cantor participated in the singing of Romanos' *kontakia*. It also appears that the vigil was a nocturnal affair that lasted until dawn. However, the occasion was the feast of none other than the patron saint of the church, so this event may have called for an exceptional vigil. These are important clues for reimagining the performance of Romanos' *kontakia*. The performance of Romanos' hymns continued for several centuries after his death and not necessarily in monastic settings but at liturgical events open to the wider Constantinopolitan community.[59]

Reimagining the Liturgical Performance of Romanos' Hymns

In the Byzantine liturgical calendar, Great Lent and Holy Week were characterised by a sombre mood that aroused compunction and provoked repentance.[60] Therefore, in reimagining the performance of Romanos' hymns, I have selected the *kontakia* from his oeuvre that perform this theme and which, according to the manuscript tradition, were sung during the course of this liturgical cycle.[61] Although the manuscript tradition

[56] Crisafulli and Nesbitt, *The Miracles of St Artemios*, 174–75.   [57] Ibid., 114–15.

[58] Ibid., 116–17. A *psaltes* was a chanter (liturgical cantor) in a Byzantine choir. See Evangelia C. Spyrakou, Οἱ Χοροὶ τῶν Ψαλτῶν κατὰ τὴν Βυζαντινὴ Παράδοση [*Singers' Choirs according to the Byzantine Tradition*], Institute of Byzantine Musicology Studies 14 (Athens: University of Athens, 2008), 69–78.

[59] Frank, 'Romanos and the Night Vigil', 66; Lingas, 'The Liturgical Place of the Kontakion', 53.

[60] As noted in the previous chapter, Great Lent was preceded by three preparatory Sundays and it culminated in Holy Week. Indeed, the Byzantine hymnal for this period, the *Triodion*, begins with these preparatory Sundays and ends on Holy Saturday. For an overview of this liturgical cycle, see Getcha, *The Typikon Decoded*, 141–232.

[61] Several of Romanos' hymns are entitled 'a compunctious *kontakion*' (κοντάκιον κατανυκτικόν) in the manuscript tradition. See, for example, the hymns *On the Prodigal Son* and *On the Rich Man and Lazarus* in Romanos le Mélode, *Hymnes. Tome III*, 234, 278. *On the Infernal Powers* in *Hymnes*.

usually assigns each *kontakion* to a particular day in the liturgical calendar, this does not necessarily reflect when each hymn was sung in sixth-century Constantinople. I recognise that our knowledge of liturgical practice and the lectionary in the sixth century is scant, owing to the fact that no liturgical books relating to Constantinopolitan worship survive from that century. The manuscript tradition for Romanos' hymns begins in the early tenth century, which is also when the manuscripts of the *Typikon of the Great Church* emerge. While these manuscripts reflect the liturgical practices of prior centuries, I acknowledge there remains uncertainty in relation to Romanos' time. The prehistory of the Byzantine liturgical calendar is still being written. Nevertheless, as a liturgical phenomenon that extended beyond the lifetime of the hymnographer, the performance of Romanos' hymns during sacred rituals is something that generations of faithful in Constantinople would experience for centuries after his death. The post-humous life of Romanos' hymnody and its liturgical trajectory underscore the relationship between performance and sacred emotions.

Out of the fifty-nine genuine *kontakia* in the manuscript tradition, it appears that almost half (twenty-seven) were sung during the Lenten liturgical cycle. Within the confines of this study, which will also explore hymns by Andrew of Crete and Kassia sung during this period, it is not possible to examine all of these hymns, even if the *kontakia* that are not concerned with compunction – such as those written for Lazarus, Palm Sunday and the Passion of Christ – are excluded. Therefore, rather than attempt to reimagine all of Romanos' hymns according to their liturgical order in the Lenten cycle, I explore these hymns according to three themes: compunction and repentance; biblical exemplars (and counter-exemplars) of compunction; and compunction in the face of eschatological judgment. By employing these three themes, I do not presume to order Romanos' hymns in a definitive way. Indeed, it is often the case that a *kontakion* will straddle more than one of these themes. Moreover, the affective texture of each of the Melodist's hymns is rarely confined to a single emotion. However, as a means of extracting the most germane elements from the richness of Romanos' oeuvre for our exploration of compunction and as a way of reimagining the resonance of his hymns during the liturgical cycle of Great Lent and Holy Week in a more organic way, this approach will stand us in good stead.

Tome IV, 242. However, a number of Romanos' *kontakia* performed in Byzantium during the liturgical cycle of Great Lent and Holy Week enkindle compunction without being furnished with this heading.

Compunction and Repentance

Repentance emerges as a leitmotif of Scripture, especially in Luke–Acts[62] and late antique Christian discourse.[63] However, repentance is a difficult concept to define.[64] The *Patristic Greek Lexicon* devotes several pages to defining repentance (μετάνοια).[65] Unlike modern audiences, which have inherited 'a somewhat distorted and incomplete view of repentance in late antiquity' as inextricably connected with ecclesiastical institutions of penitence, repentance's existential significance for Christianity went beyond penitential rites, embracing the totality of Christian life.[66] Romanos' *kontakia* enacted this inclusive conception of repentance through songs that illuminated the relationships between repentance, compunction and tears.

Of course, Romanos was drawing on a corpus of literature that had already cultivated these relationships in the Christian imagination. The Psalmist's exhortation, 'speak in your hearts and feel compunction on your beds' (λέγετε ἐν ταῖς καρδίαις ὑμῶν καὶ ἐπὶ ταῖς κοίταις ὑμῶν κατανύγητε),[67] would have been familiar to an audience that ritually experienced the Psalms in its worship.[68] In the New Testament, repentance is linked with compunction (most notably in Acts 2:37–39)[69] and with tears (most vividly in Luke 7:36–50). A number of early Christian writers, including Origen, Gregory of Nyssa and John Chrysostom, develop these links.[70] The fourth-century theologian and poet Ephrem the Syrian[71] is also worth

---

[62] See Guy D. Nave, Jr, *The Role and Function of Repentance in Luke–Acts* (Leiden: Brill, 2002).

[63] On the significance of repentance and the scriptural meaning of repentance, see Kallistos Ware, 'The Orthodox Experience of Repentance', *Sobornost* 2 (1980): 18–28. On repentance in monastic literature, see Brouria Bitton-Ashkelony, 'Penitence in Late Antique Monastic Literature', in *Transformations of the Inner Self in Ancient Religions*, ed. Jan Assmann and Guy G. Stroumsa (Leiden: Brill, 1999), 179–94.

[64] Torrance, *Repentance in Late Antiquity*, 2.   [65] Lampe, *Patristic Greek Lexicon*, 855–58.

[66] Torrance, *Repentance in Late Antiquity*, 9.   [67] Psalm 4:5.

[68] Brian Daley, 'Finding the Right Key: The Aims and Strategies of Early Christian Interpretation of the Psalms', in *Psalms in Community*, ed. Attridge and Fassler, 189.

[69] After Peter's homily leaves the crowd feeling compunction in their hearts, the Apostle calls on his listeners to repent.

[70] On Origen and Gregory of Nyssa, see Ilaria Ramelli, 'Tears of Pathos, Repentance and Bliss: Crying and Salvation in Origen and Gregory of Nyssa', in *Tears in the Graeco-Roman World*, ed. Thorsten Fögen (Berlin: De Gruyter), 367–96. For Chrysostom, see Francis Leduc, 'Penthos et larmes dans l'œuvre de Saint Jean Chrysostome', *Proche-Orient Chrétien* 41 (1991): 220–57; Laurence Brottier, *Propos sur la contrition de Jean Chrysostome: le destin d'écrits de jeunesse méconnus* (Paris: Éditions du Cerf, 2010).

[71] See the exploration of his *Homily on the Sinful Woman* (an exegesis of Luke 7:36–50) in Hannah Hunt, 'The Tears of the Sinful Woman: A Theology of Redemption in the Homilies of St Ephraim and His Followers', *Hugoye: Journal of Syriac Studies* 1, no. 2 (1998): 165–84.

citing, especially given he was 'almost certainly one of the influences on Romanos'.[72] Indeed, two centuries before Romanos' lifetime, the emergence of monasticism in Egypt and Syria underscored the spiritual significance of tears.[73] Chrysostom had written about compunction as the 'mother of tears' (δακρύων ἐστὶ μήτηρ)[74] and often linked tears and compunction in his homilies.[75] And the letters of the famous Old Men from sixth-century Gaza – Barsanuphios and John – reflect on 'weeping and compunction'.[76] Moreover, Isaac the Syrian's seventh-century writings often highlight the importance of weeping as an expression of repentance.[77]

Texts like John Chrysostom's letters *To Demetrius* and *To Stelechius, On Compunction*[78] vividly described the 'the fire [of compunction]'[79] and the 'fountains of tears'[80] that raged and streamed in his recipients' souls. However, it was during homilies like those he delivered on the occasion of Eutropius' fall from grace that emotions embedded in a text emerged and compunction entered the emotional lexicon of Christianity.[81] This rings all the more true in the performance of Byzantine hymns.

---

[72] See Lash's examination of the non-biblical influences on the sixth-century hymnographer in Lash, *On the Life of Christ*, 235.

[73] Kallistos Ware, '"An Obscure Matter": The Mystery of Tears in Orthodox Spirituality', in Patton and Hawley, eds., *Holy Tears*, 242–54.

[74] *To Demetrius*, chapter 7. See PG 47, 404 and John Chrysostom, *A Companion for the Sincere Penitent: Or, a Treatise on the Compunction of the Heart. In Two Books*, trans. John Veneer (London: Judge's-Head, St Dunstan's Church, 1728), 35.

[75] '[N]ow it's especially a time for tears and compunction, and for a prepared soul and much zeal and much firmness of purpose'. *On the Statues*, homily 17, *John Chrysostom*, trans. Wendy Mayer and Pauline Allen (New York, NY: Routledge, 2000), 106. See also *Homilies on the Gospel of St Matthew*, homily 55 on Matthew 16:24: 'And after this hymn, being filled with much compunction, and with many and fervent tears, so they proceed to sleep, snatching just so much of it as a little to refresh themselves.' St John Chrysostom, *The Homilies of S. John Chrysostom, Archbishop of Constantinople, on the Gospel of St Matthew, Translated with Notes and Indices. Part 2. Hom. 26–58* (Oxford: John Henry Parker, 1844), 754. See also *Homilies on the Epistles of Paul to the Corinthians*, homily 7 on 1 Corinthians 2:6, 7 in *Saint Chrysostom: Homilies on the Epistles of Paul to the Corinthians*, trans. Philip Schaff (New York, NY: Christian Literature Company, 1899), 74: 'For their call was from fornication unto chastity; from love of life unto sundry kinds of death; from drunkenness unto fasting; from laughter unto tears and compunction.'

[76] See, for example, letters 343 and 461 in *Barsanuphios and John: Letters*, trans. Chryssavgis, Vol. 1 (Washington, DC: Catholic University of America Press, 2006), 314; *Letters*, vol. 2, 75. The Greek text is in *Barsanuphe et Jean de Gaza: Correspondance*, edited by François Neyt and Paula de Angelis-Noah. SC 450–51 (Paris: Éditions du Cerf, 2000–2002).

[77] See Hannah Hunt, 'The Monk as Mourner: St Isaac the Syrian & Monastic Identity in the 7th C. & Beyond', in *Orthodox Monasticism Past and Present*, ed. John A. McGuckin (Piscataway, NJ: Gorgias Press, 2015), 331–42.

[78] The letters *To the Monk Demetrius: On Compunction* and *To Stelechius: On Compunction* appear in PG 47, 393–422. Any translations are my own.

[79] *To Stelechius*, chapter 1, PG 47, 411.   [80] *To Demetrius*, chapter 1, PG 47, 394.

[81] *On Eutropius*, PG 52, 391–96.

Although several of Romanos' hymns present a biblical figure as an exemplar of compunction and repentance, two of his *kontakia* are explicitly concerned with the overarching significance of this catalogue of repentant sinners: *On Repentance* and *A Prayer*.[82] They are strategically placed at the beginning and near the end of the Lenten liturgical cycle as touchstones of repentance. *On Repentance* presents the narrative of the remorseful Ninevites as an image and song of collective repentance, and *A Prayer* recapitulates various Lenten themes, such as eschatology and biblical exemplars of fallenness, compunction and repentance, in a personal plea for salvation to God. These collective and personal entreaties are contrasted with the silence of the unrepentant drowned in Romanos' *kontakion* on Noah, which was also sung during the early weeks of Lent.[83]

The performance of Romanos' hymn *On Repentance* took place during the Wednesday of the first week of the Lenten fast.[84] Beyond its immediate context of the *pannychis*, this *kontakion* was sung only a few days after Cheese-Fare Sunday – the Sunday that enacted the exile of Adam and Eve from Eden.[85] This Sunday encapsulated the climate of paradisal nostalgia and the sense of alienation from the divine that characterised the journey of Lent. One of the hymns that is found in the *Triodion* for this day dramatises Adam's lament at being banished from the 'bliss of Paradise' (Παραδείσου τῆς τρυφῆς) in the form of a soliloquy, during which he exclaims on three occasions: 'Woe is me!' (Οἴμοι).[86] The anonymous

---

[82] *On Repentance* is a 'compunctious *kontakion*' about the repentance of the Ninevites. It was sung on the Wednesday of the first week of the Lenten fast. See Romanos le Mélode, *Hymnes. Tome I*, 410–27. *A Prayer* is a 'compunctious *kontakion*' about repentance that was chanted during the Wednesday of the fifth week of the Lenten fast (a day before Andrew of Crete's *Great Kanon*). It only survives in a single manuscript, the eleventh-century Patmiacus 213. See Romanos le Mélode, *Hymnes. Tome V*, 512–25.

[83] See Georgia Frank, 'Crowds and Collective Affect in Romanos' Biblical Retellings', in *The Garb of Being: Embodiment and the Pursuit of Holiness in Late Ancient Christianity*, ed. Georgia Frank, Susan R. Holman and Andrew S. Jacobs (New York, NY: Fordham University Press, 2020), 169–90.

[84] For further background on the evolution of the *pannychis* in Constantinople, see Miguel Arranz, 'N. D. Uspensky: The Office of the All-Night Vigil in the Greek Church and in the Russian Church', *St Vladimir's Theological Quarterly* 24 (1980): 169–74.

[85] According to the fourteenth-century Byzantine historian, Nikephoros Kallistos Xanthopoulos, commemorating the exile of Adam and Eve from Eden on Cheese-Fare Sunday (the last Sunday of the pre-Lenten period) was an ancient practice. See Getcha, *The Typikon Decoded*, 160–61. Hymns narrating this biblical event can be found in three of the earliest manuscripts of the *Triodion*: Sinai Graecus 734–735, fols. 45r–49r, Vaticanus Graecus 771, fols. 30r–32r, and Grottaferrata Δβ I, fols. 28r–30v.

[86] Ware and Mother Mary, *The Lenten Triodion*, 178. This hymn is found in two of the earliest manuscripts of the *Triodion*: Sinai Graecus 734–735, fol. 46r, and Grottaferrata Δβ I, fol. 28v.

composition, *On the Lament of Adam*,[87] invited the faithful to sing the words of Adam in the refrain of the hymns as if they were the cry of all Christians: 'O Merciful, have mercy on the one who has fallen' ('Ελεῆμον, ἐλέησόν με τὸν παραπεσόντα).[88]

According to the Old Testament lectionary of Constantinople, the *Prophetologion*,[89] the worshipping faithful heard passages from Genesis during Lenten vespers, beginning on the first Monday of Lent (which liturgically began on the evening of the previous day – Cheese-Fare Sunday), and ending on Palm Sunday.[90] The narrative of the exile of Adam and Eve was read during vespers on Friday of the first week of Lent.[91] And according to Romanos' hymn *On the Victory of the Cross*,[92] the crucifixion of Christ heralds the end of this banishment for the first-created humans and indeed all the faithful:

Οὐκέτι φλογίνη   ῥομφαία φυλάττει τὴν πύλην τῆς Ἐδέμ
αὐτῇ γὰρ ἐπῆλθε,   παράδοξος δέσις,   τὸ ξύλον τοῦ σταυροῦ·
. . .
ἡμῖν τὸ ξύλον σου   ἀποδίδωσι
καθ' ἡμέραν καὶ καιρὸν   πλοῦτον ἀτίμητον·
τοὺς γὰρ πάντας εἰσάγει   πάλιν εἰς τὸν παράδεισον.[93]

The sword of flame no longer guards the gate of Eden,
for a strange bond came upon it: the wood of the Cross.
. . .
To us your Tree gives back,
every day and moment, wealth beyond price,
for it brings us all
          again to Paradise.[94]

---

[87] For the Greek text of this late fifth-century, early sixth-century hymn, see Paul Maas, *Frühbyzantinische Kirchenpoesie: I. Anonyme Hymnen des V–VI Jahrhunderts* (Berlin: De Gruyter, 1931), 16–20.

[88] For an English translation of this hymn by Ephrem Lash, see: https://web.archive.org/web/20150702103638/http://www.anastasis.org.uk:80/adam's_lament.htm (retrieved 1 September 2018). For an exploration of how the voice of Adam and the voice of the Christian were fused in the performance of such hymns, see Krueger, *Liturgical Subjects*, 186–91.

[89] Høeg, Zuntz and Engberg, *Prophetologium*.

[90] The *Prophetologion* itself emerged in the eighth century but reflected earlier lectionary practices in Constantinople. See Sysse Gundrun Engberg, 'The *Prophetologion* and the Triple-Lection Theory – the Genesis of a Liturgical Book', *Bollettino della Badia Greca di Grottaferrata* (series 3) 3 (2006): 67–92; James Miller, 'The Prophetologion: The Old Testament of Byzantine Christianity?', in *The Old Testament in Byzantium*, ed. Magdalino and Nelson, 55–76.

[91] See the readings for the first and second weeks of Lent in volume one (fasciculus secundus, 1940) of Høeg, Zuntz and Engberg, *Prophetologium*, 150–54.

[92] According to the manuscript tradition, the liturgical context of *On the Victory of the Cross* was not Holy Friday but the Wednesday of mid-Lent. See Romanos le Mélode, *Hymnes. Tome IV*, 282.

[93] Ibid., 284, 310.   [94] Prelude 1 and strophe 18. See Lash, *On the Life of Christ*, 155, 163.

The refrain subtly echoes the metanarrative of repentance and salvation that recurs throughout Romanos' *kontakia*, highlighting the moment of epiphany when the journey of homecoming begins.

Although the narrative structure of *On Repentance* was the Old Testament story of how the Ninevites' fasting and repentance delivered their city from impending doom, its broader liturgical and Lenten context framed the meaning of the compunction and repentance it enacted. Moreover, Romanos juxtaposes this story from a bygone era with his contemporary reality of the people of Constantinople in the prelude of the *kontakion*,[95] inviting all to the 'infirmary of repentance' (ἰατρεῖον τῆς μετανοίας) in the first strophe:

δεῦτε,
προφθάσωμεν,   κἀκεῖθεν ῥῶσιν   ταῖς ψυχαῖς ἡμῶν λάβωμεν·
ἐν αὐτῷ γὰρ ἡ πόρνη ὑγίανεν,   ἐν αὐτῷ ἀπέθετο
   καὶ ὁ Πέτρος τὴν ἄρνησιν,
ἐν αὐτῷ τὸ ἐγκάρδιον   ἄλγος Δαυὶδ ἔθραυσεν,
ἐν αὐτῷ καὶ Νινευῆται   ἰατρεύθησαν.
Μὴ οὖν ὀκνῶμεν,   ἀλλ' ἀναστῶμεν
   καὶ δείξωμεν τὸ τραῦμα   τῷ Σωτῆρι,   καὶ λάβωμεν ἔμπλαστρον·
ὑπὲρ πάντα γὰρ πόθον   προσδέχεται ἡμῶν   τὴν μετάνοιαν.

come,
let us act in anticipation and let us receive from there strength for our souls;
for there the harlot became healthy,
there also Peter put away his denial,
there David broke down the pain of his heart,
and there the Ninevites were cured.
Let us not be indolent, but let us rise up,
let us show our wound to the Saviour, let us receive a salve;
for above every desire,
   he accepts our repentance.

The medical imagery presents sin as a sickness of the soul and repentance as its remedy. In inviting the faithful to the infirmary of spiritual healing, Romanos momentarily strays from his storybook. He repeatedly invokes the hortative voice and weaves the story of the Ninevites together with other stories of repentance from the Old and New Testaments. The unifying threads in these narratives of repentance are tears and compunction. Indeed, 'tears are cherished, desired and longed for by the Saviour' (δάκρυα· ἔστι

---

[95] 'Lord, show compassion even now on your people and your city' (Κύριε σπλαγχνίσθητι καὶ νῦν ἐπὶ λαὸν καὶ πόλιν σου).

γὰρ καὶ φίλτατα καὶ ἐράσμια τῷ ῥύστῃ καὶ ποθούμενα),[96] they 'cleansed the filth of [the city]' (τὸν ῥύπον αὐτῆς ἐκπλύναντες)[97] and they can paradoxically overcome the omnipotence of God:

ἡδέως γὰρ   ὑπὸ δακρύων   ὁ οἰκτίρμων συνέχεται,
τῶν δακρύων δὲ τῶν ἐκ τοῦ πνεύματος,   οὐ τῶν ἐκ τοῦ σώματος,
   ὧν αἱ θλίψεις παραίτιοι·
καὶ νεκροὺς γὰρ δακρύομεν   καὶ ἐκ πληγῶν κλαίομεν·
ἡ γὰρ σάρξ πηλὸς ὑπάρχει   ῥέων ἄπαυστα.
Κλαύσωμεν τοίνυν   ἀπὸ καρδίας,
   ὃν τρόπον Νινευῆται   κατανύξει   τὸν οὐρανὸν ἤνοιξαν
καὶ ὤφθησαν τῷ ῥύστῃ,   καὶ ἐδέξατο αὐτῶν   τὴν μετάνοιαν.[98]

for truly the compassionate one is pleasantly constrained by tears,
by tears that are from the soul, not from the body,
tears which are partly caused by afflictions.
For we not only weep over the dead but also cry from wounds;
for our flesh is clay, flowing with unceasing tears.
Therefore, let us weep from the heart,
in which manner the Ninevites, with compunction, opened heaven
and they were seen by the deliverer,
   and he accepted their repentance.

Romanos does not portray tears of compunction as incorporeal; he suggests their source – the innermost depths of the human person – differs from that of other tears, such as tears of sorrow or tears of pain. *On Repentance* depicts compunction and tears as having the power to purify a city and to summon God's mercy. In presenting repentance as an infirmary, the hymn's imagery echoes Gregory of Nyssa's portrayal of 'a tear as blood from the wounds of the soul' (τῶν τῆς ψυχῆς τραυμάτων ὥσπερ αἷμα τὸ δάκρυον)[99] leading to repentance.[100]

Encouraging the faithful to weep from their hearts like the Ninevites of old, Romanos' hymn, *On Repentance*, enacts the collective feeling and cosmic implications of a city's compunction and repentance. Although the final strophe reverts to the first-person singular, ending with a

---

[96] Strophe 2.   [97] Strophe 5.   [98] Ibid.
[99] Gregory of Nyssa, *Funeral Oration on the Empress Flacilla* in PG 46, 880C and *Gregorii Nysseni Opera* IX, ed. Andreas Spira (Leiden: Brill, 1967), 477. Quoted in Kimberley Christine Patton, '"Howl, Weep and Moan, and Bring it Back to God": Holy Tears in Eastern Christianity', in Patton and Hawley, eds., *Holy Tears*, 261.
[100] It also points to what the word compunction originally signified. Before Christianity transposed its meaning, κατάνυξις denoted physical pain rather than a metaphorical piercing of the heart. See Michael S. Driscoll, 'Compunction', in *Catholic Dictionary of Spirituality*, ed. Michael Downey (Collegeville, MN: Liturgical Press, 1995), 193.

personal prayer for repentance, the previous strophes dramatise the salvation of the Ninevites and God's compassion in the face of their compunction. Without diminishing the personal significance of repentance for each of the faithful, Romanos' *kontakion* sought to shape an emotional community that felt compunction and understood the sacred dimension of tears that flowed from this emotion.[101] The congregation's singing of the refrain – 'he accepts our repentance' – and its variations, their familiarity with the *kontakion* and its story, which was sung every year in the first week of Lent, and their experience of the *pannychis*, became their musical, textual and ritual scripts. However, they were also liturgical scripts through which the faithful besought the tears of compunction that saved the Ninevites.

This theme is more pronounced in Romanos' *A Prayer*, which four weeks later would invite the faithful to cry out and ask God for tears that 'purify [the soul] through compunction'.[102] To underscore why this catharsis of tears is vital, Romanos invoked the nuptial metaphor of the soul's union with the Creator, which echoed the allegorical interpretation of the Song of Songs that Origen and Gregory of Nyssa had espoused:

> Ῥερύπωται ἡ ψυχή μου
> ἐνδεδυμένη τὸν χιτῶνα τῶν πταισμάτων μου·
> . . .
> λαμπρὰν στολήν με ἔνδυσον   ἀξίαν τοῦ γάμου σου,
> ὁ θέλων πάντας τοὺς ἀνθρώπους σωθῆναι.[103]

> My soul has been defiled
> having been clothed in a garment of my misdeeds
> . . .
> Clothe me in radiant raiment that is worthy of your wedding,
> *You who desire all people to be saved.*

The context for this personal plea is an intricate image presented by the prelude of the *kontakion* in the form of a dialogue between self and soul. Romanos encourages the faithful to become introspective and remember events from the past and the future as they partake in the affective mystagogy of hymnody:

---

[101] However, no single emotion could define such a community – emotional communities were built on a constellation of emotions. See Rosenwein, *Emotional Communities*, 26.
[102] Strophe 2.   [103] Ibid.

Τοῦ φοβεροῦ δικαστοῦ   τὴν ἐξέτασιν
ἐν τῇ ζωῇ σου, ψυχή,   ἐνθυμήθητι,
καὶ μνήσθητι τῶν στεναγμῶν τοῦ τελώνου,   τῶν ὀδυρμῶν τῆς πόρνης,
κραυγάζουσα ἐν κατανύξει·
«Ταῖς εὐχαῖς τῶν ἁγίων   ἱλασμόν μοι παράσχου,
ὁ θέλων πάντας τοὺς ἀνθρώπους σωθῆναι».[104]

O my soul, during your life, ponder the scrutiny of the fearful judge and
remember the sighings of the publican, the lamentations of the harlot,
crying out in compunction:
'Through the prayers of the saints grant me forgiveness,
You who desire all people to be saved'.

The refrain of *A Prayer* would have become the entreaty of the faithful as
the *kontakion* was sung and it echoed the Ninevites' song of repentance,
which the congregation sang on their behalf: '[the Saviour] accepts our
repentance' (προσδέχεται ἡμῶν τὴν μετάνοιαν).[105] The mimicry of emotion and its potential for contagion would have been provoked by Romanos' use of crowds to present collective emotions, such as the Ninevites'
tears of compunction.[106]

Repentance and tears emerge as the essential characteristics of the
biblical exemplars that have paved the way to the experience of divine
benevolence:

Πολλοὶ διὰ μετανοίας
τῆς παρὰ σοῦ φιλανθρωπίας ἠξιώθησαν·
τελώνην στενάξαντα   καὶ πόρνην δακρύσασαν   ἐδικαίωσας.[107]

Many through repentance
have been made worthy of your love towards humanity:
You justified the sighing tax collector and the weeping harlot.

This hope of salvation would have been juxtaposed with the sombre reality
evoked by the *troparion*[108] that, according to the *Typikon of the Great
Church*, was chanted in Hagia Sophia on the same day:

Ἀνυπόστατος, Κύριε, ἡ ὀργὴ τῆς ἐπὶ ἁμαρτωλοὺς ἀπειλῆς σου, καὶ οὐκ
ἐσμὲν ἄξιοι ἀτενίσαι καὶ αἰτῆσαι παρὰ σοῦ τὸ ἔλεός σου. μὴ τῷ θυμῷ σου,
μὴ τῇ ὀργῇ σου ἀπολέσῃς ἡμᾶς, οὓς ἐκ γῆς τῇ χειρί σου ἔπλασας.[109]

---

[104] *A Prayer*, prelude.   [105] *On Repentance*, strophe 1.
[106] Elaine Hatfield, Megan Carpenter and Richard L. Rapson, 'Emotional Contagion as a Precursor to
Collective Emotions', in *Collective Emotions*, ed. Christian von Scheve and Mikko Salmela
(Oxford: Oxford University Press, 2014), 108–22.
[107] *A Prayer*, strophe 1.   [108] See Elizabeth M. Jeffreys, 'Troparion', in *ODB*, 2124.
[109] Mateos, *Le Typicon de la Grande Église: Tome II*, 48. The translation into English is my own.

O Lord, the wrath of your threat on sinful persons cannot be withstood, and we are not worthy to gaze upon and entreat from you your mercy. Do not destroy us whom you fashioned from the earth by your hand, neither in your anger nor in your wrath.

The dialectic of creation and the eschaton is perpetuated. This was reiterated centuries later in the *Triodion*. For example, in Sinai Graecus 734–735, fol. 59r, and Grottaferrata Δβ I, fol. 114v, there is a *troparion* that recalls the exile from Eden and the salvation of the Cross:

Ξύλου γευσάμενος, Ἀδὰμ μὴ προσηκόντως, τῆς ἀκρασίας τοὺς καρποὺς πικρῶς ἐτρύγησεν, ὑψωθεὶς δὲ ἐν ξύλῳ τοῦτον ἐλυτρώσω, Οἰκτίρμον, τῆς καταδίκης τῆς χαλεπῆς· διό σοι ἀναβοῶμεν· Δίδου ἡμῖν, ἐγκρατεύεσθαι Δέσποτα, ἀπὸ καρποῦ φθοροποιοῦ, καὶ πράττειν σου τὸ θέλημα, ὅπως εὕρωμεν ἔλεος.

Having tasted the tree, Adam unfittingly gathered the bad mixture of the fruits, but you O Merciful One, being raised on the cross, redeemed him from the grievous condemnation; wherefore we cry out to you: 'Grant to us, Master, to abstain from the deadly fruit, and to do your will, so that we may find mercy'.

The Byzantine experience of hymnody was scaffolded by the affective mysticism of the Lenten liturgical cycle, synchronically, in the unfolding of compunction in a particular performance, and diachronically, in the acquisition of an emotional repertoire.

It is difficult to unearth the iconography that the faithful in Constantinople would have seen while singing the hymns of Romanos. Remnants from the artistic tradition that produced images of Christ and the Theotokos before the outbreak of the iconoclastic crisis that engulfed Byzantium are rare.[110] Nevertheless, the age of Justinian was a fecund one for Christian art and architecture.[111] An icon of Christ that survives from the first half of the sixth century, which is of Constantinopolitan provenance, is found at the monastery of St Catherine in the mountains of the Sinai Peninsula. The strong duality of this icon of Christ, which seems to combine two different styles and facial expressions into the one icon, portrays 'a duality within God himself: the paradoxical coexistence of mercy and judgment'.[112] If the

---

[110] For historical background and context on the cult of images and icons before Iconoclasm, see Leslie Brubaker and John Haldon, *Byzantium in the Iconoclast Era, c. 680–850: A History* (Cambridge: Cambridge University Press, 2011), 9–68.

[111] See the array of sources collected in Mango, *The Art of the Byzantine Empire*, 55–119.

[112] Maximos Constas, *The Art of Seeing: Paradox and Perception in Orthodox Iconography* (Alhambra, CA: Sebastian Press, 2014), 68.

faithful were able to gaze upon such an icon of Christ during the singing of hymns, this juxtaposition of mercy and judgment may have highlighted the emotional arc of Romanos' *On Repentance* and *A Prayer*.[113]

Themes of divine mercy and judgment were also evoked in Romanos' *On Earthquakes and Fires*, which the manuscript tradition ascribes to the Wednesday of the third week of Lent.[114] The hymn enjoins repentance and arouses compunction by vividly alluding to historical events of destruction – the Nika revolt of 532 and various earthquakes – which are described as a means of placing 'faintheartedness' (ἀθυμίαν) at 'the table of grace' (τὴν τράπεζαν τῆς χάριτος)[115] and an example of God's mysterious compassion: 'Inwardly the master is merciful, while he outwardly appears inclined to anger' (Ἔνδοθεν ὁ δεσπότης φιλάνθρωπος, ἔξωθεν ὀργίλος·).[116] Romanos did not construct a terrifying image of God's judgment seat. Towards the end of *On Earthquakes and Fires,* the hymnographer presents the sacred space of Hagia Sophia as an embodiment of the heavenly kingdom, 'as imitating heaven, the divine throne, which grants eternal life'.[117] The mosaics of Christ and the Theotokos in Hagia Sophia, which survive to this day, were restored after the end of Iconoclasm and may represent a later stage in the evolution of Byzantine art.[118] Although Romanos' hymns were sung for centuries after his death, his *kontakia* and the *Christ Pantokrator* icon are contemporary, exhibit thematic parallels and represent a reimagining of what the faithful may have heard and seen during the performance of his hymns.

The intermedial connections between hymnography and iconography were integral to Byzantine worship, which constituted a 'metaesthetic iconotext'[119] – a 'liturgical synergy of images and words' that sought to

---

[113] Although it is unclear whether this icon would have been seen in the churches of Constantinople, it is fair to assume that icons of Christ and the Theotokos did adorn sacred spaces of worship. In Hagia Sophia, Paul the Silentiary tells us that Christ's image on the altar cloth was like that of the *Christ Pantokrator*. 'The forearm and hand are thus laid bare. He seems to be stretching out the fingers of the right hand, as if preaching his immortal words, while in his left hand he holds the book of divine message—the books that tells us what he, the Lord, accomplished with provident mind when his foot trod the earth.' *Ekphrasis of Hagia Sophia*, lines 775–80. For the Greek text, see Veh, *Prokop: Werke*, 344–46. (Volume 5 also contains Paul the Silentiary's works.) The English translation is from Mango, *The Art of the Byzantine Empire*, 89.

[114] For the text of the hymn, see Romanos le Mélode, *Hymnes. Tome V*, 470–98. While the manuscript tradition may assign this hymn to the third week of Lent, it may have been intended as a panegyric to Justinian in Romanos' lifetime.

[115] Strophe 14.   [116] Strophe 5.   [117] Strophe 23.

[118] See Photios' *Homily XVII* for the unveiling of the image of the Virgin and Child delivered on 29 March 867 in Hagia Sophia in Laourdas, Φωτίου Ὁμιλίαι [*The Homilies of Photios*], 164–72; Mango, *The Homilies of Photius*, 286–96.

[119] Olkinuora, *Byzantine Hymnography*, 269.

Figure 1:   *Christ Pantokrator,* encaustic on board, Monastery of St Catherine, Mt Sinai.
By permission of Saint Catherine's Monastery, Sinai, Egypt

render biblical persons or events present.[120] Despite the scarcity of sources
for the icons that would have been found in the churches of Constantinople before the advent of Iconoclasm, the pictorial rhetoric of hymns
provided the faithful with a vast array of images. Indeed, 'listening, as well
as seeing, smelling, touching' during worship had the power to inscribe
images and memories in their hearts.[121] Hymns, homilies and prayers
helped the Byzantines construct 'an inner world of images' and opened
the potential for performance to reach out towards the divine.[122] Through
ekphrasis and *enargeia*,[123] hymnody could turn listeners into spectators,

[120] Ibid., 205.   [121] Harrison, *The Art of Listening*, 61.   [122] Ibid., 62–63.
[123] As Ruth Webb notes, *enargeia* (ἐνάργεια) is the quality of language that appeals to the imagination
and is a defining quality of ekphrasis. See Webb, 'Imagination and the Arousal of the Emotions',

engender a feeling of presence and arouse emotions. Romanos' use of
ekphrasis and *enargeia* was not merely an attempt to persuade his audience;
it sought to blur the boundaries between past and present, between self
and other. This will become a particularly relevant premise as we explore
Romanos' exemplars of compunction.

Biblical Exemplars of Compunction

As the faithful journeyed through Great Lent and Holy Week, Romanos'
hymns presented them with biblical exemplars of compunction, retelling
scriptural stories and welcoming them into these narratives. The parable of
the prodigal son, the story of the harlot who washed Christ's feet with her
tears and other narratives that juxtaposed biblical heroes with counter-
ideals, such as the foolish virgins and Judas, were enriched with melody
and dramatic dialogue as the hymnographer explored the emotions of his
protagonists and dramatised their repentance – or obduracy.

However, Romanos' hymnography did not simply enrich biblical texts.
His hymns sought to harness the iconic nature of the liturgy to incite a
profound experience that could shape Christian personhood.[124] The singing of these hymns by the faithful signified a liturgical imitation of these
biblical exemplars, where the speech acts of Romanos' protagonists could
become the song and confession of the congregation, and where emotions
could become intersubjective.[125] Singing the words of these biblical exemplars and entering the liturgical world of these scriptural stories, the faithful
prayed for tears and yearned to feel the compunction that were embodied
in poetry, melody and sacred drama.

I will explore two hymns that were performed during Great Lent and
Holy Week – *On the Prodigal*[126] and *On the Harlot*[127] – while briefly
alluding to other relevant *kontakia*, such as *On the Ten Virgins*, *On Peter's*

112–27. See also Olkinuora, *Byzantine Hymnography*, 210–12; Webb, 'Spatiality, Embodiment
   and Agency in Ekphraseis of Church Buildings', in Pentcheva, ed., *Aural Architecture in
   Byzantium*, 165.
[124] See Taft, *Through Their Own Eyes*, 148–54; Tkacz, 'Singing Women's Words', 275–328; Krueger,
   'Romanos the Melodist and the Early Christian Self', 255–74.
[125] On the intersubjective dimension of Byzantine worship in sixth-century Constantinople, see
   Schibille, *Hagia Sophia and the Byzantine Aesthetic Experience*, 32–37.
[126] This is a 'compunctious *kontakion*' about repentance and forgiveness that, according to the
   Patmiacus 213 manuscript, was chanted during the Second Sunday of Lent. For the Greek text
   of the hymn, see Romanos le Mélode, *Hymnes. Tome III*, 234–60. For the English translation, see
   Lash, *On the Life of Christ*, 101–11.
[127] This hymn was chanted during Holy Wednesday. For the Greek text see Romanos le Mélode,
   Hymnes. Tome III, 20–42. For the English translation, see Lash, *On the Life of Christ*, 77–84.

Denial and, as a stark contrast, *On Judas*. The first hymn that presented the faithful with a biblical exemplar of compunction during the Lenten cycle was *On the Prodigal*. Although it is unclear from the manuscript tradition whether Romanos' *On the Prodigal* was performed on the Second Sunday of Lent or on the first of the three preparatory Sundays preceding Lent, before the fourteenth century in Constantinople the Second Sunday of Lent had no particular theme.[128] Moreover, the *Typikon of the Great Church* does not assign Luke 15:11–32 (the parable of the prodigal son) as the Gospel reading for that Sunday.[129] Instead, this biblical passage is prescribed for the first of the three preparatory Sundays preceding Lent – 'the Sunday before Carnival Sunday'.[130]

Further evidence that this Sunday commemorated the parable of the prodigal son is found in two early manuscripts of the *Triodion*, which dedicate a number of hymns to the theme of the prodigal for this day.[131] One of the hymns common to both manuscripts ends by inviting the faithful to sing the words of the prodigal son:

> σοὶ γὰρ Κύριε· ἐν κατανύξει κραυγάζω. Ἥμαρτον Πάτερ εἰς τὸν οὐρανὸν καὶ ἐνώπιόν σου.[132]

> to you, O Lord, in compunction I cry out: Father, I have sinned against heaven and in your sight.[133]

The hymn *On the Prodigal* begins by adopting a similar strategy, asking the congregation to identify their 'senseless deeds' (ταῖς ἀτόποις μου πράξεσι) with those of the prodigal son who befouled 'the first robe of grace' (τὴν πρώτην καταστολὴν τῆς χάριτός) – a baptismal image that is developed further in the fourth strophe – with 'the stains of passions' (παθῶν ταῖς κηλῖσιν).[134] As the prodigal son 'came to himself'[135] and arose to return to his father's house, likewise the *kontakion* calls each of the faithful back to the 'mystical table' (μυστικῆς τραπέζης)[136] – an image of the Eucharist:

> καὶ ὡς ἐκεῖνος προσπίπτω σοι   καὶ ζητῶ τὴν ἄφεσιν, Κύριε·
> διὸ μὴ παρίδῃς με,   ὁ τῶν αἰώνων δεσπότης καὶ κύριος.[137]

---

[128] Getcha, *The Typikon Decoded*, 189.
[129] Mateos, *Le Typicon de la Grande Église: Tome II*, 30. Instead, this passage from Mark 2:1–12 (the healing of the paralytic) is prescribed. It is the Hagiopolite tradition and its lectionaries that assign Luke 15: 11–32 to the Second Sunday of Lent. See Getcha, *The Typikon Decoded*, 146.
[130] Mateos, *Le Typicon de la Grande Église: Tome II*, 2.
[131] See Sinai Graecus 734–735, fol. 3 r–v, and Vaticanus Graecus 771, fol. 9 r–v.
[132] Sinai Graecus 734–735, fol. 3r; Vaticanus Graecus 771, fol. 3r.
[133] The translation is my own.   [134] Preludes 1 and 2.   [135] Luke 15:17.   [136] Prelude 2.
[137] Prelude 1.

and like him I fall down before you and seek forgiveness, Lord.
Therefore do not despise me
Master and Lord of the ages.

Romanos presents the prodigal son as a paradigm of humanity who travels to
a faraway land and – not unlike Adam – acknowledges his fallenness, feels
compunction and nostalgia, and begins the journey home. Strangely though,
the prodigal son only utters one line in the whole *kontakion* (in the third
strophe). Nevertheless, it is through the prism of his repentance that Romanos invites the faithful to see and hear every other monologue and dialogue in
the hymn, as well as the eucharistic and baptismal themes that emerge.

Unlike his hymn *On the Harlot*, which delves into the protagonist's
thoughts and feelings, Romanos here encourages the congregation to be
more circumspect and ponder the entire drama of salvation at play. In the
first and second strophes alone, the hymn employs the hortative voice or
imperative mood on several occasions, inviting the congregation to step
into the liturgical world of the *kontakion*: 'let us contemplate' (κατίδωμεν);
'hurry' (σπεύσατε); 'let us celebrate' (εὐφρανθῶμεν); 'let us hasten' (σπουδάσωμεν); 'let us banquet' (συνεστιαθῶμεν); 'let us see' (ἴδωμεν).[138]

The hymn likens the robe that the prodigal son is given upon his
repentance to 'the first robe, which the baptismal font weaves for all' (τὴν
στολὴν τὴν πρώτην ἣν ἡ κολυμβήθρα πᾶσιν ὑφαίνει).[139] This 'first robe'
symbolises the ancient glory of Adam and Eve before they were given the
'garments of skin'[140] and represents the common gift of all Christians who
have been 'baptised into Christ' and have 'put on Christ'.[141] Therefore in
encouraging the faithful to imitate the prodigal son's repentance, Romanos
unlocks the significance of his compunction for all Christians. And in
dramatising the father's compassion for his son with a monologue that does
not appear in the Lukan narrative, the hymnographer demonstrates God's
desire for all of his creation to be found worthy of forgiveness:[142]

> Ἴδον αὐτὸν καὶ παριδεῖν   οὐ στέγω τὸν γυμνωθέντα·
> οὐ φέρω βλέπειν οὕτως   τὴν εἰκόνα μου τὴν θείαν·
> ἐμὴ γὰρ αἰσχύνη   τὸ ὄνειδος τοῦ παιδός μου·
> ἰδίαν δόξαν   τὴν τοῦ τέκνου δόξαν ἡγήσομαι.[143]

---

[138] Strophes 1–2.   [139] Strophe 4.

[140] Genesis 3:21. As noted earlier, the faithful heard passages from Genesis during Lent, including the
narrative of the exile from Eden.

[141] Galatians 3:27.

[142] Romanos intimates in the first strophe that the father of the prodigal son is 'the Father of all
humankind'.

[143] Strophe 5.

I saw him and I cannot allow myself to overlook his nakedness;
I cannot bear to see my divine image like this.
For the disgrace of my child is my shame;
I will consider the glory of my child my own glory.[144]

Here, Romanos begins to allude to the salvific acts of Christ – the crucifixion, descent into Hades, and resurrection – that will mark the climax of the Lenten journey. Although it is still the beginning of the Lenten season and these events have not yet come to pass, the ritual aesthetic and performance of Byzantine hymns create a rich dialectic between what has happened before and will occur again.

Romanos' exegesis of the fatted calf and the banquet that mark the festivities for the prodigal's return collapses events that took place long ago with what will be celebrated at the end of Great Lent and Holy Week into the present liturgical moment. The human drama of the prodigal son's compunction and repentance unfolds amidst the divine drama of God's compassion, incarnation and sacrifice:

Ἕλκετε, θύσατε τὸν ζωοδότην
τὸν καὶ θυόμενον καὶ μὴ νεκρούμενον,
τὸν ζωοποιοῦντα πάντας τοὺς ἐν ᾅδῃ,
ἵνα φαγόντες ἐπευφρανθῶμεν·[145]

Drag in, sacrifice the Giver of life,
who is sacrificed and not put to death,
who gives life to those in hell,
so that as we eat we may celebrate.

The hymn's allusion to the Eucharist suggests that the celebration of the liturgy in Hagia Sophia and the other churches of Constantinople was imminent. While the liturgical context of Romanos' hymns was the *pannychis*, this particular *kontakion* was chanted in anticipation of the Sunday liturgy and its eucharistic subtext is striking. Therefore, it underscored the compunction that Emperor Justinian desired the eucharistic prayers of the liturgy to engender. More significantly, it embodied and enacted the liturgy it foreshadowed with poetry and melody.

The repentance of the prodigal climaxes not simply in reconciliation with his father but in the eucharistic celebration where all are given 'the Lover of humankind' as 'all-holy food'.[146] According to Romanos, this celebration is the nub of the parable, which gives meaning to, and is the

---

[144] The phrase 'my divine image' is an allusion to Genesis 1:26.
[144] The phrase 'my divine image' is an allusion to Genesis 1:26.   [145] Strophe 8.
[146] Strophe 9.

fulfilment of, the prodigal son's compunction. Paradoxically, it is not a bishop or priest who presides but God himself who offers and is offered at this mystical banquet:

καὶ πάντες εὐφρανθέντες   ἐμελῴδουν θεῖον ὕμνον·
ὁ πατὴρ μὲν πρῶτος   κατήρξατο τῶν παρόντων,
«Γεύσασθε, λέγων,   καὶ ἴδετε ὅτι Χριστός εἰμι».[147]

and as all were celebrating, they sang a godly hymn.
The Father, first of those present, began.
'Taste', he said 'and see that I am good.'[148]

The speaker in the hymn invites the faithful to internalise the very communion they were anticipating:

«Τὸ πάσχα τὸ ἡμέτερον
ἐτύθη νῦν   Ἰησοῦς Χριστός,
ὁ τῶν αἰώνων   δεσπότης καὶ κύριος».[149]

'Our Passover has now been sacrificed, Jesus Christ,
   Master and Lord of the ages.'

On the Prodigal ends with a prayer to the Logos to accept 'through compassion' all those who, like the prodigal son, cry out with compunction: 'Give us tears, as you did the harlot [and] as you did the publican'.[150] Once again, Romanos brings other scriptural characters into his story, offering these figures as paradigms of repentance. Moreover, in an unexpected twist to the familiar biblical narrative, Romanos adds a new ending to the Lukan account. The prodigal son's disgruntled elder brother, who in the Gospel story refuses to enter the banquet and celebrate his younger brother's return, is persuaded by the love of the father to partake in the supper and sing with joy.[151]

Several weeks after the performance of this *kontakion*, Romanos' hymn *On the Harlot*[152] was sung during Holy Wednesday, days before the crucifixion and burial of Christ. This liturgical positioning deepens the

---

[147] Strophe 10.
[148] 'Taste and see that the Lord is good' (Psalm 33:9) is arguably the earliest communion hymn of the Byzantine liturgy. See Dimitri E. Conomos, *The Late Byzantine and Slavonic Communion Cycle: Liturgy and Music* (Washington, DC: Dumbarton Oaks, 1985), 6–16.
[149] Strophe 10.   [150] Strophe 22.   [151] Strophe 21.
[152] *On the Harlot* was based on the biblical passage from Luke 7:36–50 about the sinful woman who washed Christ's feet with her tears and wiped them with her hair. However, according to the *Typikon of the Great Church*, the Gospel reading prescribed for that day was the same – albeit shorter – narrative from Matthew 26:6–16. See Mateos, *Le Typicon de la Grande Église: Tome II*, 70. The same story is recounted in Mark 14:3–9.

significance of the harlot washing Jesus' feet with tears and anointing him
with myrrh by interweaving her act of repentance with the actions 'grant-
ing the breath of life to all the faithful' (τοῖς πιστοῖς πᾶσι πνοὴν ζωῆς
χορηγοῦντα)[153] – Christ's death and resurrection. Moreover, it is not
without reason that this hymn performed on Holy Wednesday is liturgically nestled between two other pedagogic hymns by Romanos – *On the
Ten Virgins*[154] and *On Peter's Denial*[155] – and a third hymn, *On Judas.*[156]
Whereas the harlot's repentance and 'Peter's tears'[157] conquer Christ, the
foolish virgins lack 'tears, compunction and mercy' (δάκρυα, κατάνυξιν
καὶ ἐλεημοσύνην),[158] and Judas is unable to repent: 'the murderer did not
feel compunction' (οὐ κατενύγη ὁ φονεύς).[159] The latter serve as counter-
ideals that are a stark contrast to the biblical exemplars who 'rouse [their]
tears as intercession to [Christ]'.[160]

Romanos' *On the Harlot* enlarges the Lukan narrative, exploring the
interiority of the harlot who, 'with compunction' (ἐν κατανύξει),[161] closely
follows Christ's footsteps:

> Τὴν φρένα δὲ τῆς σοφῆς   ἐρευνῆσαι ἤθελον
> καὶ γνῶναι πῶς ἔλαμψεν   ἐν αὐτῇ ὁ Κύριος[162]
>
> I wish to search the mind[163] of the wise woman
> and to know how Jesus came to shine in her.

To underscore the appeal of his protagonist as an exemplar worthy of
emulation, Romanos juxtaposes the harlot's tears and repentance with his
own inability to feel compunction by briefly entering the hymn at the end
of the first strophe: 'but I, though I quail, remain in the filth of my deeds'
(ἐγὼ δὲ καὶ πτοούμενος ἐπιμένω τῷ βορβόρῳ τῶν ἔργων μου).[164] This
authorial intrusion into the hymn also serves as a device that could move
the congregation to introspection and compunction. Romanos mediates

---

[153] *On the Harlot*, strophe 1.
[154] This is a *kontakion* that was chanted during Holy Tuesday. However, it appears that Romanos
composed two versions of this hymn on the same topic for the same day: Romanos le Mélode,
Hymnes. Tome III, 322–64; *Hymnes. Tome V*, 296–326.
[155] A *kontakion* chanted during Holy Thursday. *Hymnes. Tome IV*, 111–42; Lash, *On the Life of
Christ*, 129–38.
[156] An 'alternative *kontakion* for Holy and Great Thursday'. *Hymnes. Tome IV*, 68.
[157] *On Peter's Denial*, strophe 20.   [158] Prelude 6, Romanos le Mélode, *Hymnes. Tome III*, 328.
[159] *On Judas*, strophe 3.   [160] *On Peter's Denial*, prelude 2.   [161] *On the Harlot*, prelude 2.
[162] Strophe 4.
[163] Romanos' choice of the Homeric Greek word (φρένας) did not simply mean the mind as the seat of
the mental faculties, but also the heart as the seat of the passions. See H. G. Liddell and R. Scott,
A Greek–English Lexicon (Oxford: Clarendon Press, 1996), 1954.
[164] Strophe 1.

the repentance of his protagonist and the obstinacy of his sinful self by opening a space of participation for the faithful and offering them a choice between exemplar and counterexample.[165]

However, Romanos' intrusion is only fleeting. The hymn soon shifts back to the voice of the harlot – which is absent from the Gospels – and her first-person narrative: 'I am going to him, because it is for me he has come' (Ἀπέρχομαι πρὸς αὐτόν, δι' ἐμὲ γὰρ ἤλυθεν).[166] Romanos dramatises his protagonist's repentance through the vocalisation of her emotions and the transformation of her desire. Often, it is dramatic dialogue – such as her extra-biblical encounter with the perfume-seller[167] – or even a soliloquy that unveils her emotions:

Πῶς σοι ἀτενίσω   τοῖς ὄμμασιν
   ἡ πάντας ἀπατῶσα   τοῖς νεύμασιν;
Πῶς σε δυσωπήσω   τὸν εὔσπλαγχνον
   ἡ σὲ παροργίσασα   τὸν κτίστην μου;[168]

How may I, who have trapped all with my glance, gaze on you?
How may I, who have enraged you, my Creator, entreat you, the
   Compassionate?

Before the harlot's repentance, her lascivious gaze could incite wanton eroticism. Similarly, expensive perfume would have been a tool of her seduction. However, both are transformed when Romanos' protagonist asks for forgiveness:

Ἀλλὰ δέξαι τοῦτο τὸ μύρον   πρὸς δυσώπησιν, Κύριε,
καὶ δώρησαί μοι ἄφεσιν   τῆς αἰσχύνης
τοῦ βορβόρου τῶν ἔργων μου.[169]

But accept this sweet ointment as entreaty, my Master,
and grant me forgiveness from the shame of
   the filth of my deeds.

The transformation of licentious perfume into the fragrance of salvation manifests the harlot's interiority and the metamorphosis of passion that is about to unfold. The hymn suggests a relationship between the sensorium and the emotions. The honing of the harlot's senses enable her to perceive 'Christ's words like sweet drops of fragrance raining down' (ῥήματα τοῦ Χριστοῦ καθάπερ ἀρώματα ῥαινόμενα).[170] Her desire for erotic fulfilment

---

[165] See Krueger's reflections on Romanos as a 'Byzantine Christian Everyman' in *Liturgical Subjects*, 41–44.
[166] Strophe 5, line 1.   [167] Strophes 9–11.   [168] Prelude 2, lines 3–6.
[169] Prelude 2, lines 7–9.   [170] Strophe 1, lines 1–2.

is redefined and reconfigured when she encounters Jesus, 'the loveliest and creator of what is lovely, whose form the harlot longed for before she saw him' (ὁ ὡραιότατος καὶ τῶν ὡραίων ὁ κτίστης, οὗ τὴν ἰδέαν πρὶν ἴδη ἡ πόρνη ἐπόθησεν).[171] Tears of compunction transform her into 'the wise woman' and engender a mystical eroticism for Christ, which is evoked using affective stylistics that echo the *epektasis*[172] of the human to the divine:

ἀφίημι τούς ποτε,   τὸν γὰρ νῦν πάνυ ποθῶ,
καὶ ὡς φιλοῦντά με   μυρίζω καὶ κολακεύω·
κλαίω, στενάζω καὶ πείθω δικαίως ποθῆσαί με
ἀλλοιοῦμαι πρὸς τὸν πόθον   τοῦ ποθητοῦ,
καὶ ὡς θέλει φιληθῆναι,   οὕτω φιλῶ τὸν ἐραστήν μου.[173]

I am leaving those who were once mine, because now I long greatly for him.
And as the One who loves me, I anoint him and caress him,
I weep and I groan and I urge him fittingly to long for me.
I am changed to the longing of the One who is longed for,
and, as he wishes to be kissed, so I kiss my lover.

The harlot's longing for 'the One who is longed for' only intensifies into a more ardent desire after she is 'wounded by the vision of the One whose nature is invisible' (ἐτρώθην πρὸς τὴν ἰδέαν τοῦ ἔχοντος φύσιν ἀνεί-δεον).[174] It is reminiscent of the nuptial imagery in the Song of Songs, which was interpreted by Rabbinic commentary and early Christianity as the love between Christ and the Church but also as the love between Christ and the soul made in his image.[175] Romanos boldly applies this typology of the mystical wedding to the longing of the harlot for Christ and her perception of his divine beauty, suggesting that an erotic yet spiritual bond emerges between them.

Although Romanos does not explicitly present Christ as the bridegroom in this hymn, this theme emerges in his hymn *On the Ten Virgins* and in the hymns sung at the beginning of Holy Week that were composed and performed alongside his *kontakia* as part of the *Triodion* after his lifetime.

---

[171] Strophe 4, line 3.
[172] In the writings of Gregory of Nyssa – such as his *Homilies on the Song of Songs* and *The Life of Moses* – *epektasis* is the perpetual ascent of the human person towards God in an unlimited progress. The 'desire of the soul that is ascending never rests content with what has been known' – it is 'always journeying toward the infinite by way of higher things'. See Homily 8 in Gregory of Nyssa, *Homilies on the Song of Songs*, 261.
[173] Strophe 5.   [174] Strophe 11, line 4.
[175] See the discussion on affective mysticism in Chapter 2. See also Bernard McGinn, '*Unio Mystical* Mystical Union', in *The Cambridge Companion to Christian Mysticism*, ed. Amy Hollywood and Patricia Z. Beckman (Cambridge: Cambridge University Press), 200–10.

The first prelude of Romanos' *On the Ten Virgins* begins with the entreaty:
'Let us love the bridegroom' (Τὸν νυμφίον, ἀδελφοί, ἀγαπήσωμεν).[176] And
according to Sinai Graecus 734–735, fol. 143r, Grottaferrata Δβ I,
fol. 156v, and Vaticanus Graecus 771, fol. 152r, one of the hymns that
was sung by the faithful at the beginning of Holy Week warned about the
bridegroom who is coming in the middle of the night:

> Ἰδοὺ ὁ Νυμφίος ἔρχεται ἐν τῷ μέσῳ τῆς νυκτός, καὶ μακάριος ὁ δοῦλος, ὃν
> εὑρήσει γρηγοροῦντα, ἀνάξιος δὲ πάλιν, ὃν εὑρήσει ῥαθυμοῦντα. Βλέπε
> οὖν ψυχή μου, μὴ τῷ ὕπνῳ κατενεχθῇς, ἵνα μὴ τῷ θανάτῳ παραδοθῇς, καὶ
> τῆς βασιλείας ἔξω κλεισθῇς . . .[177]

> Behold the Bridegroom comes in the middle of the night and blessed is the
> servant whom He shall find watching, but unworthy is he whom He shall
> find in slothfulness. Beware, then, O my soul, and be not overcome by sleep,
> lest thou be given over to death and shut out from the Kingdom . . .[178]

At the beginning of Holy Week, Romanos' *On the Ten Virgins* and the
Triodion evoked the nuptial metaphor of the Song of Songs, inviting the
faithful to identify with the wise virgins. These hymns were closely
followed by *On the Harlot*, which presented the faithful with the harlot's
speech acts of compunction and repentance.

By dramatising the compunction of biblical exemplars, Romanos' *kontakia* became poetic and musical embodiments of the tears and repentance
of his protagonists. Poetry, dramatic dialogue and melody vividly described
the emotions of scriptural heroes and their somatic manifestations. And as
they sang the words of these protagonists, Romanos beckoned the congregation to enter the liturgical narrative:

Τὸν νοῦν ἀνυψώσωμεν,   τὴν φρένα ὑφάψωμεν,   τὸ πνεῦμα μὴ σβέσωμεν,
   τῇ ψυχῇ διαναστῶμεν   καὶ σπουδάσωμεν σχεδὸν συμπαθεῖν τῷ ἀπαθεῖ·[179]

Let us raise up our minds, let us set our hearts on fire, let us not quench the spirit,
Let us rise up in soul and let us hasten to share the Passion of the Dispassionate.

Hearing and singing Romanos' *kontakia*, the faithful could step into the
liturgical world of the hymn and desire the compunction evoked amidst
the mystagogy of holy ritual. The biblical exemplars examined above, such

---

[176] Romanos le Mélode, *Hymnes. Tome III*, 324.
[177] The text appears in the earliest manuscripts of the *Triodion* but also in later redactions such as
Τριῴδιον Κατανυκτικόν, περιέχον ἅπασαν τὴν ἀνήκουσαν αὐτῷ ἀκολουθίαν τῆς ἁγίας καὶ
μεγάλης Τεσσαρακοστῆς (Rome: [n.p.], 1879), 619. Hereafter, I cite the 1879 edition of the
Triodion printed in Rome as Τριῴδιον Κατανυκτικόν.
[178] Ware and Mother Mary, *The Lenten Triodion*, 511.
[179] *On Peter's Denial*, strophe 1, lines 1–2.

as the prodigal and the harlot, reaffirmed the link between compunction and repentance, presenting the faithful with scriptural heroes they could emulate – in stark contrast to Judas, who did not feel compunction.

Compunction and the Eschaton

The final theme that will guide my exploration of compunction in Romanos' hymns is the eschaton. *On the Second Coming* is the most explicitly eschatological hymn by Romanos.[180] However, *On the Infernal Powers* and *On the Victory of the Cross* are also noteworthy *kontakia* that touch upon this theme.[181] Although the eschaton often denoted the last things – the end of the world and its final judgment by God – in Byzantine Christian thought, the eschaton was not simply a future occurrence but a reality anticipated in the liturgy and experienced in the Eucharist.[182] Indeed, a tension emerges between an eschatology that has already been inaugurated by the Incarnation, death and resurrection of Christ, and a future eschatology that will be consummated in the life of the age to come.[183] According to Maximus' *On Ecclesiastical Mystagogy*, the performance of the liturgy enacts the eschaton, collapsing past, present and future into liturgical time.[184]

This is not to say that Christians were nonchalant about the end of history or their own death. Speculation on the Last Judgment as a historical event was common in the sixth century.[185] But irrespective of whether the apocalypse was imminent, the sense of mortality and death, and the prospect of either salvation or condemnation, were surely compunction's bedfellows:

---

[180] Romanos le Mélode, *Hymnes. Tome V*, 232–67; Lash, *On the Life of Christ*, 221–30. This *kontakion* was chanted during the second of the three preparatory Sundays before Lent (Carnival Sunday). On the assignment of this hymn to Carnival Sunday in relation to the Second Coming, see Krueger, *Liturgical Subjects*, 33–34.

[181] *On the Infernal Powers* is a 'compunctious *kontakion*' that was chanted during the Thursday of the fifth week of Lent. Romanos le Mélode, *Hymnes. Tome IV*, 242–61. Although Maas and Trypanis entitle this hymn *On the Crucifixion*, I find Grosdidier des Matons' title – *On the Infernal Powers* – more apposite.

[182] Meyendorff, *Byzantine Theology*, 218–20. For early Christianity, the eschaton became a protean concept. See Brian Daley, *The Hope of the Early Church: A Handbook of Patristic Eschatology* (Cambridge: Cambridge University Press, 1991), 1–5.

[183] See Georges Florovsky, 'The Patristic Age and Eschatology: An Introduction', in *Aspects of Church History: Volume Four in the Collected Works of Georges Florovsky* (Belmont, MA: Nordland Publishing Company, 1975), 63–78; Baghos, 'St Basil's Eschatological Vision'.

[184] See chapter 24 in Berthold, *Maximus Confessor*, 206–13. For the Greek text, see Boudignon, *Maximi Confessoris Mystagogia*, 55–71. The 'proclamation of the Gospel' marks the 'end of history' and all that follows takes place in 'the age to come'. Louth, 'The Ecclesiology of Saint Maximus', 114.

[185] Daley, *The Hope of the Early Church*, 179–84.

Κατάνυξις κυρία ἐστίν, ἀμετεώριστος ὀδύνη ψυχῆς μηδεμίαν ἑαυτῇ παρ-
ηγορίαν παρέχουσα, μόνην δὲ τὴν ἑαυτῆς ἀνάλυσιν καθ' ὥραν
φανταζομένη.[186]

True compunction is undistracted pain of soul, which takes for itself no
consolation, each hour imagining only its death.[187]

Romanos draws on this distant yet looming event by cultivating liturgical
compunction through his hymns, not simply as a preparation for future
death and judgment, but as a mode of interacting with an unfurling reality
that was proleptically internalised in the hearts of the faithful through
sacred ritual. He warns the faithful that '[t]he eschaton is near' (Ἡ ἐσχάτη
ἐγγύς) and invites them to engage in a dialogue with their interiority:
'Why are you idle, my humble soul?'[188]

The liturgical positioning of *On the Second Coming* amplified the
remembrance of death and eschatological mood that Romanos' *kontakion*
sought to engender. Not only was it sung during the Sunday of Last
Judgment, when the Gospel passage prescribed by the *Typikon of the Great
Church* (Matthew 25:31–46) narrated this event in a parable[189] – it was
sung a day after the Saturday of the Dead.[190] The biblical passage for this
day (Luke 21:8–36)[191] was also about the eschaton, predicting calamity
and war, and urging the faithful to be watchful, lest the day come and they
be caught unawares. Similarly, Romanos' hymn *On the Second Coming*
opens with a powerful evocation of apocalyptic imagery, a biblical pastiche
drawn from a number of scriptural sources:[192]

> Ὅταν ἔλθῃς, ὁ Θεός,   ἐπὶ γῆς μετὰ δόξης,
>   καὶ τρέμουσι τὰ σύμπαντα,
>   ποταμὸς δὲ τοῦ πυρὸς   πρὸ τοῦ βήματος ἕλκει,
>   καὶ βίβλοι διανοίγονται   καὶ τὰ κρυπτὰ δημοσιεύονται,
> τότε ῥῦσαί με   ἐκ τοῦ πυρὸς τοῦ
>   καὶ ἀξίωσον   ἐκ δεξιῶν σού με στῆναι,
>   κριτὰ δικαιότατε.[193]

---

[186] John Klimakos, *Ladder of Divine Ascent*, PG 88, 808A. Although this is a seventh-century text, it
was representative of the early Christian tradition of asceticism from the fourth century through to
the sixth century. See Torrance, *Repentance in Late Antiquity*, 158–75.
[187] The translation is my own.
[188] *On the Ten Virgins*, strophe 1, lines 5 and 1, Romanos le Mélode, *Hymnes. Tome V*, 298.
[189] Mateos, *Le Typicon de la Grande Église: Tome II*, 2.
[190] According to the *Typikon of the Great Church* and the *Typikon of St Alexios the Stoudite*, this
commemoration emerged as early as the ninth century and was a remembrance of all the departed.
See Getcha, *The Typikon Decoded*, 147–48.
[191] Mateos, *Le Typicon de la Grande Église: Tome II*, 2.
[192] Matthew 25:31, Daniel 7:10, Revelation 21:12, Matthew 3:12, Matthew 25:33, 2 Timothy 4:8.
[193] Prelude.

> When you come upon the earth, O God, in glory,
> And the whole universe trembles,
> while a river of fire flows before the seat of judgment,
> and books are opened and all secrets are disclosed,
> then deliver me from the unquenchable fire
> and count me worthy to stand at your right hand,
>   *Judge most just.*

Although the hymn initially presents judgment as a forthcoming event, a tension emerges between the end of time and its liturgical proximity. As the faithful sang of the eschaton, the immediacy of the fear and compunction they were incited to feel became apparent: 'accused by my conscience, I quake and tremble' (φρίττω καὶ πτοοῦμαι ὑπὸ τῆς συνειδήσεως).[194]

The refrain of the *kontakion* that the congregation would have sung – 'Judge most just' – echoed throughout the hymn as a glimmer of hope and mercy amidst the tears and apocalyptic chaos that prevailed. Moreover, the image of Christ's fearful coming is juxtaposed with the 'ineffable beauty of the Bridegroom' (τὸ κάλλος ἐκεῖνο τὸ ἄφραστον τοῦ νυμφίου)[195] and the grace of the bridal chamber.[196] Romanos reminds his audience that 'blessed will be the one who endures and loves [Christ]' (μακάριος ἔσται δὲ ὁ φέρων καὶ στέργων σε),[197] and immortality will be an 'unutterable joy' (χαρὰν τὴν ἀνεκλάλητον) that is 'without end, without change' (ἀτελεύτητον, ἄτρεπτον).[198] However, he advises the faithful to cultivate 'the fruit of repentance' (τὸν τῆς μετανοίας καρπὸν) now rather than cry with 'vain repentance' (μετάνοιαν ματαίαν) at the hour of judgment.[199] Despite the various portrayals of destruction and suffering, the compunction and repentance the hymn arouses and beseeches is cast in a positive light as a medicine to 'heal the wound of sin'[200] and as a participation in the 'mercy, grace and forgiveness'[201] of God:

> Νῦν οὖν τοῦ σωτῆρος   πάντες δεηθῶμεν   βοῶντες· «Δὸς κατάνυξιν
> τοῖς δούλοις σου, κύριε,   ἵν' εὕρωμεν ἄνεσιν,
>   κριτὰ δικαιότατε».[202]

> And now let us all entreat the Saviour as we cry, 'Give compunction
> to your servants, Lord, that we may find pardon,
>   *Judge most just*.

However, the optimistic dénouement of the hymn did not dispel the damnation that awaited the unrepentant. Two other hymns by Romanos,

---

[194] Strophe 1, line 3.   [195] Strophe 17, line 5.   [196] Strophe 18, lines 2 and 9.
[197] Strophe 14, line 9.   [198] Strophe 21, lines 8 and 5.   [199] Strophe 22, lines 8 and 7.
[200] Strophe 23, lines 6–7.   [201] Strophe 22, line 9.   [202] Strophe 23, lines 8–10.

On the Infernal Powers and *On the Victory of the Cross*, reminded the faithful of the eschaton and the exigency of repentance by plunging them into the underworld, before returning to the salvific power of Christ's crucifixion.

Chanted in the fifth week of the Lenten period, *On the Infernal Powers* begins with an eschatological tone but quickly recapitulates the imagery of healing that other *kontakia* such as *On Repentance* and *On the Second Coming* had evoked earlier in the pre-Lenten and early Lenten phase. The dialogue between self and soul is provoked by the imminence of death:

Ψυχή μου, ψυχή μου, ἀνάστα· τί καθεύδεις;
Τὸ τέλος ἐγγίζει καὶ μέλλεις θορυβεῖσθαι
ἀνάνηψον οὖν, ἵνα φείσηταί σου Χριστὸς ὁ Θεός,
ὁ πανταχοῦ παρὼν καὶ τὰ πάντα πληρῶν.[203]

O my soul, my soul, wake up—why do you sleep?
The end draws near and you will be thrown into confusion,
come to your senses then, so that Christ the God spares you,
He who is everywhere and filling all things.

However, Romanos quickly draws the attention of the congregation to the infirmary of Christ, which is a source of health for all of humanity.[204] This sanctuary of healing that Christ's crucifixion has inaugurated becomes the undoing of the powers of hell and causes the devil to cry out in agony as the scene shifts to the underworld:

«Τί ποιήσω τῷ υἱῷ τῆς Μαριάμ;
Κτείνει με ὁ Βηθλεεμίτης, ὁ πανταχοῦ παρὼν καὶ τὰ πάντα πληρῶν.
Ὁ κόσμος ὅλος ἐπλήσθη τῶν αὐτοῦ ἰαμάτων,
κἀγὼ τὰ ἔνδοθεν πονῶ ...»[205]

'What shall I do to the son of Mary?
The Bethlehemite is killing me,
He who is everywhere and filling all things.
The world has been filled with his healings,
but I, my insides suffer ...'

The dramatic dialogue that ensues between the devil and his infernal companions is reminiscent of that which takes place between Hades and Satan in a hymn by Romanos that was sung in the middle of Lent.

In *On the Victory of the Cross*, Christ's crucifixion has paradoxically left Hades bitterly wounded and afraid, but Satan insists that this is nothing

---

[203] *On the Infernal Powers*, prelude.   [204] Strophe 1, lines 1–2.
[205] Strophe 1, lines 6–7, strophe 2, lines 1–2.

more than trickery: 'Who has misled you?'[206] When the latter realises his
error, he grieves with the former, bemoaning their fall and Adam's return:
'Now therefore, Hades, groan and I will harmonize with your wails'.[207]
The tree that they had 'carpentered up there for Mary's Child' to 'do away
with the second Adam' has suddenly become a 'holy trunk' and 'fair haven'
for 'thieves, murderers and publicans and harlots'.[208] Against the backdrop
of an underworld dirge, the faithful sing a song of triumph as they behold
the most unlikely of heroes – the thief – steal the 'unravished pearl' from
the Cross, and use it as a key to enter 'again into Paradise'.[209]

In the middle of Lent, according to the *Typikon of the Great Church* and
Theodore the Stoudite's eighth-century *Oration on the Veneration of the
Precious and Life-Giving Cross in Mid-Lent*, the faithful venerated the wood
of the Cross during the feast and its vigil.[210] Although the ceremonial
grandeur of the patriarchal and royal procession of the Cross – complete
with honour guard, incense and candles – occurred after the vigil, the
sensual act of kissing the Cross, which would have been illuminated by the
candlelight of Hagia Sophia or a nearby monastery and celebrated in *On
the Victory of the Cross*, brought the faithful intimately close to the
embodiment of sacrifice and regeneration they sang about:

> For in your Cross we all boast.
> To it let us nail our hearts,
> that on it we may hang our instruments
> And sing to you, the Lord of all, from the songs of Sion.[211]

Christ's crucifixion also embodied the compunction that Romanos' hymns
sought to arouse by evoking a constellation of biblical narratives that
framed the Lenten journey. It recalled the exile from Eden, the imminence
of death and the prospect of judgment, but it also engendered salvation,
created a sanctuary for Romanos' biblical exemplars and was the source of
healing that tears of compunction desired. Finally, it linked the last things
with the first things through the melody and poetry of the refrain – 'again

---

[206] Strophe 4. The story of *On the Victory of the Cross* was a familiar one. The apocryphal *Gospel of
Nicodemus* had gradually embedded the tale of Christ's Orphic and Herculean descent into Hades
and the character of Satan in the Christian imagination of Late Antiquity. By Romanos' lifetime,
they were 'part of the resurrection celebrations throughout the empire'. See Frank, 'Dialogue and
Deliberation', 171.

[207] Strophe 16, line 1.   [208] Strophes 2 and 16.   [209] Strophe 17.

[210] Theodore the Stoudite's oration declares that 'on this day the all-holy cross is worshipped and the
resurrection of Christ is proclaimed. Today the life-giving tree is worshipped and the entire cosmos
is reawakened to praise'. PG 99, 693. Quoted in Pelikan, *The Spirit of Eastern Christendom*, 139.
See also Taft and Kazhdan, 'Cult of the Cross', in *ODB*, 551–53.

[211] Strophe 18, lines 3–6.

to Paradise' – which invited the faithful to return to the bliss of Eden
where the story began.

The Musical Dimension of Romanos' *Kontakia*

While I have already touched on the musical dimension of Romanos'
refrains, it is worth considering the overall melodic significance of his
kontakia. Such an exploration is fraught with difficulty and
I acknowledge that it might elicit more questions than conclusions, but
it will provoke us to consider the role of music in the relationship between
performance and compunction. According to the manuscript tradition,
each of Romanos' *kontakia* was composed in one of the eight modes of
Byzantine music.[212] In the case of *On the Victory of the Cross*, Grosdidier
de Matons' survey of the manuscripts indicates that it was composed in the
grave mode[213] and with a unique melody that did not follow a contrafactum.[214] However, it is difficult to reimagine the emotive universe of
Byzantium, and it is unclear what feelings this mode of Byzantine music
may have elicited. The questions of whether music expresses emotion and
what emotions music arouses are complex and have puzzled philosophers
since antiquity.[215]

Contemporaneous perceptions of the characteristics of each of the eight
modes of music in Byzantium are extant. One such example is the
following poem on the grave mode:

> O fitting melody for the heavily armed phalanx,
> You have received the calling of deepness, which you bear,
> You, the simple mode, which holds the title of Grave,
> Loved by the one who hates thoughts to be expressed with shouts.
> Although you roar out a song of men, O second of third modes,
> While you are manifold, your friends are people of simplicity.[216]

---

[212] For background on the origins of the system of modes, see Stig Simeon Ragnvald Frøyshov, 'The
Early Development of the Liturgical Eight-Mode System in Jerusalem', *St Vladimir's Theological
Quarterly* 51 (2007): 139–78.

[213] The grave mode is one of the eight modes (*Oktoechos*) of Byzantine sacred music. The grave mode
belonged to the enharmonic genus.

[214] Romanos le Mélode, *Hymnes. Tome IV*, 282.

[215] Stephen Davies, 'Emotions Expressed and Aroused by Music', in *Handbook of Music and Emotion:
Theory, Research, Applications*, ed. Patrik N. Juslin and John A. Sloboda (Oxford: Oxford
University Press, 2010), 15–43.

[216] See Frank Desby, 'The Modes and Tunings in Neo-Byzantine Chant' (PhD dissertation,
University of Southern California, 1974), 27. Desby quotes Greek verses that were probably
added to the *Oktoechos* after the ninth century and which describe the sound of each of the modes.
His source is Grottaferrata Heirmologion II (a thirteenth-century manuscript). I have modified
Desby's translation.

This poetic reflection on the grave mode of Byzantine music conjures feelings associated with conflict and war before juxtaposing them with quiet emotions of contemplation. Yet the pathway it paves to the musical dimension of Romanos' *kontakion* is slippery at best. It is more fruitful to explore the way in which Romanos' *kontakia* were set to music.[217]

The liturgical expression of the sixth-century *kontakion* would have privileged text over music. Although melismatic elements cannot be discounted and do emerge centuries later in the *Psaltika*, it is more likely that Romanos' music was syllabic, enhancing the rhetoric of the homily and encouraging the congregation to sing the refrain.[218] The repetition of the refrain may have attenuated the musical impact of the hymn but, by the same token, the tune may have been contagious, instantly appealing and memorable.[219] Romanos' refrain formed an intrinsic part of the cognitive ecology of his hymns, creating an emotive universe where the human heart – as the nexus of mind, body and soul – could dwell in a liturgical world. The refrain's melody would have embellished the emotional turns of the text and enriched its dramatic resonance. The refrain's choral character would have facilitated the participation of the congregation in the singing of the *kontakia*, inviting the faithful to step into a liturgical world wherein intricate themes, various scriptural and apocryphal characters, as well as the incarnate Logos, coexisted in the drama of salvation.

The soundscape of the sacred space where the *kontakion* was performed would have contributed to the affective mystagogy of the liturgical event and elicited the faithful's immersion in this atmosphere. This would have especially been the case if the *kontakion* was performed in the cathedral of Hagia Sophia, whose sonic architecture engendered rich reverberation. Indeed, the building acted as a kind of 'musical instrument', with the magnificent dome emitting sound waves 'like an acoustic waterfall' on the faithful below.[220]

Although it is difficult to understand today how the melody per se was emotionally meaningful so many centuries ago in Byzantium, the affective mystagogy of hymnody evoked an emotional and liturgical community.

---

[217] See Alexander Lingas, 'Sunday Matins in the Byzantine Cathedral Rite: Music and Liturgy' (PhD dissertation, University of British Columbia, 1996), 7.

[218] Wellesz, *A History of Byzantine Music*, 202; Jørgen Raasted, 'Zur Melodie des Kontakions Ἡ παρθένος σήμερον', *Cahiers de l'Institut du Moyen-Âge Grec et Latin* 59 (1989): 233–46; Koder, 'Imperial Propaganda', 286–90.

[219] Moreover, the choice of grave mode may have kindled the musical memory of the audience, recalling other hymns that were composed in the same mode.

[220] Pentcheva, 'Performing the Sacred', 125.

As we saw in the previous chapter, hymnody exemplified Maximus the Confessor's eschatological vision of liturgical worship, where the 'spiritual delight of divine songs' (πνευματικὴν τῶν θείων ἀσμάτων τερπνότητα) moved souls 'toward the unfading and blessed love of God'.[221] In the mystery of worship, the faithful sang hymns with the angels and entered 'an unconfused unity' (ἀσύγχυτον ἕνωσιν) where all were joined to each other.[222] This was not a vision of liturgical theology and hymnody unique to Maximus. Several monastic foundation documents depict 'the angelic choir singing continuously in heaven above, accompanied by (or alternating with) the human choir below'.[223]

The affective resonance of the particular mode of Byzantine music that characterised Romanos' various *kontakia* may be elusive, but the overall purpose of sacred song was evident. Even before Maximus' *On Ecclesiastical Mystagogy*, Basil the Great spoke of liturgical music as a remedy for depraved passions and pedagogy for the soul. For Basil, such music did not enkindle the sensuality that could incite these passions. Rather, by mixing 'the sweetness of melody with doctrine' and providing 'a common surgery for souls', hymnody could edify the faithful and elicit blessed emotions.[224] Of course, music could just as easily have aroused depraved passions:

> For passions, which are the offspring of servility and baseness, are produced by [the music of corrupt songs]. On the other hand, we must employ that class of music that is better and leads to the better, which David, the sacred Psalmist, is said to have used to ease the madness of the king.[225]

Similarly, Basil's brother, Gregory of Nyssa, suggested that liturgical singing is not the music of the lyric poets. Sacred song combines 'the sweetness of honey' with 'divine words' in a way that moderates the passions through the 'proper rhythm of life' that leads to 'the more sublime state of life'.[226]

---

[221] *On Ecclesiastical Mystagogy*, chapter 11. See Boudignon, *Maximi Confessoris Mystagogia*, 40.

[222] *On Ecclesiastical Mystagogy*, chapter 24, ibid., 60. On the notion of singing with the angels, see chapter 13, ibid., 42.

[223] Dubowchik, 'Singing with the Angels', 281.

[224] *Homily on Psalm 1*, translated in McKinnon, *Music in Early Christian Literature*, 65. A translation of the entire homily appears in Basil the Great, *Exegetical Homilies*, 151–54. For the Greek text, see PG 29, 209–12.

[225] Basil the Great, *Address to Youth. On How They Might Benefit from Classical Greek Literature* (Sydney: St Andrew's Orthodox Press, 2011), 52. I have modified the translation. For the Greek text, see PG 31, 581D.

[226] Heine, *Treatise on the Inscriptions of the Psalms*, 91–92. For the Greek text, see *Gregorii Nysseni. In inscriptiones Psalmorum: In sextum Psalmum: In ecclesiasten homiliae*, ed. J. McDonough and P. Alexander, GNO 5 (Leiden: Brill, 1986), 33–34.

While it may be difficult to reimagine the emotive universe of Byzantium's sacred music, a few insights can be retrieved. The refrain that the faithful sang could destabilise personhood, inviting them to enter the world of Romanos' stories and feel the emotions of his protagonists. This was facilitated and amplified by the affective mystagogy of hymnody and the potential for sacred song to serve as a kind of pedagogy for the soul, edifying the congregation and eliciting blessed emotions.

Concluding Remarks

In retelling and amplifying the sacred stories that defined the Byzantines, Romanos' *kontakia* sought to frame and shape an emotional and liturgical community in Constantinople. The Melodist's compunctious hymns presented sin as a sickness of the soul and repentance as its remedy. The rhetoric of these hymns sought to evoke compunction and its purifying power, spurring the faithful to enter the infirmary of spiritual healing. *Kontakia* became liturgical scripts for the faithful, teaching them to yearn for tears of compunction and entreat God to bestow his compassionate mercy. Moreover, the performance of these hymns took place in a liturgical environment, where icons and other sacred media contributed to the experience of liturgical emotions.

Through the singing of hymns, the passions of the singer's soul could mirror the text. Poetry and music showed forth the compunction of the prodigal, the harlot and other scriptural figures. Amidst an overarching narrative of exile, incarnation and salvation that framed the Lenten journey, Romanos' hymns presented the hidden desires of scriptural characters, inviting the faithful to become part of the sacred drama unfolding before them and cry the tears of compunction that marked his protagonists' repentance. They also cultivated compunction by dramatising the eschaton as a culmination of history that Christ's incarnation, death and resurrection had already inaugurated – a liturgical reality that hymnody and the mysticism of the Eucharist embodied in the performance of poetry and melody.

The faithful were invited to partake in this liturgical performance through the singing the refrain. However, even if a member of the congregation had no talent in singing, the action of listening to the sacred narrative and melody of a hymn, and hearing the voices of its biblical exemplars, opened a shared world of 'aural images' that were impressed upon the heart.[227] In this way, the liturgical world that hymnody created,

---

[227] Harrison, *The Art of Listening*, 8.

the emotions its protagonists felt, and the tears of compunction they cried, could be internalised by the faithful. The songs of Romanos' protagonists were not just the utterances and affections of scriptural characters or a hymnographer, they could become the voices and emotions of the faithful. After all, the Melodist's hymns cultivated and mediated liturgical emotions that were collective yet personal.[228]

---

[228] See McKinnon's excerpt from Basil the Great's *Letters* (207, 3) in *Music in Early Christian Literature*, 68–69: 'Among us the people arise at night and go to the house of prayer; in pain, distress and anguished tears they make confession to God, and finally getting up from prayer they commence the singing of psalms . . . all in common as if from one mouth and one heart offer the psalm of confession to the Lord, while each fashions his own personal words of repentance.' Although Basil is referring to psalmody, hymnody harnessed and amplified this liturgical tradition. For the Greek text, see PG 32, 764.

CHAPTER 4

Andrew of Crete

Born in Damascus around 660, Andrew of Crete was a homilist and hymnographer whose journey through Byzantium included sojourns in Jerusalem, Constantinople and Crete. He died in 740 on the island of Lesbos. Although it is generally agreed that he was educated in Jerusalem, served as a deacon at Hagia Sophia and ordained a bishop in Gortyna, there are aspects of his life that either remain the subject of scholarly debate or continue to be elusive because of the vagueness of his vita.[1] Athanasios Papadopoulos-Kerameus published the vita in 1888, editing two of the surviving manuscripts on Mt Athos: the tenth-century codex 79 of Vatopedi Monastery (the earliest extant manuscript) and the fifteenth-century codex 148 of Dionysiou Monastery.[2] However, Panagiotes Skaltses' recent critical edition of the *Life of St Andrew of Crete* analyses nine of the twelve manuscripts of the vita that are extant, correcting a number of errors in the nineteenth-century edition and referencing various patristic texts alluded to in the vita.[3]

The *Life of St Andrew* was originally written by an obscure figure known as Niketas, possibly as early as the eighth century, though some argue that he lived in the tenth century.[4] Some aspects of Niketas' account, such as

---

[1] The more recent explorations of Andrew's vita by Alexander Kazhdan and Marie-France Auzépy are valuable but the critical study undertaken by Siméon Vailhé remains indispensable. Vailhé, 'Saint André de Crète', *Échos d'Orient* 5 (1902): 378–87; Auzépy, 'La carrière d'André de Crète', *BZ* 88 (1995): 1–12; Kazhdan, *A History of Byzantine Literature (650–850)* (Athens: National Hellenic Research Foundation, 1999), 37–41.

[2] Athanasios Papadopoulos-Kerameus, ed., 'Life of St Andrew of Crete', in Ἀνάλεκτα Ἱεροσολυμιτικῆς Σταχυολογίας, Vol. 5 (St Petersburg: Kirschbaum, 1898), 169–79.

[3] Panagiotes Skaltses, ed., 'Βίος τοῦ ἐν ἁγίοις Πατρὸς ἡμῶν Ἀνδρέου τοῦ Ἱεροσολυμίτου, ἀρχιεπισκόπου Κρήτης [Life of our Father among the Saints Andrew of Jerusalem, Archbishop of Crete]', in Ο Ἅγιος Ἀνδρέας Ἀρχιεπίσκοπος Κρήτης ο Ἱεροσολυμίτης, Πολιούχος Ερεσού Λέσβου. Πρακτικά Επιστημονικού Συνεδρίου (1–4 Ιουλίου 2003) (Mytilene: Holy Metropolis of Mytilene, 2005), 367–94.

[4] See John F. Haldon, *Byzantium in the Seventh Century: The Transformation of a Culture* (Cambridge: Cambridge University Press, 1990), 79; Kazhdan, *A History of Byzantine Literature*, 37. See also the commentary on this issue in the introduction to the critical edition by Skaltses, 'Βίος', 367–69.

Andrew of Crete's presence at the Sixth Ecumenical Council, are questionable. Moreover, some crucial details about the life of the saint are absent from the vita. Nevertheless, the account provides a sketch of key milestones in Andrew's life. Interestingly, the *Life of St Andrew* contains an hagiographical parallel with the vita of Romanos the Melodist. Echoes of Romanos miraculously receiving the gift of sacred song can be heard in the narrative of Andrew being granted the gift of speech when he was eight years old. According to Andrew's vita, his voice was liberated and his speech became 'articulate' (ἔναρθρον) after he partook of the 'life-giving body and blood' (ζωοποιοῦ σώματος καὶ αἵματος) of Christ on the first day of his eighth year.[5] The hagiographer interprets the seven years of muteness as a kind of divine pedagogy, 'ordaining the good way of life in silence' (προτυπουμένων τῆς ἐν ἡσυχίᾳ χρηστῆς διαγωγῆς) and suggests the eighth year manifests 'the eighth and first day without evening' (τὴν ὀγδόην καὶ πρώτην ἀνέσπερον ἡμέραν) – the life of the age to come.[6] Romanos' gift of song and Andrew's gift of speech betoken the Byzantine view of hymnography as vatic and its performance as a manifestation of divine mysteries.[7]

Some further brushstrokes of Andrew's life can be ascertained with some confidence. Andrew's early association with the church of the Anastasis in Jerusalem, where he became a monk and was educated, explains why some historical sources refer to him as Andrew of Jerusalem. However, either in 685 or soon thereafter, Andrew journeyed to Constantinople, where he attained important ecclesiastical offices, administered an orphanage and tended to the poor. He was elected to the archiepiscopal see of Crete around 711. Over the course of his career, his compositions were largely liturgical songs, but his panegyrical and festal homilies should not be overlooked, especially given they are also liturgical. Nevertheless, the corpus of homilies attributed to Andrew is problematic:

> confusion concerning Andrew's actual corpus will remain until a systematic study has been made of all the homilies both on stylistic and contextual grounds.[8]

---

[5] Skaltses, 'Βίος', 382; Papadopoulos-Kerameus, 'Life of St Andrew', 171.   [6] Ibid.

[7] See the poetry of Gregory the Theologian who deliberately invoked the Holy Spirit, not the Muses of Greek mythology. McGuckin, 'Poetry and Hymnography', 648.

[8] Mary B. Cunningham, 'Andrew of Crete: A High-Style Preacher of the Eighth Century', in *Preacher and Audience: Studies in Early Christian and Byzantine Homiletics*, ed. Mary Cunningham and Pauline Allen (Leiden: Brill, 1998), 268. Cunningham has also translated several of Andrew's homilies in *Wider than Heaven: Eighth-Century Homilies on the Mother of God* (Crestwood, NY: St Vladimir's Seminary Press, 2008), 71–138. For the Greek text of the homilies attributed to Andrew of Crete, see PG 97, 805–1304.

His surviving hymns were largely composed in the same genre – *kanon* – and were devoted to liturgical feasts such as the nativity of the Theotokos, the resurrection of Lazarus and the celebration of Mid-Pentecost.[9] The epic hymn known as the *Great Kanon* is his magnum opus.

Andrew of Crete lived during a tempestuous but momentous chapter in the history of Byzantium. The late seventh and early eighth centuries ushered in a period of social, political and religious upheaval that transformed Byzantine culture.[10] The Roman Empire was facing the threat of an emergent Arab caliphate and losing its imperial control of a changing political landscape in the Balkans. Moreover, the discord engendered by the theological controversies of Monothelitism (the question of whether Christ had a single will) and Iconoclasm was so profound that it threatened to unravel the harmony of church and state.[11]

The Byzantine conflict over icons may have been a political struggle, but it was also a theological crisis connected with the Christological controversies that divided Christianity in the fifth and sixth centuries.[12] So critical was the defence of icons for Byzantine theology that, according to John of Damascus, who was contemporary with Andrew, it would either uphold or break every link in the great chain of images that began with the Creator of all images and Christ as the 'image of the invisible God'.[13] This 'cosmology of icons' linked Creator and creation 'through a comprehensive schema of images' and enshrined icons within a 'hierarchical metaphysical reality' that included humanity, Scripture and typological images – such as the burning bush or Melchizedek – which prefigured

---

[9] PG 97, 1305–44.

[10] See Haldon, *Byzantium in the Seventh Century*, 436–58; Andrew Louth, 'Byzantium Transforming (600–700)', in *The Cambridge History of the Byzantine Empire c. 500–1492*, ed. Jonathan Shepard (Cambridge: Cambridge University Press, 2008), 221–48.

[11] Cunningham, 'Andrew of Crete', 267. On Monothelitism and its context, see John Meyendorff, *Imperial Unity and Christian Divisions* (Crestwood, NY: St Vladimir's Seminary Press, 1989), 333–80. On the theological apologia for icons during the iconoclastic conflict, see Jaroslav Pelikan, *Imago Dei: The Byzantine Apologia for Icons* (Princeton, NJ: Princeton University Press, 2011).

[12] Ibid., 70. The foreword by Judith Herrin to the new edition of Pelikan's lectures (which were originally delivered in 1987) provides an overview of more recent developments in scholarship on Iconoclasm. For an examination of the historical and cultural context of Iconoclasm, see Brubaker and Haldon, *Byzantium in the Iconoclast Era*.

[13] Colossians 1:15. John of Damascus' examination of the six links in the great chain of images appears in his third *Apologetic Oration on the Holy Icons*, 16–23. See Bonifatius Kotter, ed., *Die Schriften des Johannes von Damaskos III. Contra imaginum calumniatores orationes tres* (Berlin: De Gruyter, 1975), 125–30 (PG 94, 1337–44). The third oration is translated by Andrew Louth in *Three Treatises on the Divine Images* (Crestwood, NY: St Vladimir's Seminary Press, 2003), 81–158 (see 95–100 for the six kinds of images).

what was to come in the history of salvation.[14] Although icons were the sixth and final link in this great chain of images, they were explicitly linked to the first five classes of image in such a way that the iconoclastic disavowal of icons was 'tantamount to a rejection not only of one link but of the entire chain of images'.[15]

Hymnody for Andrew of Crete was also part of this great chain of images.[16] On the one hand, it was a verbal icon that enacted a rewritten Bible. On the other hand, it paraded before the faithful exemplars and counter-ideals that were scriptural reflections of the soul. Indeed, Andrew of Crete alludes to this phenomenon by describing David's composition of Psalm 50 as the creation of an image:

Δαυῒδ ποτὲ ἀνεστήλωσε, συγγραψάμενος ὡς ἐν εἰκόνι, ὕμνον, δι' οὗ τὴν πρᾶξιν ἐλέγχει, ἣν εἰργάσατο κραυγάζων· Ἐλέησόν με· σοὶ γὰρ μόνῳ ἐξήμαρτον, τῷ πάντων Θεῷ, αὐτὸς καθάρισόν με.[17]

David once composed a hymn, setting forth, as in an image, the action he had done; and he condemned it, crying: 'Have mercy upon me, for against you only have I sinned, God of all, cleanse me'.[18]

Likewise, the *Great Kanon* is a poetic meditation on and vivid description of the 'godly deeds' and 'evil deeds' of each person's life.[19] This ekphrasis is performed in a reflexive way, summoning images of various biblical figures and asking the faithful to examine their own feelings and ponder their own actions as they contemplated the adventures of these figures. The singer's soul, which can be a reflection of – or reflected in – the images appearing in Andrew of Crete's poetic universe, is ultimately presented as an image of God that has been discoloured and tainted by sin, yet which can be

---

[14] Pelikan, *Imago Dei*, 175–81.   [15] Ibid., 182.

[16] As Mary Cunningham has argued, Dionysius the Areopagite's philosophy helped to shape Andrew of Crete's understanding of 'the way in which divine truth may be apprehended, even if only dimly, by means of types, imprints or images that take the form of mental images or words. It is also worth noting that he sees this process as happening not only in the context of penitential prayer, ascetic exercise or rational enquiry, but above all through participation in the liturgical celebration of the Church. Deification, he implies, occurs in the lives of the Christian faithful when they join in the timeless but also commemorative celebration of the liturgy'. Cunningham, 'The Impact of Pseudo-Dionysius the Areopagite on Byzantine Theologians', in *A Celebration of Living Theology: A Festschrift in Honour of Andrew Louth*, ed. Justin A. Mihoc and Leonard Aldea (London: Bloomsbury, 2014), 57.

[17] This strophe, which is from the seventh ode of the *Great Kanon*, appears in two of the earliest manuscripts of the *Triodion*: Sinai Graecus 734–735, fol. 79v, and Grottaferrata Δβ I, fol. 13v. It is also in the post-Byzantine examples of the received tradition, such as Τριῴδιον Κατανυκτικόν, 482.

[18] The English translation is my own.

[19] From the first ode, strophes 7–8: Sinai Graecus 734–735, fol. 69r–v. Τριῴδιον Κατανυκτικόν, 463.

restored to its original beauty through tears of compunction.[20] On several occasions throughout the *Great Kanon*, Andrew of Crete entreats the faithful to visually experience the divine mystery: 'See now, see that I am God: give ear, my soul, to the Lord as He cries to you' (Ἴδετε ἴδετε, ὅτι ἐγώ εἰμι Θεός, ἐνωτίζου ψυχή μου, τοῦ Κυρίου βοῶντος)[21] – and later in the same ode: 'Know and see that I am God, who searches hearts' (Γνῶτε καὶ ἴδετε, ὅτι ἐγώ εἰμι Θεός, ὁ ἐρευνῶν καρδίας).[22] The desire for visual communion continues later in the hymn: 'O Master and Lord, may my tears be to me as Siloam, so that I also may wash clean the eyes of my soul and with my mind behold You, the light before the ages' (Σιλωὰμ γενέσθω μοι τὰ δάκρυά μου, Δέσποτα Κύριε, ἵνα νίψωμαι κἀγώ, τὰς κόρας τῆς καρδίας, καὶ ἴδω σε νοερῶς, τὸ φῶς τὸ πρὸ αἰώνων).[23]

Byzantine Hymnography and the *Kanon*

A revised critical history of the *kanon* is desirable.[24] Although Wellesz and Grosdidier de Matons have explored the history and significance of the genre, some of their assumptions were erroneous.[25] More recent studies have shown that *kanons* might have emerged as early as fourth-century Jerusalem and that they never supplanted the other prominent genre of hymnography – the *kontakion* – in the seventh and eighth centuries.[26] In Constantinople, the strophic poems known as *kanons* coexisted with *kontakia* in the liturgical season of Lent and the broader calendar of worship, allowing the faithful to experience the performance of hymns belonging to both these genres during the cycle of sacred feasts and fasts.

The nine odes of a *kanon* are modelled on the nine biblical canticles found in the fifth-century Codex Alexandrinus and other early

---

[20] This theme emerges in the second ode of the *Great Kanon*.

[21] Second ode, strophe 1. Sinai Graecus, fol. 71v; Grottaferrata Δβ I, fol. 8r; Τριώδιον Κατανυκτικόν, 467.

[22] Sinai Graecus 734–735, fol. 72r; Grottaferrata Δβ I, fol. 8v; Τριώδιον Κατανυκτικόν, 468.

[23] Fifth ode, strophe 21, Sinai Graecus 734–735, fol. 76v; Grottaferrata Δβ I, fol. 11v; Τριώδιον Κατανυκτικόν, 477.

[24] Krueger, *Liturgical Subjects*, 245 (footnote 7).

[25] Wellesz, *A History of Byzantine Music*, 198–239; Grosdidier de Matons, 'Liturgie et hymnographie', 31–43.

[26] Stig Simeon Ragnvald Frøyshov, 'The Georgian Witness to the Jerusalem Liturgy: New Sources and Studies', in *Inquiries into Eastern Christian Worship: Selected Papers of the Second International Congress of the Society of Oriental Liturgies, Rome, 17–21 September 2008*, ed. Bert Groen, Steven Hawkes-Teeples and Stefanos Alexopoulos (Leuven: Peeters, 2012), 237–40; Lingas, 'The Liturgical Place of the Kontakion', 50–57.

manuscripts of the Septuagint Bible.[27] The canticles, which sometimes vary from nine to fifteen, provided early Christianity with a series of liturgical songs for worship throughout the week, based on the songs of righteous biblical figures that were sung in thanksgiving following the occurrence of a miracle, such as the crossing of the Red Sea:

(1)   The Song of Moses and Miriam (Exodus 15:1–19)
(2)   The Song of Moses at the end of his life (Deuteronomy 32:1–43)
(3)   The Prayer of Hannah (1 Kingdoms [1 Samuel] 2:1–10)
(4)   The Prayer of Habakkuk (Habakkuk 3:1–19)
(5)   The Prayer of Isaiah (Isaiah 26:9–20)
(6)   The Prayer of Jonah (Jonah 2:3–10)
(7)   The Prayer of Azariah (Daniel 3:26–56)
(8)   The Song of the Three Youths in the furnace (Daniel 3:57–88)
(9)   The songs of the Virgin (Magnificat) and Zacharias (Luke 1:46–57, 68–79).[28]

These canticles were sung during the *orthros*, the office of matins prescribed for daybreak. Their use as a complete cycle during this office has its origins in the vigil that began on Saturday evening, before becoming a fixed element of the *orthros*.[29]

Hymnographers who composed *kanons* would often allude to each of these familiar biblical canticles as they wrote new texts for various liturgical festivals. An example of a *kanon* that follows the thematic structure of the biblical canticles is the paschal *kanon* for the feast of the Resurrection in the *Pentekostarion*. In the first ode, the crucifixion and resurrection of Christ echo the passage from death to life that Moses and the Israelites experienced when they escaped the wrath of Pharaoh by crossing the Red Sea. However, Andrew of Crete's *Great Kanon* faintly echoes the thematic structure of the biblical canticles, and only insofar as it loosely follows the biblical narrative of salvation. Although the first ode explores the actions of Adam and Eve, and while the ninth ode plucks various narratives from the Gospels, the seven other odes in between sometimes blur the chronology of the Old Testament narrative, interweaving the stories of various scriptural figures.

---

[27] On the emergence of the biblical canticles, see James Miller, '"Let Us Sing to the Lord": The Biblical Odes in the Codex Alexandrinus' (PhD dissertation, Marquette University, 2006).

[28] The Magnificat was sung every day and three canticles were performed on Sundays. See Krueger, *Liturgical Subjects*, 141.

[29] Robert F. Taft, *The Liturgy of the Hours in East and West: The Origins of the Divine Office and Its Meaning for Today* (Collegeville, MN: Liturgical Press, 1986), 198–99, 277–83.

The salient purpose of Andrew's composition is to arouse compunction, which is why it goes beyond the framework of the canticles, beginning with the narrative of Adam and Eve, juxtaposing figures such as Cain and Abel, and summoning a litany of biblical characters who exemplify repentance. As we will see, the biblical canticles were only one of the textual and musical threads that wove the odes of the *Great Kanon* into an epic narrative of repentance against the backdrop of divine providence, illustrating the iconic nature of liturgical action. Indeed, the *Great Kanon* exhibits only some of the characteristics of its genre. As with other *kanons*, the *Great Kanon* consists of nine odes, though there are numerous examples of *kanons* where the second ode is omitted. Each ode begins with a model stanza, an *heirmos* (εἱρμός), that serves as the musical and metrical model for each of the stanzas that will follow. However, unlike other *kanons*, the *Great Kanon* does not link the odes together using an acrostic that reflects on the feast during which the *kanon* was to be sung. Moreover, whereas a *kanon* would usually contain around four stanzas after the *heirmos* of each ode, the *Great Kanon* devotes many more stanzas to each, resulting in an epic poem of 250 stanzas. Its lengthy performance allowed the faithful to meditate on its recurring themes and panoply of characters. In this regard, the *Great Kanon* creatively appropriates the monastic literary genre of chapters (κεφάλαια), fusing the ascetic themes of this genre with the biblical contemplation of the *kanon*.[30]

A characteristic element of the *Great Kanon* and the Middle Byzantine *kanon* repertoire is repetition.[31] Three aspects of Andrew's poem exhibit this characteristic: the thematic repetition of compunction and repentance in each ode; the invocation of familiar biblical exemplars who reinforce the penitential tone of the *kanon*; and the infrequent use of a refrain in some odes. Although this repetitive dimension of the *Great Kanon* may seem tedious to a modern audience, it is typical of the memory culture of Byzantium, which cultivated a visual narrative for the mind and persuaded the soul to 'remain vigilant in the fight against oblivion'.[32] Andrew's poem illustrates how the *kanon* – with its musical rhythm and choral nature – enacted and embodied the feeling of

---

[30] Doru Costache, 'Reading the Scriptures with Byzantine Eyes: The Hermeneutical Significance of St Andrew of Crete's Great Canon', *Phronema* 23 (2008): 53.

[31] Jaakko Olkinuora, 'Revisiting the *Great Canon* by Andrew of Crete', forthcoming in the publication of the proceedings of the 2016 International Congress of the Society of Oriental Liturgy in Armenia.

[32] Amy Papalexandrou, 'The Memory Culture of Byzantium', in James, ed., *A Companion to Byzantium*, 110.

compunction within a meaningful practice, encouraging the faithful to participate in the performance of the hymn, enter its poetic and musical universe, and internalise the emotions it evoked.

Manuscripts, Editions and Translations

Unearthing the original text of the *Great Kanon* that Andrew of Crete wrote in eighth-century Byzantium is a difficult task. As there is no extant manuscript from the lifetime of Andrew, the edition of the text that scholars often use is the one that appears in the *Triodion* published in Italy after the fall of Constantinople.[33] It is similar to the version of the text in the *Patrologia Graeca*.[34] These editions contain Andrew of Crete's composition, but it is interlaced with additional prayers and hymns that are not found in the earliest manuscripts of the *Triodion*. However, there is currently no critical edition of the *Great Kanon* based on the manuscript tradition of the *Triodion*. Although the liturgical reforms of the Stoudite monks in the ninth and tenth centuries enshrined the *Great Kanon* in the *Triodion* alongside a cornucopia of other hymns to create the cycle of Lenten offices, ensuring its transmission to posterity, this created a herculean task for any scholar who wishes to find and examine the many *Triodion* manuscripts that contain the text of Andrew's poem.[35]

The manuscript tradition begins with Sinai Graecus 734–735, fols. 69r–83v, a tenth-century *Triodion* of Constantinopolitan provenance, which represents the earliest witness to Andrew's composition and its performance during the fifth week of Lent.[36] This manuscript is linked to two other manuscripts of the *Triodion* from the eleventh century: Vaticanus Graecus 771, fol. 18v, and Grottaferrata Δβ I, fols. 7v–16r.[37] Although the publication of this hymnal in Italy after the fall of Constantinople represents the received tradition and the final stage of the evolution of the *Triodion* during the twilight of Byzantium, the liturgical performance of the *Great Kanon* began during the Middle Byzantine period. This study reimagines the performance of Andrew's composition as a centrepiece of the Lenten journey for the Byzantine faithful during this time.

---

[33] Τριώδιον Κατανυκτικόν, 463–91. This nineteenth-century edition printed in Rome exemplifies the received tradition and is based on the earliest editions of the *Triodion* printed in Venice at the beginning of the sixteenth century. See Krueger, *Liturgical Subjects*, 172.

[34] PG 97, 1329–85.

[35] For an overview of how this liturgical book was compiled, see Ware and Mother Mary, *The Lenten Triodion*, 38–43; Getcha, *The Typikon Decoded*, 35–39.

[36] Quinlan, *Sin. Gr. 734–735*, 16–41; Krueger, *Liturgical Subjects*, 174.

[37] Quinlan, *Sin. Gr. 734–735*, 39–40.

Whether the performance of the *Great Kanon* emerged in an urban, monastic or cathedral setting and where in Byzantium this first occurred, are difficult questions to answer. There is no explicit mention of the *Great Kanon* in the *Typikon of the Great Church*, but this is unsurprising since the *kanon* was not a characteristic practice of the cathedral rite of Hagia Sophia. However, the singing of *kanons* in Hagia Sophia is suggested by the Jerusalem Stavrou 40 manuscript, which mentions the chanting of *kanons* during Great Lent.[38] The eleventh-century rubrics of Alexios the Stoudite and the twelfth-century Sinai Graecus 1096 manuscript of the *Typikon of St Sabas Monastery* prescribe the *Great Kanon* for matins on the Thursday of the fifth week of Lent.[39] This is also the case in the *Synaxarion of the Monastery of the Theotokos Evergetis* near Constantinople and the twelfth-century *Typikon of the Monastery of Christ the Saviour* at Messina.[40] Both these texts also prescribe reading portions of the *Life of St Mary of Egypt* at certain points before and during the singing of the *Great Kanon*.[41] Indeed, the singing of the *Great Kanon* was only linked with the recitation of the *Life of St Mary of Egypt* after the eleventh century in Byzantium.[42] While variation over the centuries and across geographies is inevitable, and although some details remain elusive, it is clear that the *Great Kanon* became a canonical feature of Great Lent and the *Triodion*. It is difficult to outline how this occurred.

It is not only the modern scholar who encounters this difficulty as she or he explores the sources of Byzantine liturgical practice and its evolution. The eleventh-century monk known as Nikon of the Black Mountain experienced perplexity a millennium ago when faced with a similar task:

---

[38] See Mateos, *Le Typicon de la Grande Église: Tome II*, 10.

[39] For the rubrics of Alexios the Stoudite, see Getcha, *The Typikon Decoded*, 175. See fol. 171v of Sinai Gr. 1096 for the prescription of the *Great Kanon*. For an examination of Sinai Gr. 1096, see Galadza, 'Greek Liturgy in Crusader Jerusalem: Witnesses of Liturgical Life at the Holy Sepulchre and St Sabas Lavra', *Journal of Medieval History* 43, no. 4 (2017): 421–37. The *Great Kanon* is also prescribed for the same day in the twelfth-century Sinai Graecus 1094, fols. 81v–82r: https://loc.gov/item/00271076411-ms/ (retrieved 1 March 2019). On the *Typikon of St Sabas Monastery*, see André Lossky, 'Le Typikon byzantin: Édition d'une version grecque partiellement ineditée: Analyse de la partie liturgique' (ThD dissertation, St Sergius Institute, 1987).

[40] Robert H. Jordan, *The Synaxarion of the Monastery of the Theotokos Evergetis: March–August, the Movable Cycle* (Belfast: Belfast Byzantine Enterprises, 2005), 434–37; M. Arranz, *Le Typicon du monastère du Saint-Sauveur à Messine*. OCA 185 (Rome: Pontificum Institutum Orientalium Studiorum, 1969), 222.

[41] In the former, four portions are read after the recitation of the second and third *kathismata* (the divisions of the Psalter) and after the third and sixth odes of the *kanon*. In the latter, three portions are read. For the Greek text of the *Life of St Mary of Egypt*, see PG 87, 3697–726. I have used the English translation by Maria Kouli in Alice-Mary Talbot, ed. *Holy Women of Byzantium: Ten Saints' Lives in English Translation* (Washington, DC: Dumbarton Oaks, 1996), 65–94.

[42] Getcha, *The Typikon Decoded*, 196–97; Krueger, *Liturgical Subjects*, 244–45.

I came upon and collected different *typika*, of Stoudios and of Jerusalem, and one did not agree with the other, neither Studite with another Studite one, nor Jerusalem ones with Jerusalem ones. And, greatly perplexed by this, I interrogated the wise ones and the ancients, and those having knowledge of these matters and seasoned in things pertaining to the office of ecclesiarch and the rest, of the holy monastery of our holy father Sabas in Jerusalem . . .[43]

After Nikon considered all these traditions, he distilled them to create his own set of rubrics. At first glance, this exemplifies the diversity of liturgical practices that existed in Byzantium, but upon closer inspection it is a testament to how intrinsic fidelity to tradition became a unifying thread in the development of Byzantine liturgical practice, 'much as a writer fully in command of his mother tongue and its literary forms brings forth from his storehouse what is at once old and new'.[44]

Therefore, while my examination of Andrew of Crete's *Great Kanon* explores the text in the editions of the *Triodion* printed in Venice and Rome after the fall of Constantinople, as well as the text in the *Patrologia Graeca*, I also reference the text in Sinai Graecus 734–735, Vaticanus Graecus 771 and Grottaferrata Δβ I. I have also consulted Giannouli's reconstruction of the *Great Kanon* based on the thirteenth-century commentaries of Akakios Sabaites.[45] Although Akakios' version of Andrew's composition exhibits some notable variations from the early *Triodion* manuscripts, especially with the regard to the ordering of the strophes, none of the differences significantly change the nub of the *Great Kanon*. Most importantly, I have sought to reimagine its performance in Byzantium and explore what it signified for the faithful. While it might be difficult to reconstruct the performance of this text at a particular point in time and in a specific church or monastery, reimagining the *Great Kanon* as a recurring hymn within the framework of the Lenten experience is feasible.

The English translations of the *Great Kanon* are my own. However, I have consulted two existing translations of the Greek text. The first translation of the *Great Kanon* is by Ware and Mother Mary.[46] The second

---

[43] This excerpt from the preface to Nikon of the Black Mountain's *Taktikon* is quoted and translated in Robert F. Taft, 'Mount Athos: A Late Chapter in the History of the Byzantine Rite', *DOP* 42 (1988): 179.

[44] Ibid.

[45] Antonia Giannouli, *Die Beiden Byzantinischen Kommentare zum Großen Kanon des Andreas von Kreta: Eine Quellenkritische und Literarhistorische Studie* (Vienna: Verlag der Österreichischen Akademie der Wissenschaften, 2007), 182–224.

[46] *The Lenten Triodion*, 378–415.

is by Sister Katherine and Sister Thekla.[47] Provided there is no stark
disparity between the editions and manuscripts, I will limit my footnote
references of the Greek text to the manuscripts I have examined and the
1879 edition of the *Triodion* published in Rome. While Vaticanus Graecus
771 is one of the earliest witnesses to the singing of the *Great Kanon* during
the fifth week of Lent, it does not contain the text of Andrew's composition but simply the title of what is to be chanted, the author and mode of
Byzantine music – plagal second – and a direction to 'search for it in the
beginning of the *Tropologion* (ζήτει εἰς τὴν ἀρχή τοῦ τροπολογίου)'.[48] In
numbering the strophes of the *Great Kanon*, I have considered the *heirmos*
of each ode to be a kind of prelude and counted the stanza that follows
each *heirmos* as the first strophe.

The Liturgical Context of the *Kanon*

The fourteenth-century ecclesiastical historian Nikephoros Kallistos
Xanthopoulos posits that Andrew composed the *Great Kanon* in his
twilight years as a first-person narrative of repentance.[49] Getcha has
recently reiterated this theory, agreeing with the view of Ivan Karabinov
that Andrew wrote this liturgical poem with this intention in mind.[50]
Whether this was indeed the case is difficult to discern. It certainly is not a
view that is corroborated by the vita that Niketas wrote in the ninth
century, and it is not a theory that is borne out by the text of the *Great
Kanon*, which only contains oblique references to the numerous sins and
the desire for repentance.[51] In any case, in the liturgical tradition of
Byzantium, Andrew's composition became a 'compunctious *kanon*'
(κανών κατανυκτικός) that was experienced during Great Lent.[52] This

---

47 *St Andrew of Crete. The Great Kanon. The Life of St Mary of Egypt* (Whitby: The Greek Orthodox
Monastery of the Assumption, 1980), 29–64.
48 Fol. 118v. The *Tropologion* was an anthology of hymns compiled in the eighth century as a revised
hymnal for the Holy City. Manuscripts Sinai Gr. NE ΜΓ 5 and Sinai Gr. NE ΜΓ 56 (eight to ninth
century) are the oldest known Greek *Tropologia* from Jerusalem. However, it is difficult to ascertain
which *Tropologion* Vaticanus Graecus 771 references.
49 Getcha cites the *Synaxarion* of Xanthopoulos in *The Typikon Decoded*, 174–75.   50 Ibid.
51 The argument in a recent article by Panteleimon Tsormpatzoglou that the composition of the text
occurred after the Monothelite synod of 712 is not convincing. The article suggests that the
dogmatic strophes in the *Great Kanon* show Andrew's concern for confessing the true dogma of
the Orthodox Church. However, dogmatic strophes are a standard feature of *kanons* – the *Great
Kanon* is not exceptional in this regard. See Tsormpatzoglou, 'Ο Ανδρέας Κρήτης (660–740) και ο
πιθανός χρόνος συγγραφής του Μεγάλου Κανόνος [Andrew of Crete (660–740) and the likely
composition date of the Great Kanon]', *Byzantina* 24 (2004): 7–42.
52 This is how it is entitled in Sinai Graecus 734–735, fol. 69r, and Grottaferrata Δβ I, fol. 7v.
Vaticanus Graecus 771 calls it 'the *Great Kanon*' (Μέγας Κανών), fol. 118v.

designation facilitated the practice of compunction by calling to mind a
wider corpus of compunctious literature and its themes of tears, repentance and the Last Judgment. The *Great Kanon* therefore also belongs to
the genre of compunctious poetry, which sought to arouse contrition.[53]

As a liturgical hymn that became part of the *Triodion*, the *Great Kanon*
was sung in the fifth week of Lent during the *orthros*.[54] The *orthros* was
'a daybreak service' that represented one of the 'original hours of both the
cathedral and monastic offices'.[55] It was preceded by vespers and, if the
occasion was a significant liturgical event, the *pannychis*, and it culminated
in the Divine Liturgy. An inherent characteristic of the ninth-century
orthros adopted by the Stoudite monastery in Constantinople is the *kanon*.
While it is unclear whether the *Great Kanon* was one of the *kanons* that
were chanted in Hagia Sophia during Great Lent in the Middle Byzantine
period, the boundaries that separated lay congregations and monastic
communities were porous.[56] In the final centuries of Byzantium, the
kanons of the monastic *orthros* were 'celebrated beyond the monastery
throughout the Orthodox world' and became a cornerstone of morning
prayer for monastic and non-monastic communities alike.[57]

Although the *Great Kanon* was sung in its entirety during the fifth week
of Lent in tenth-century Byzantium, if not earlier, it was also separated
into four sections and chanted at compline during the first week of Lent,
though only after the eleventh century.[58] The singing of *kanons* in monasteries was a choral performance. The *Typikon of the Monastery of St John
the Forerunner on Pantelleria*, the *Typikon of the Monastery of St John
Stoudios in Constantinople* and the *Small Catechesis* of Theodore the
Stoudite contain evidence that the entire choir sang the *kanon*.[59] The
choral performance of hymns was also de rigueur at the Evergetis Monastery near Constantinople.[60] Despite consisting of 250 strophes, the genre
of the *Great Kanon* lent itself to choral performance. Indeed, the sporadic

---

[53] Giannouli, 'Catanyctic Religious Poetry', 86–109.   [54] Krueger, *Liturgical Subjects*, 131.
[55] Robert F. Taft, 'Orthros', in *ODB*, 1539.
[56] Mateos suggests that the *Typikon of the Great Church* might indirectly allude to the singing of the
Great Kanon in Hagia Sophia during Lent. *Le Typicon de la Grande Église: Tome II*, 10–11.
[57] Krueger, *Liturgical Subjects*, 172.   [58] Ibid., 244–45.
[59] See Dubowchik, 'Singing with the Angels', 282–89; Krueger, *Liturgical Subjects*, 166–67.
[60] See Christian Troelsgård, 'Kanon Performance in the Eleventh Century, Evidence from the
Evergetis Typikon Reconsidered', in *Byzantium and Eastern Europe: Liturgical and Musical
Links – In Honour of the 80th Birthday of Dr Miloš Velimirović*, ed. Nina Gerasimova-Persidkaia
and Irina Lozovaia (Moscow: State Conservatory of Moscow 'Piotr Tjajkowskij', 2004), 44–51;
Robert H. Jordan and Rosemary Morris, *The Hypotyposis of the Monastery of the Theotokos Evergetis,
Constantinople (11th–12th Centuries): Introduction, Translation and Commentary* (Farnham:
Ashgate, 2012), 60–61.

use of a refrain in the *Great Kanon* is also a device that encourages the congregation to participate in the singing of its strophes.

The theological dimension of liturgical worship sheds light on the significance of the choral performance of the *kanon*. Byzantine monastic foundation documents depicted earthly worship in monasteries as an imitation of heavenly worship. The notion of the angelic choir singing in heaven, accompanied by the human choir singing on earth, echoes the liturgical theology that emerged during the lifetime of Romanos the Melodist and as early as the fourth-century Cappadocian Fathers.[61] In his *Oration on Theophany*, Gregory the Theologian describes the liturgical celebration of the feast as one that embraces heaven and earth:

Μετὰ ποιμένων δόξασον, μετὰ ἀγγέλων ὕμνησον, μετὰ ἀρχαγγέλων χόρευσον. Ἔστω κοινὴ πανήγυρις οὐρανίων καὶ ἐπιγείων δυνάμεων. Πείθομαι γὰρ κἀκείνας συναγάλλεσθαι καὶ συμπανηγυρίζειν σήμερον, εἴπερ εἰσὶ φιλάνθρωποι καὶ φιλόθεοι, ὥσπερ ἃς Δαβὶδ εἰσάγει μετὰ τὸ πάθος συνανιούσας Χριστῷ, καὶ προσυπαντώσας καὶ διακελευομένας ἀλλήλαις τὴν τῶν πυλῶν ἔπαρσιν.[62]

Give glory with the shepherds, sing praise with the angels, dance with the company of archangels! Let there be a common festival for the powers of heaven and earth! For I believe that they, too, are rejoicing and holding festival along with us today, if it is true that they are friends of both humanity and God, like those David portrays as 'ascending on high' with Christ after his passion, going out to meet him and urging each other to 'lift high the gates'.[63]

As we saw in Chapter 2, this is also the case in Byzantine liturgical commentaries. The affective mystagogy of hymnody and its evocation of an emotional and liturgical community traversed the divide between earthly and heavenly. Not unlike Romanos' *kontakia*, the *Great Kanon* echoed the eschatological communion of liturgical worship that Maximus the Confessor envisioned in his commentary *On Ecclesiastical Mystagogy*.

Reimagining the Performance of the *Great Kanon*

Before the first ode of the *Great Kanon* in the *Triodion*, the text briefly outlines the order of service and, in doing so, provides a few clues about how we can begin to reimagine its performance:

[61] Dubowchik, 'Singing with the Angels', 281.
[62] Oration 38, 17. Claudio Moreschini, ed., *Grégoire de Nazianze: Discours 38–41.* SC 358 (Paris: Éditions du Cerf, 1990), 144. See also PG 36, 332AB.
[63] Daley, *Gregory of Nazianzus*, 126.

On Wednesday evening, about the fourth hour of the night, we assemble in
church and the priest says, 'Blessed is our God . . .'; and we continue with
the prayer 'O heavenly King . . .' . . . After that we read the Six Psalms and
then, after the Great Litany, we sing as usual 'Alleluia' and the Hymns to
the Holy Trinity in the Tone of the week . . . Next we read the first part of
the *Life of St Mary of Egypt*, written by St Sophronios, Patriarch of
Jerusalem. Psalm 50 is read, and then, after the great litany, 'O Lord, save
your people . . .' we begin to sing the *Great Kanon*, slowly and with
compunction.[64]

Aside from rubricating how the ritual is performed, these words are also
the 'anthropological and cosmological context in which the service is
celebrated'.[65] Andrew's poem inhabited the space between vespers and
liturgy – matins, which marked the anticipation of the Incarnation against
the backdrop of exile from Eden.[66] The *Great Kanon* followed the contrite
atmosphere created by the incense and candles of vespers, the singing of
Psalm 103 and the closing of the royal doors, which betokened the very act
of creation but also the paradisal nostalgia engendered by the fall of Adam
and Eve. Before the *Great Kanon* was sung, the faithful followed the
journey of Mary of Egypt into the desert, contemplating how the most
notorious of harlots could become the holiest of desert-dwellers. The
theme of repentance continued with the recitation of Psalm 50. Finally,
the faithful began to sing the nine odes of the *kanon*, 'slowly and with
compunction'.

The nine odes of the *Great Kanon* invoke an array of biblical narratives
and scriptural characters. The list below summarises the main content of
each ode, though it should be noted that some biblical figures – such as the
prodigal son or the harlot who repented at Christ's feet – only make a
cameo in one or two strophes.

---

[64] I have used the translation in Ware and Mother Mary, *The Lenten Triodion*, 377. The Greek text
appears in the 1879 edition printed in Rome – Τριώδιον Κατανυκτικόν, 462–63. In the editions
printed in Venice in the sixteenth century, it does not end with the words 'slowly and with
compunction' but rather 'with a contrite heart and voice' (μετὰ συντετριμμένης καρδίας καὶ
φωνῆς). See, for example, Andrea Cunadi, ed. Τριώδιον (Venice: de Sabio, 1522), 285–86. These
rubrics do not appear in the early manuscripts of the *Triodion*, such as Sinai Graecus 734–735,
Vaticanus Graecus 771 and Grottaferrata Δβ I. Elements of these rubrics – the reading of the *Life of
St Mary of Egypt* and Psalm 50 – appear in the eleventh-century (or early twelfth-century) *Evergetis
Synaxarion*, which influenced later monastic liturgical regulations. See Jordan, *The Synaxarion of
Theotokos Evergetis*, 434–37; Jordan and Morris, *The Hypotyposis*, 3–5. While I have not investigated
when and where these rubrics first appear in the manuscript tradition of the *Triodion*, Getcha
suggests it would have been from the thirteenth century onwards – *The Typikon Decoded*, 37.
[65] Nellas, *Deification in Christ*, 163.   [66] Cabasilas, *Commentary on the Divine Liturgy*, 26–27.

(1)   Adam and Eve, Cain and Abel, the parable of the Prodigal Son.
(2)   The generations from Cain to Noah, the narratives of the cataclysmic flood and tower of Babel, the harlot who repented at Christ's feet.
(3)   Sodom and the tale of Lot, Abraham and Jacob.
(4)   Jacob, Esau and Job.
(5)   Joseph and his brothers, Moses and the Samaritan woman who spoke with Jesus by the well.
(6)   The exodus from Egypt, Joshua, Samuel and David.
(7)   Kings and prophets from David to Ahab.
(8)   Elijah, Elisha, Jeremiah and Jonah.
(9)   Various narratives and characters from the Gospels, including the Publican and the Pharisee, the harlot who repented at Christ's feet and the thief who asked Jesus for forgiveness on the Cross.

Although a few New Testament figures appear briefly in the first eight odes, the overall prominence of the Old Testament in Andrew's composition is notable.

Andrew of Crete's knowledge of the Old Testament in eighth-century Byzantium, when manuscripts of the entire Old Testament were rare, is remarkable.[67] While Byzantine lectionaries for Great Lent habituated the faithful with various narratives from the Old Testament, the books of Genesis, Proverbs and Isaiah dominated the readings.[68] Other Old Testament narratives, such as the stories of Job, Jeremiah or the three youths in the furnace, would have been familiar. These narratives either formed part of the Holy Week lectionary or eight of the nine biblical canticles.[69] However, Andrew takes the faithful on a journey beyond these familiar stories, creatively rewriting biblical texts into an existential and soteriological narrative that elicits introspection and arouses compunction.[70] Whereas Romanos the Melodist usually devotes an entire *kontakion* to one biblical figure or scriptural narrative, Andrew's *Great Kanon* guides the faithful through an astounding constellation of stories and characters, inviting them to consider their part in the sacred drama that unfolds and doing so against an eschatological backdrop.

On the same day that Andrew of Crete's *Great Kanon* was sung, before the performance of the *orthros*, Romanos' *On the Infernal Powers* was chanted during the *pannychis*. This *kontakion* begins with a dialogue

---

[67] Krueger, *Liturgical Subjects*, 145.   [68] Miller, 'The Prophetologion', 67.
[69] Høeg, Zuntz and Engberg, *Prophetologium*, 602–3.
[70] Doru Costache, 'Byzantine Insights into Genesis 1–3: St Andrew of Crete's Great Canon', *Phronema* 24 (2009): 38.

between self and soul that is provoked by the nearness of death.[71] The juxtaposition of condemnation and salvation plays on the tension between the present life and the life of the age to come. Romanos' hymn seeks to arouse tears of compunction and repentance by enacting the eschaton, collapsing past, present and future into sacred time. Andrew of Crete's *Great Kanon* continues this strategy on an epic scale, summoning a vast assembly of scriptural exemplars in its flight through the biblical account of God's people and the salvific acts of Christ.

Scriptural Exemplars of Compunction

In the same way that the nine biblical canticles on which *kanons* were usually modelled would call to mind the entire scriptural story of salvation, the biblical characters Andrew of Crete summons traverse the Old and New Testaments. The scriptural exemplars of repentance and wickedness that Andrew musters are images and narratives that seek to enkindle compunction:

> Μωσέως παρήγαγον, ψυχή τὴν κοσμογένεσιν, καὶ ἐξ ἐκείνου, πᾶσαν ἐνδιάθετον, γραφὴν ἱστοροῦσάν σοι, δικαίους καὶ ἀδίκους ... Τῆς νέας παράγω σοι, Γραφῆς τὰ ὑποδείγματα, ἐνάγοντά σε, ψυχὴ πρὸς κατάνυξιν.[72]

> I have put before you, my soul, Moses' account of the creation of the world and all the recognised Scriptures that tell you the story of the righteous and the wicked ... I bring you, O my soul, examples from the New Testament, to lead you to compunction.

This striking strophe suggests the hymnographer's ekphrastic strategy was to immerse the faithful in biblical narratives, taking them on a liturgically imagined journey through salvation history and conjuring a raft of scriptural exemplars as companions. Andrew begins his litany of exemplars with the first-created humans, Adam and Eve. But this scriptural story becomes the story of the faithful as they sing the *Great Kanon*. The liturgical performance of the text destabilises the 'I' of subjectivity. The fall and exile of Adam and Eve from Eden becomes their own alienation from divine grace. Having 'rivalled in transgression Adam the first-created human', the faithful could ponder their own estrangement from the 'everlasting

---

[71] 'O my soul, my soul, wake up—why do you sleep?'
[72] Ninth ode, strophes 2, 4. Sinai Graecus 734–735, fol. 81v, Grottaferrata Δβ I, fol. 15r. Τριώδιον Κατανυκτικόν, 488–89.

kingdom' and could feel the paradisal nostalgia and mortality that the 'garments of skin' represent.[73] The nakedness of Adam and Eve, their loss of the ancestral robe of beauty and their garments of skin, become images of the congregation's own fallenness and desire for Edenic bliss:

Διέρρηξα, νῦν τὴν στολήν μου τὴν πρώτην, ἣν ἐξυφάνατό μοι, ὁ Πλασ-τουργὸς ἐξ ἀρχῆς, καὶ ἔνθεν κεῖμαι γυμνός.[74]

Now I have rent my first robe, which the Creator wove for me from the beginning, and thence I lie naked.

In the odes that follow, the *Great Kanon* continues to present Old Testament examples of virtuous and iniquitous figures to elicit compunction.

Perhaps the most striking figure is King David who is one of the scriptural characters appearing in the seventh ode.[75] Although the hymn notes his murderous and adulterous actions in the fourth strophe, it later celebrates David's repentance, which is interwoven with the singer's own desire for forgiveness: 'but in pity restore to me joy, as David sings'.[76] David's composition of the Psalms is a detail that would have been familiar to the congregation. The importance and centrality of the Psalms in the cycle of Byzantine worship is evident.[77] Perhaps the most well-known Psalm was the fiftieth, which spoke of David's repentance. However, according to Athanasius of Alexandria, when the faithful sang these words, the text became the song of their own repentance.[78] Psalm 50 may have been in use as early as the fourth century at the beginning of matins and, by the late sixth century, it was the prelude to the nine biblical canticles that were sung in Palestinian and Syrian monasteries.[79] Therefore, the recitation or singing of Psalm 50 during the performance of the *Great Kanon* – as a prelude to the hymn – and in the *orthros* more generally,

---

[73] First ode, strophe 3. Sinai Graecus 734–735, fol. 69r. Τριῴδιον Κατανυκτικόν, 463. On the significance of God clothing Adam and Eve in 'garments of skin' after the fall, see Nellas, *Deification in Christ*, 43–91.

[74] Second ode, strophe 8. Sinai Graecus 734–735, fol. 70v. Τριῴδιον Κατανυκτικόν, 465.

[75] Sinai Graecus 734–735, fols. 78v–80r, Grottaferrata ΔΒ I, fols. 13r–14r. Τριῴδιον Κατανυκτικόν, 481–84.

[76] Seventh ode, strophe 17. Sinai Graecus 734–735, fols. 79v–80r, Grottaferrata ΔΒ I, fol. 14r. Τριῴδιον Κατανυκτικόν, 483. This is an allusion to Psalm 50:14.

[77] Daley, 'Finding the Right Key', 189.

[78] *Letter to Marcellinus*, PG 27, 24B; Athanasius of Alexandria, *The Life of Antony and the Letter to Marcellinus*, 111; Georgia Frank, 'The Memory Palace of Marcellinus: Athanasius and the Mirror of the Psalms', in *Ascetic Culture: Essays in Honour of Philip Rousseau*, ed. Blake Leyerle and Robin Darling Young (Notre Dame, IN: University of Notre Dame Press, 2013), 114.

[79] Krueger, *Liturgical Subjects*, 150.

would have resonated in the minds of the faithful when the seventh ode of Andrew's composition was sung. Amidst the various biblical exemplars of repentance brought before the faithful, the *Great Kanon* invokes Psalm 50 as the quintessential prayer of compunction and forgiveness, which has already been sung and recited on numerous occasions and will recur throughout the liturgical cycle of Great Lent.

From time to time, the loosely chronological sequence of Old Testament biblical exemplars in the first eight odes is interrupted. In the first ode, amidst the narratives of Adam and Eve, and Cain and Abel, Andrew of Crete invokes the figure of the prodigal son as a universal figure of sinfulness and yet a model of repentance for the faithful to emulate:

Εἰ καὶ ἥμαρτον Σωτήρ, ἀλλ᾽ οἶδα ὅτι φιλάνθρωπος εἶ, πλήττεις συμπαθῶς, καὶ σπλαγχνίζῃ θερμῶς, δακρύοντα βλέπεις, καὶ προστρέχεις ὡς Πατήρ, ἀνακαλῶν τόν Ἄσωτον.[80]

Although I have sinned, O Saviour, yet I know that you are the lover of humankind, you chastise mercifully, and fervently show compassion, you see the one who weeps and hasten as the Father, recalling the prodigal son.

The repentance of the prodigal son would have already been celebrated earlier in the Lenten cycle when the hymns prescribed for that liturgical event, especially a *kanon* devoted to the prodigal, probably composed by Theodore the Stoudite or his brother, called on the faithful to identify with this scriptural exemplar of compunction.[81] Andrew of Crete's poem once again invites the faithful to feel what the prodigal felt when he became so alienated from divine grace in faraway lands that he was lost even to himself, content to dine with swine rather than his kith and kin. Yet, remembering the royal dignity of his paternal home, compunction rekindled the flame of his relationship with God and 'he came to himself' (εἰς ἑαυτὸν δὲ ἐλθών).[82] This moment of compunction marks the prodigal's emergence from the abyss of alienation into a wakefulness that desires restoration. It becomes a call for the faithful singing the *Great Kanon* to take up the words of the prodigal and yearn for the prodigal's salvation, by beginning their own return to the bliss of Eden.

After making a few brief cameos in the earlier odes, the scriptural figure of the harlot emerges in the ninth ode as another protagonist for Andrew of Crete. Whereas in the second ode the harlot's tears are equated with the

[80] First ode, strophe 12. Sinai Graecus 734–735, fol. 69v. Τριώδιον Κατανυκτικόν, 464.

[81] Sinai Graecus 734–735, fols. 3v–5v. On the *kanon* by a Stoudite hymnographer, see *Liturgical Subjects*, 173–76.

[82] Luke 15:17.

scented oil, the final ode of the hymns simply recalls the account from the Gospel and chides the soul for not imitating the woman's repentance:

Τὴν Πόρνην ὦ τάλαινα, ψυχή μου οὐκ ἐζήλωσας, ἥτις λαβοῦσα, μύρου τὸ ἀλάβαστρον, σὺν δάκρυσιν ἤλειψε, τοὺς πόδας τοῦ Κυρίου, ἐξέμαξε δὲ ταῖς θριξί, τῶν ἀρχαίων ἐγκλημάτων, τὸ χειρόγραφον ῥηγνύοντος αὐτῇ.[83]

O my wretched soul, you have not emulated the harlot who took the alabaster jar of myrrh, and with her tears anointed the feet of the Lord. She wiped them with her hair, and he tore up for her the manuscript of ancient crimes.

By juxtaposing the power of tears to annul past iniquities with the soul's inertia, the *Great Kanon* evokes a powerful comparison between repentance and obdurate sinfulness. Unlike Romanos the Melodist, who in his hymn *On the Harlot* enlarges the scriptural narrative, exploring the interiority of his protagonist and her compunction, Andrew is content simply to place the harlot alongside an array of biblical icons of repentance. However, in doing so, he asks the faithful to consider whether they can identify with the models of righteousness or the unrepentant figures from the Old and New Testaments appearing throughout his hymn.

While this poetic menagerie of biblical exemplars and counter-ideals may seem repetitive – the 250 strophes of the *Great Kanon* far exceeds the length of any other *kanon* sung during the liturgical year – Andrew's hymn enacts a unified narrative from beginning to end. His composition invites the faithful to journey through history with the righteous and the wicked, asking them to consider their own place in the divine drama of salvation. Indeed, the poem could be reconsidered as an example of Byzantine ekphrasis, which vividly describes a vision of human repentance against the backdrop of biblical stories and invites 'a contemplation of God through the eyes of the soul'.[84]

Similarly, the hagiographical *Life of St Mary of Egypt*, which in late Byzantium was read during the performance of the *Great Kanon*, calls the faithful to envision the footsteps of Mary as she travels into the desert and emulate her tears of compunction. Indeed, when Mary is prevented from entering a church in Jerusalem during 'the holy feast of the Exaltation of the Cross' by an invisible force, her evocative description of feeling compunction in the text echoes the refrain of Romanos the Melodist's hymn *On the Harlot*:

---

[83] Ninth ode, strophe 18. Sinai Graecus 734–735, fol. 82v, Grottaferrata Δβ I, fol. 15v. Τριῴδιον Κατανυκτικόν, 490.

[84] Olkinuora, 'Revisiting the *Great Canon*', forthcoming.

Only then did I realize the cause which prevented me from laying eyes on the life-giving cross, for a salvific word touched the eyes of my heart, showing me that it was the filth of my deeds that was barring the entrance to me. Then I began to cry, lamenting and beating my breast, raising sighs from the depths of my heart.[85]

The liturgical significance of reading this text in an ecclesiastical setting is to invoke the presence of the saint in the assembly of the faithful 'in a sacramental manner', so that she can walk with them and they with her on the path of repentance.[86] However, it also renders the harlot a universal figure of repentance who recurs throughout the hymnography of the *Triodion*. The *Great Kanon* deploys this liturgical motif by asking the faithful to go beyond a superficial emulation of its scriptural exemplars of repentance. The first-person narrative of the hymnographer could become the words of the Byzantine faithful who took up the song of the righteous that had gone before them. The 'courage [of] Jacob', the 'tears of the harlot', and the plight of 'the woman with the issue of blood' could become their own feelings through sacred song and liturgical mysticism.[87]

The Musical and Performative Tradition of the *Kanon*

The musical and performative tradition of the *kanon* amplified its affective mystagogy and encouraged all the faithful to experience a communion of saints. Setting words to familiar music, such as a contrafactum, enjoined the faithful to sing the *kanon* together with the choir of chanters and wove an emotional link with other melodies and texts in the *Triodion*. Moreover, the melodic style of the *Great Kanon* was not the triumphal first mode[88] of the resurrection *kanon* that was chanted during the paschal matins, but the more solemn plagal second mode,[89] which recurs often in Lenten hymnody. The Byzantine poem describing characteristics of the plagal second mode that appears in the *Oktoechos* is intriguing but somewhat vague: 'You are the pleasing song, the melodic

---

[85] *Life of St Mary of Egypt*, chapter 23. Talbot, *Holy Women of Byzantium*, 82. PG 87, 3713B. Note the similarity between 'the filth of my deeds' (ὁ βόρβορος τῶν ἔργων μου) and the refrain of Romanos' hymn.

[86] Nellas, *Deification in Christ*, 167.

[87] Fourth ode, strophe 9; second ode, strophe 5; eighth ode, strophe 16. Sinai Graecus 734–735, fols. 74r, 70v, 81r. The quoted strophe from the second ode is not in Grottaferrata Δβ I – see fols. 10r and 14v for the other two references. Τριώδιον Κατανυκτικόν, 473, 466, 486.

[88] One of the eight modes of Byzantine sacred music, which belonged to the diatonic genus.

[89] The plagal second mode belonged to the chromatic genus.

sweetness, the singing cicada. Who, O Second Plagal, cannot love you?'[90] Moreover, these lines are found in a thirteenth-century manuscript from Grottaferrata and may not reflect Middle Byzantine views of the ethos of this particular mode of Byzantine music. However, as previously noted, it is as difficult to argue that there is one mode of Byzantine music that evokes compunction as it is to reimagine the emotive universe of liturgical chant. It is more fruitful to explore the way in which the text of the *kanon* was set to music.

While the musical tradition of the *kanon* constituted an important aspect of its performance, it is not the only consideration that should be borne in mind in reimagining the performance of Andrew's composition and how the faithful participated in the liturgical event unfolding before them. The liturgical experience of hymns and the emotions it may have engendered has a synesthetic dimension. Each of the liturgical aspects of performance, be it iconography, music, or the text of the hymn, enhances the meaning of each of the other kinds of liturgical expression. It is the unity of these different elements that defines the experience of the faithful. Although it is not always certain what iconography the faithful would have seen during the performance of the *Great Kanon*, it was likely that several of the biblical exemplars of repentance would have been visible in the monastery or urban church where it was sung, especially given the crisis of Iconoclasm had come to an end when the *Triodion* was compiled. While the feelings of the faithful as they gazed upon these icons are impossible to know, the *Life of St Mary of Egypt* describes how the protagonist felt when she looked upon the Virgin Mary:

> In my mind I would stand in front of the icon of the Mother of God, my guarantor, and I would weep before her, asking her to chase away those thoughts that assailed my miserable soul ... When I had shed enough tears and had beaten my breast as hard as I could, I used to see the light shining everywhere around me.[91]

The effect of this interaction between text, music and image during the performance of the hymn would have enhanced the impact of *Great Kanon* and its arousal of compunction.

Although we are beginning to understand the soundscape of Hagia Sophia, there are a multitude of Byzantine churches where Andrew's hymn might have been performed and very few, if any of them, possessed the

---

[90] Desby, 'The Modes and Tunings', 27. I have modified the translation.
[91] Chapter 28. Talbot, *Holy Women of Byzantium*, 86.

sonic architecture of Constantinople's cathedral. However, since the *Great Kanon* – as with all *kanons* – follows a tradition where the odes are modelled on contrafacta, it is possible to approach the musical significance of the *Great Kanon* without considering the musical notation of *kanons* that emerges in late Byzantium.

The liturgical expression of the *kanon* privileged text over music. It was not melismatic chant but a syllabic melody where the 'great number of contrafacta effectively dilute through repetition the purely musical impact of each Byzantine model melody'.[92] Its choral character facilitated popular participation in the singing of the hymns. However, the potential for the faithful to participate in the singing of a *kanon* does not of itself reveal the musical significance of the melody of the *Great Kanon*. The contrafacta of any *kanon* should be examined in the wider liturgical context of the church calendar, as a part of the musical constellation that the performance of all the various hymns constitutes. Beyond the tight-knit relationship between words and melody in any given *kanon*, the associations that might emerge between melodies of *kanons* in the fullness of the liturgical cycle are pivotal. In the case of the *Great Kanon*, the liturgical framework of Great Lent and the *kanons* performed during this period are particularly relevant.

The choice of contrafactum on which the melody of each mode was modelled may have kindled the musical memory of the audience, recalling the events of one of the Sundays from the preparatory period of the Lenten cycle. The mode and contrafactum of the *Great Kanon* was also the model melody for the first *kanon* for Carnival Sunday in the *Triodion*:

> Βοηθὸς καὶ σκεπαστής, ἐγένετό μοι εἰς σωτηρίαν, οὗτός μου Θεός, καὶ δοξάσω αὐτόν, Θεὸς τοῦ Πατρός μου, καὶ ὑψώσω αὐτόν· ἐνδόξως γὰρ δεδόξασται.[93]

> He has become my helper and protector unto salvation, this is my God and I will glorify him. He is the God of my father, and I will exalt him, for he has gloriously triumphed.

This is not without reason or rhyme, especially since the remembrance of death and the imminence of the Last Judgment were often the stimulants of compunction. The melodic echo of the contrafactum would have produced an aural iconicity – a visual and sonic intertextuality – that

---

[92] Lingas, 'Sunday Matins', 7.
[93] Sinai Graecus 734–735, fol. 22r, Vaticanus Graecus 771, fol. 14r, Grottaferrata Δβ I, fol. 2v. Τριώδιον Κατανυκτικόν, 34.

elicited a panoramic liturgical experience of biblical characters and events. The text is also reminiscent of the Song of Moses, which was the first biblical canticle:

> The Lord is my strength and song,
> And He has become my salvation;
> He is my God, and I will praise Him;
> My father's God, and I will exalt Him.[94]

This poetic and musical intertextuality creates a multifaceted image of compunction that is not limited to one *kanon* or one day of Great Lent and Holy Week. While history divides and orders the narrative of salvation and its scriptural characters in the Bible, time and place become somewhat blurred in the performance of the *Great Kanon*. As with other Byzantine hymns, its affective mystagogy erodes the logical, historical and existential distinctions between the tears that the prodigal or the harlot wept and what the faithful are called to feel.

Passions and Compunction in the *Great Kanon*

As a mystical vision, Andrew of Crete's poem brought together a variety of biblical characters, scattered across time and place, and the congregation into liturgical union amidst a divine drama that unfolds in an eschatological climate and yet within 'the hidden person of the heart'.[95] According to the *Great Kanon*, the salvation of the human person is not merely a matter for the soul but for the flesh also:

> Δεῦρο τάλαινα ψυχή, σὺν τῇ σαρκί σου τῷ πάντων Κτίστῃ, ἐξομολογοῦ καὶ ἀπόσχου λοιπόν, τῆς πρὶν ἀλογίας, καὶ προσάγαγε Θεόν, ἐν μετανοίᾳ δάκρυα.[96]

> Come wretched soul, with your flesh, to the Creator of all. Make confession to Him and abstain henceforth from your past brutishness, and offer to God tears in repentance.

Andrew of Crete does not render asunder the psychosomatic unity of the human person – the sins of his protagonists have wounded 'soul and body' and left them 'stripped naked of God' – nor does he perceive repentance to be anything other than an embodied phenomenon that has spiritual and

---

[94] Exodus 15:2.   [95] 1 Peter 3:4.
[96] First ode, strophe 2. Sinai Graecus 734–735, fol. 69r, Grottaferrata ΔΒ I, fol. 7v. Τριώδιον Κατανυκτικόν, 463.

somatic markers.[97] Indeed, the fallen nature of humanity is often illustrated with physical metaphors:

Μορφώσας μου, τὴν τῶν παθῶν ἀμορφίαν, ταῖς φιληδόνοις ὁρμαῖς, ἐλυμη-
νάμην τοῦ νοῦ τὴν ὡραιότητα.

With my lustful desires I have formed within myself the deformity of the
passions and disfigured the beauty of my mind.[98]

However, as the *Great Kanon* suggests, and as one of Andrew's contem-
poraries, Isaac the Syrian, remarked, tears 'mark the boundary between the
bodily and the spiritual state, between the state of subjection to the
passions and that of purity'.[99]

The significance of the passions for the human person in Byzantine
thought is not restricted to either soul or body but the unity of the two.
Whereas passions that were unruly and depraved could disfigure the
beauty of the mind, liturgical song sought to arouse blessed emotions that
could excite the mind, elicit tears and begin to restore the original glory of
the human person.[100] The *Great Kanon* often dramatises the darker side of
emotions, portraying these as passions enslaved by the idolatry of materi-
alism. However, the 'swine's meat' and the 'flesh-pots' of Egypt are
juxtaposed with 'the food of heaven' to depict a pleasure that is either
wedded to or divorced from a heavenly freedom.[101] Passions are not
without their blessed counterparts, such as the pleasure of the marriage
bed.[102] Indeed, by liberating the soul from the oppressive forces that can
pervert the passions, their vital energy can be discovered:

Ὡς Μωσῆς ὁ μέγας τὸν Αἰγύπτιον νοῦν, πλήξασα τάλαινα, οὐκ ἀπέκτεινας
ψυχή, καὶ πῶς οἰκήσεις λέγε, τὴν ἔρημον τῶν παθῶν, διὰ τῆς μετανοίας;[103]

---

[97] First ode, strophes 11 and 3. Sinai Graecus 734–735, fol. 69v, 69r. Although strophe 11 is in
Grottaferrata Δβ I, fol. 7v, strophe 3 from the first ode does not appear in this manuscript.
Τριώδιον Κατανυκτικόν, 464, 463.

[98] Second ode, strophe 20. Sinai Graecus 734–735, fol. 70v, Grottaferrata Δβ I, fol. 8r. Τριώδιον
Κατανυκτικόν, 466.

[99] Ascetical homily 14. See Isaac the Syrian, *The Ascetical Homilies*, trans. Dana Miller (Boston, MA:
Holy Transfiguration Monastery, 1984), 82.

[100] This theme emerges as early as in Basil the Great's *Homilies on the Psalms*. For the relevant excerpts,
see McKinnon, *Music in Early Christian Literature*, 65–67.

[101] Sixth ode, strophe 7. Sinai Graecus 734–735, fol. 77r, Grottaferrata Δβ I, fol. 12r. Τριώδιον
Κατανυκτικόν, 478.

[102] Ninth ode, strophe 12. Sinai Graecus 734–735, fol. 82r, Grottaferrata Δβ I, fol. 15v. Τριώδιον
Κατανυκτικόν, 489.

[103] Fifth ode, strophe 9 (strophe 8 in the Sinai Graecus manuscript and strophe 20 in the Grottaferrata
manuscript). Sinai Graecus 734–735, fol. 76r, Grottaferrata Δβ I, fol. 11v. Τριώδιον
Κατανυκτικόν, 476.

O miserable soul, you have not struck and killed the Egyptian mind, as did Moses the great. Tell me then, how will you go to dwell in the wilderness of the passions, through repentance?[104]

Andrew does not propose the obliteration of the passions. He suggests the passions are not depraved by nature but can become so through evil desire and a life divorced from asceticism.

Indeed, passions can engender a transformation of the human person. The emotion that emerges as the catalyst of repentance and the key to forgiveness for many of Andrew's protagonists is compunction. The second strophe of the first ode of the *Great Kanon*, which was quoted earlier, distinguishes between the related feelings of compunction and repentance. As in the seventh-century *Ladder of Divine Ascent*, compunction and repentance represent two different actions, albeit intertwined:

Κατέχων κάτεχε τὴν μακαρίαν τῆς ὁσίας κατανύξεως χαρμολύπην· καὶ μὴ παύσῃ τῆς ἐν αὐτῇ ἐργασίας, ἄχρις οὗ μετάρσιον ἐκ τῶν ἐντεῦθεν τῷ Χριστῷ καθαρὸν παραστήσῃ σε·[104]

Hold fast to the blessed and joyful sorrow of holy compunction and do not cease labouring for it until it lifts you high above the things of the world to present you, a cleansed offering, to Christ.[105]

Whereas repentance is a radical change of mind, compunction is the emotion that incites this action by accentuating the fallenness of the human person and kindling a desire for restoration. Compunction could open the door of repentance and lead to an inner renewal: 'wash me clean, O Saviour, by my tears'.[106] Moreover, while compunction may be a precondition for repentance, the inverse can also take place:

Τοῦ Μανασσῆ, ἐπεσώρευσας, τὰ ἐγκλήματα τῇ προαιρέσει, στήσασα ὡς βδελύγματα πάθη, καὶ πληθύνουσα ψυχή, προσωχθίσματα. Ἀλλ' αὐτοῦ τὴν μετάνοιαν, ζηλοῦσα θερμῶς, κτῆσαι κατάνυξιν.[107]

By deliberate choice, my soul, you have incurred the guilt of Manasseh, setting up the passions as idols and multiplying abominations. But with fervent heart emulate his repentance and acquire compunction.

---

[104] PG 88, 804BC.
[105] John Klimakos, *The Ladder of Divine Ascent*, trans. Colm Luibhéid and Norman Russell (New York, NY: Paulist Press, 1982), 137.
[106] Ibid.
[107] Seventh ode, strophe 15. Sinai Graecus 734–735, fol. 79v, Grottaferrata Δβ I, fol. 14r. Τριῴδιον Κατανυκτικόν, 483.

Compunction displays teleological dimensions, performing a restoration of humanity.[108] This theme of restoration is prominent in the second ode of the *Great Kanon*, where the image of God in which humankind was created is identified with a comely form of the human person, and depraved passions represent the disfigurement of this beauty. However, tears of compunction can heal the deformity of the human person and clothe her/him with the blessed raiment of Eden:

> Κατέχρωσα, τῆς πρὶν εἰκόνος τὸ κάλλος, Σῶτερ τοῖς πάθεσιν, ἀλλ᾽ ὡς ποτὲ τὴν δραχμήν, ἀναζητήσας εὑρέ.[109]

> I have discoloured with the passions the beauty of the image of old, O Saviour, but having sought me, as once you had sought the lost coin, find me.

Andrew of Crete enjoined a transfiguration of the human person through compunction and a mystical imitation of scriptural heroes: 'Like the Harlot I cry to you, I have sinned ... Accept my tears as sweet ointment, O Saviour'.[110] This metamorphosis was consummated in the eucharistic climax of the liturgy, which *orthros* – the framework of the *Great Kanon* – anticipated. Feeling liturgical emotions was an extension of the Eucharist, a perpetuation of the mystery where creation communicated with the uncreated and was deified.[111] And it was within the affective mystagogy of liturgical prayer that compunction was sought:

> Οὐ δάκρυα, οὐδὲ μετάνοιαν ἔχω, οὐδὲ κατάνυξιν, αὐτός μοι ταῦτα Σωτήρ, ὡς Θεὸς δώρησαι.[112]

> I have no tears, no repentance, no compunction; but as God, O Saviour, bestow them on me.

Within the sacred drama that unfolded in the performance of the *Great Kanon*, human feelings could become liturgical feelings and wield salvific power through divine grace.

---

[108] On the teleological theme of the soul as a realm of potentialities, see Niklaus Largier, 'The Plasticity of the Soul: Mystical Darkness, Touch, and Aesthetic Experience', *MLN* 125, no. 3 (2010): 536–51.

[109] Second ode, strophe 21. Sinai Graecus 734–735, fol. 71r, Grottaferrata Δβ I, fol. 8r. Τριῴδιον Κατανυκτικόν, 466.

[110] Second ode, strophe 22. Ibid.

[111] See the analysis of Cabasilas' *Commentary on the Divine Liturgy* in Taft, *Through Their Own Eyes*, 155–58.

[112] Second ode, strophe 25. Sinai Graecus 734–735, fol. 71r, Grottaferrata Δβ I, fol. 8r. Τριῴδιον Κατανυκτικόν, 466.

Concluding Remarks

For the Byzantine faithful, the singing of the *Great Kanon* became a liturgical act that could mirror, shape and transform the passions of the singer's soul. The hymn unveiled emotions that could become the feelings of the congregation through sacred song. It presented the hidden desires of biblical characters and invited the faithful to become part of the sacred drama unfolding before them. In hymnody, desire was not abolished but united with the otherness of the divine and invited into an ever-intensifying, all-consuming participation with 'the Creator of the ages' who 'united in himself the nature of humankind' (ἥνωσεν ἑαυτῷ, τὴν τῶν ἀνθρώπων φύσιν).[113]

Andrew of Crete contributed to the writing of a new chapter in the history of liturgical emotions, asking the faithful to journey into his poetic world of biblical stories, contemplate the characters therein and transform their passions. The *Great Kanon* plunged emotion into the mystical knowledge of the eschaton by portraying 'tears of compunction' (δάκρυα κατανύξεως) and the repentance they heralded as dismantling the psychological armour that disrupted the faithful from experiencing the 'Trinity beyond all being' (Ὑπερούσιε Τριάς).[114] Compunction became meaningful in the liturgical performance of the hymn, which traversed time and space as it guided the soul through scriptural landscapes in a dreamlike journey. As Anastasios of Sinai declared, 'as many dreams as you will see producing in you compunction, and correction, and conversion, and fear of God, love only these'.[115] But whereas dreaming was an experience where discursive thought was suspended, hymnody was a controlled dream that deconstructed the binaries of rational and irrational, inner and outer, sensory and intelligible. The call of the *Great Kanon* was an entreaty to shake off delusion and enter the liturgically imagined narrative of salvation.

The performance of the *Great Kanon* exemplified the mystical dimension of liturgical feeling and has intriguing implications for the history of emotions in Byzantium. If emotions were understood within the context of a Christian anthropology that viewed humankind as created in the image and likeness of God, then emotions were not simply constructed within a social and cultural milieu but within a liturgical event. Emotions

---

[113] Fifth ode, final strophe. Sinai Graecus 734–735, fol. 76v, Grottaferrata Δβ I, fol. 12r. Τριώδιον Κατανυκτικόν, 477.

[114] First ode, penultimate strophe. Sinai Graecus 734–735, fol. 70r. Τριώδιον Κατανυκτικόν, 465.

[115] *Questions and Answers*, 72 in *Quaestiones et Responsiones*, ed. Marcel Richard and Joseph A. Munitiz CCSG 59 (Turnhout: Brepols, 2006), 125. The English translation is my own.

were imbued with a theological quality, evoking the mystical unity of the faithful as members of the body of Christ and, as elements of this unity, participating in the grace of the Incarnation and a communion of saints.

As Andrew's magnum opus came to inhabit the *Triodion* and the sacred rituals of Great Lent, it played a role in creating an affective and mystical space where compunction could be perceived and felt. Liturgical emotion was not a disavowal of the physical and cognitive dimensions of emotions. The emotions of the *Great Kanon* invariably have somatic markers and are characterised by 'upheavals of thought'[116] – 'awaken my mind and turn me back'[117] – but they are given shape and form in humanity's encounter with the divine:

> Τὰ κρύφια τῆς καρδίας μου, ἐξηγόρευσά σοι τῷ Κριτῇ μου, ἴδε μου τὴν ταπείνωσιν, ἴδε καὶ τὴν θλίψιν μου, καὶ πρόσχες τῇ κρίσει μου νῦν, καὶ αὐτός με ἐλέησον ὡς εὔσπλαγχνος ὁ τῶν Πατέρων Θεός.[118]

> The secrets of my heart have I confessed to You, my Judge, see my abasement, see my affliction, and attend to my judgment now, and in Your compassion have mercy upon me, O God of our fathers.

Although the *Great Kanon* evokes the deep longing that binds the faithful to their Creator, Judge and Saviour in a personal relationship, it refracts this longing through an intricate prism of an eschatological communion where biblical figures come together, inviting the congregation to sing with the prodigal, the harlot and the thief, and to feel compunction collectively yet personally in liturgical time and space.

---

[116] See Nussbaum, *Upheavals of Thought*, 1–18.
[117] Eighth ode, strophe 1. Sinai Graecus 734–735, fol. 80r, Grottaferrata Δβ I, fol. 14r. Τριῴδιον Κατανυκτικόν, 485.
[118] Seventh ode, strophe 2. Sinai Graecus 734–735, fol. 78v, Grottaferrata Δβ I, fol. 13r. Τριῴδιον Κατανυκτικόν, 482.

CHAPTER 5

Kassia

Of all the hymnographers whose works appear in the liturgical books of Byzantium, only one hymnographer – Kassia – was a woman.[1] She was born around the year 810 in Constantinople and died around 865, though there is still some conjecture about whether she was born as early as 800 or 805 and whether she lived beyond the first half of the ninth century.[2] Although Byzantinists have occasionally viewed the ninth century as a transitional period that saw the end of Iconoclasm and the beginning of what is known as the Macedonian revival, it was a time of political, cultural and ecclesiastical innovation.[3] Kassia personified this spirit of innovation. As the daughter of a distinguished member of the imperial court with the rank of *kandidatos*, she had access to an excellent education.[4] Theodore the Stoudite extols her erudition in the following way:

Οἷα ἡμῖν καὶ αὖθις ἐφθέγξατο ἡ κοσμιότης σου ὁμοῦ μὲν σοφά, ὁμοῦ δὲ καὶ συνετά, ὥστε με εἰκότως ἐστὶ ξενολογεῖσθαι καὶ εὐχαριστεῖν τῷ Κυρίῳ, ἐπὶ κόρῃ ἀρτιφυεῖ τηλικαύτην γνῶσιν ἐνορῶνταν, οὐ μὲν οὖν κατὰ τὰς πάλαι (πολλοῦ γὰρ ἀποδέομεν καὶ ἄπειρον καὶ ἄνδρες καὶ γυναῖκες τῆς ἐκείνων σοφίας καὶ παιδεύσεως οἱ νῦν), ὅμως δ' οὖν ὅτι κατὰ τὸ παρὸν ὑπερῆρας ὅτι μάλιστα καὶ κόσμος σοι ὁ λόγος, πάσης ἐπικήρου εὐπρεπείας ὡραιότερος.[5]

---

[1] Topping, *Sacred Songs*, 207.

[2] Kazhdan, *A History of Byzantine Literature*, 316–17; Anna M. Silvas, 'Kassia the Nun c. 810–c. 865: An Appreciation', in *Byzantine Women: Varieties of Experience AD 800–1200*, ed. Lynda Garland (Aldershot: Ashgate, 2006), 17.

[3] See the collection of papers in Leslie Brubaker, ed., *Byzantium in the Ninth Century: Dead or Alive? Papers from the Thirtieth Spring Symposium of Byzantine Studies, Birmingham, March 1996* (Aldershot: Ashgate, 1998).

[4] Theodore the Stoudite's first epistle to Kassia is addressed to Kassia *Kandidatissa*. Georgios Fatouros, ed. *Theodori Studitae epistulae*, Vol. 2 (Berlin: De Gruyter, 1992), 339.

[5] Second epistle of Theodore to Kassia in ibid., 501.

Once more your decorum has expressed to us things so wise and understanding that it is right for me to be astonished and give thanks to the Lord
when I see such knowledge in a maiden lately sprung. While you have not
surpassed those of old, of whose wisdom and education we in this gener-
ation, both men and women, fall far short—and immeasurably so—you
have done so with regard to those of the present, since the fair form of your
discourse has far more beauty than a mere specious prettiness.[6]

During the second wave of Iconoclasm that gripped Byzantium, she
suffered a beating for flouting the edicts against icons.[7] She desired the
monastic life from her youth and founded a monastery of her own on
Xerolophos, the seventh hill of Constantinople, possibly toward the end of
Iconoclasm, in 843.[8] Her literary talent and close ties with the Stoudite
monastery and its abbot, Theodore, were instrumental in enshrining her
compositions in the Byzantine hymnal that Theodore, his brother Joseph
and their successors assembled.[9]

Kassia is also regarded as the author of various gnomic epigrams, which
are pithy meditations on the ethical life of a Christian.[10] Although we will
not examine the epigrams attributed to Kassia and their social commentary
closely, they disclose how highly she regarded the monastic life, which for
her was not a place of refuge from society but the embodiment of the
Christian philosophy that was 'a shining lamp to all' (λύχνος φαίνων τοῖς
πᾶσι).[11] Like the composition of hymns, it was unusual for a woman to
write epigrams in such a male-dominated literary field. Perhaps this was an
advantage for Kassia and accounts for her originality. Although her epigrams follow 'an old and venerated tradition of moralizing in verse',
Kassia's contribution to this tradition creatively fused secular and religious
maxims in what one scholar has dubbed 'an osmosis of ancient wisdom
and monastic truth' that revitalised and transformed the genre and made it
relevant for the Byzantines.[12] An example of this is the following epigram,
which at first glance appears to comment on stupidity:

---

[6] The translation is from Silvas, 'Kassia the Nun', 35.
[7] See the second epistle of Theodore the Stoudite to Kassia in Fatouros, *Theodori Studitae epistulae*,
501. See also the discussion in Niki Tsironis, ed. Κασσιανή ἡ ὑμνῳδὸς (*Kassiane the Hymnodist*)
(Athens: Phoinika, 2002), 18–19.
[8] Tripolitis, *Kassia*, xv.   [9] Krueger, *Liturgical Subjects*, 164–65.
[10] On the question of whether these epigrams are truly the work of Kassia, see Marc D. Lauxtermann,
Byzantine Poetry from Pisides to Geometres: Text and Context (Vienna: Verlag der Österreichischen
Akademie der Wissenschaften, 2003), 248–52. The Greek text of these epigrams is available in
Tsironis, Κασσιανή, 79–89. Several of these are translated into English by Anna Silvas in 'Kassia the
Nun', 23–27.
[11] Quoted in Silvas, 'Kassia the Nun', 23.   [12] Lauxtermann, *Byzantine Poetry*, 241.

Γνῶσις ἐν μωρῷ πάλιν ἄλλη μωρία·
γνῶσις ἐν μωρῷ κώδων ἐν ῥινὶ χοίρου.[13]

Knowledge in a fool is another form of folly;
knowledge in a fool is a bell on a pig's snout.[14]

The scriptural resonance of the Greek word for knowledge that Kassia employs suggests she is alluding to spiritual wisdom, not intellect. Echoing the Pauline maxim that 'the wisdom of this world is foolishness', the epigram points to the emptiness of knowledge that is divorced from spiritual wisdom.[15]

Although these epigrams were probably a form of catechism for her nuns and perhaps any friends of the monastery, their circulation in Constantinople is unclear.[16] Nevertheless, they engage in a unique kind of commentary on social structures, friendship and women. One epigram bespeaks a refashioning of gender that, as we will see, is also apparent in her most famous hymn:

Φῦλον γυναικῶν ὑπερισχύει πάντων·
καὶ μάρτυς Ἔσδρας μετὰ τῆς ἀληθείας.[17]

Esdras is witness that the race of women
together with truth prevails over all.

While it is tempting to translate this epigram as a feminist manifesto – a literal translation would be: 'the race of women prevails over everything' – it cannot be divorced from its scriptural context. The basis of the epigram is a line from 1 Esdras 3:12, which is the statement that King Darius finds most persuasive in a debate over what is superior: 'women prove superior, but above all things truth is victorious' (ὑπερισχύουσιν αἱ γυναῖκες, ὑπὲρ δὲ πάντα νικᾷ ἡ ἀλήθεια). Kassia changes the biblical verse into an avowal of women's strength that is wedded to Christian anthropology.

According to the anthropology of the Byzantine patristic tradition, gender 'could not define the identity and experience of people who have been spiritually transformed'.[18] As the fourth-century hermit Amma Sarra enigmatically remarked, 'according to my nature I am a woman, but not

---

[13] Tsironis, Κασσιανή, 88.   [14] The English translation is my own.
[15] 1 Corinthians 3:19. See also the discussion in Lauxtermann, *Byzantine Poetry*, 269.
[16] Silvas, 'Kassia the Nun', 23.
[17] Ibid., 26. Silvas cites the Greek text and provides the English translation.
[18] Doru Costache, 'Living above Gender: Insights from Saint Maximus the Confessor', *JECS* 21, no. 2 (2013): 277.

according to my thoughts'.[19] This is also evident in the eschatological anthropology of Gregory of Nyssa, who argued that gender, and even the sexually differentiated body, would vanish in the life of the age to come.[20] However, this does not imply that an androgynous state is the destiny of deified human nature. As Gregory's fellow Cappadocians Basil the Great and Gregory the Theologian suggested, the eschaton will bring about the restoration of human nature through its complete participation in divine life, where 'the virgin of either gender is the bride of Christ'.[21] Given how deeply present emotion and gender are in the performance of Kassia's most famous hymn, these insights will be important to consider as we explore the compunction of the woman who repented at the feet of Christ.[22]

Reflecting on Kassia's life and times, it is difficult to ignore the much-debated question of whether she participated in the bride show for Emperor Theophilos. The famous encounter between Kassia and Theophilos deserves brief interrogation because it raises the matter of gender and its complexity in the Byzantine world, which I will explore later in this chapter in the context of tears.[23] Whether Kassia participated in the bride show is also an example of the difficulty in recovering the life history of Kassia and other women writers from Byzantium. It has led to one modern historian characterising Kassia as a 'pious but pert poetess' who proves that educated women really did exist in Constantinople.[24]

Symeon Logothetes' tenth-century *Chronographia* tells the story of a bride show that took place in 830 for Emperor Theophilos. According to

[19] Quoted ibid. See *The Sayings of the Desert Fathers: The Alphabetical Collection*, trans. Benedicta Ward (Kalamazoo, MI: Cistercian Publications, 1975), 230.

[20] Verna E. F. Harrison, 'Male and Female in Cappadocian Theology', *Journal of Theological Studies* 41, no. 2 (1990): 441; Ilaria Ramelli, 'Tears of Pathos', 380.

[21] See the exploration of Basil the Great's *Homily on Psalm 114* (PG 29, 492C) and Gregory the Theologian's *Oration 37*, chapters 10–13 (PG 36, 293–300), and other texts in Harrison, 'Male and Female in Cappadocian Theology', 451, 463.

[22] While I acknowledge Judith Butler's theory of gender performativity, it is difficult to reconcile a second-order discourse with what the performance of gender signified in Byzantine thought. Butler's work may prove a useful point of departure for some, but I will explore compunction and the performance of gender through liturgical and theological lenses. For an example of a scholar rereading Byzantine hymns as a way of constructing and performing gender, see Ashley Purpura, 'Beyond the Binary: Hymnographic Constructions of Orthodox Gender Identities', *Journal of Religion* 97, no. 4 (2017): 524–46. Purpura admits that Butler did not have Byzantine Christianity in mind when she wrote, but suggests that modern gender theory offers the opportunity to reconsider the performance of gender identity in Orthodox ritual.

[23] On gender in Byzantium, see Liz James, ed., *Women, Men, and Eunuchs: Gender in Byzantium* (New York, NY: Routledge, 1997); Bronwen Neil and Lynda Garland, eds., *Questions of Gender in Byzantine Society* (Farnham: Ashgate, 2013).

[24] Steven Runciman, 'Women in Byzantine Aristocratic Society', in *The Byzantine Aristocracy: IX to XIII Centuries*, ed. Michael Angold (Oxford: British Archaeological Reports, 1984), 15.

the text, it is during this extravagant event, orchestrated by Theophilos' matchmaking mother, Euphrosyne, that the beautiful and witty Kassia defies the Emperor:

Εὐφροσύνη ἀποστείλασα ἐν πᾶσι τοῖς θέμασιν ἤγαγε κόρας εὐπρεπεῖς πρὸς τὸ νυμφοστολῆσαι Θεόφιλον, τὸν υἱὸν αὐτῆς. ἀναγαγοῦσα δὲ ταύτας ἐν τῷ παλατίῳ εἰς τὸν λεγόμενον Μαργαρίτην τρίκλινον δέδωκε τῷ Θεοφίλῳ χρυσοῦν μῆλον, εἰποῦσα, ὅτι εἰς ἥν ἀρεσθῇς, ἐπίδος τοῦτο αὐτῇ. ἦν δέ τις ἐξ εὐγενῶν ἐν αὐταῖς κόρη ὀνόματι Ἰκασία, ὡραιοτάτη πάνυ· ἥν ἰδὼν Θεόφιλος καὶ ὑπεραγασθεὶς αὐτὴν τοῦ κάλλους ἔφη, ὡς ἄρα διὰ γυναικὸς ἐρρύη τὰ φαῦλα. ἡ δὲ μετ' αἰδοῦς πως ἀντέφησεν· ἀλλὰ διὰ γυναικὸς πηγάζει τὰ κρείττονα. ὁ δὲ τῷ λόγῳ τὴν καρδίαν πληγεὶς ταύτην μὲν εἴασε, Θεοδώρᾳ δὲ τὸ μῆλον ἐπέδωκεν ... καὶ ἡ μὲν εἰρημένη Ἰκασία τῆς βασιλείας ἀποτυχοῦσα μονὴν κατεσκεύασεν, εἰς ἥν καὶ ἀποκειραμένη ἀσκοῦσα καὶ φιλοσοφοῦσα καὶ Θεῷ μόνῳ ζῶσα διετέλεσε μέχρι τέλους ζωῆς αὐτῆς.[25]

Euphrosyne, dispatching a servant to gather contestants, gathered comely maidens to find a bride for her son Theophilos. Bringing them into the palace, into the so-called Hall of the Pearl, she gave to Theophilos a golden apple, saying that he should in turn give it to her who was pleasing to him. Among them was a certain noble maiden who was surpassingly beautiful called Kassia. Upon seeing her Theophilos, who was exceedingly pleased by her beauty said, 'truly through a woman flow the wicked things'. With modesty, she retorted, 'but through a woman flow abundantly the better things'. Wounded in the heart by this statement, he put her aside and gave the apple to Theodora ... and Kassia, failing to become an empress, built a monastery where she was tonsured, practising asceticism and philosophy until the end of her life.[26]

The text does not clarify whether Kassia was devastated by Theophilos' rejection or simply had no imperial ambition. It does not draw a causative link between the rebuff and her decision to build a monastery. Indeed, an epistle that Theodore the Stoudite wrote to Kassia reveals she yearned to become 'the bride of Christ' (νύμφη Χριστοῦ) from childhood.[27]

Upon closer analysis, Symeon Logothetes' account of the event is dubious and Kassia's participation in Theophilos' bride show is questionable. Even the historicity of the bride shows in Byzantium is a contentious

[25] Symeone the Logothete, *Chronikon*, in *Symeonis Magistri et Logothetae Chronicon*, ed. Staffan Wahlgren (Berlin: De Gruyter, 2006), 216–17 (chapter 130).

[26] The English translation is my own. Although her name is Ἰκασία in the Greek text, Kassia's name is spelled in a number of ways in various primary sources: Kasia, Eikasia, Ikasia and Kassiane. See Kazhdan, *A History of Byzantine Literature*, 315.

[27] Fatouros, *Theodori Studitae epistulae*, 339.

issue.[28] The earliest extant account of Theophilos' bride show is from the tenth century and has all the trappings of a tale concocted after the restoration of icons in 843 to besmirch the reputation of an iconoclast emperor.[29] The repartee between the emperor and Kassia, which alludes to the biblical figures of Eve and Mary and their respective roles in the drama of salvation, is a direct quotation from a homily on the Annunciation attributed to John Chrysostom.[30] Since it is doubtful that both interlocutors were aware of this text, and given that there is no mention of Kassia's involvement in the bride show in the ninth-century sources, including the three surviving letters Theodore wrote to Kassia, it appears that revisionism is afoot.[31]

Other scholars have defended the credibility of Kassia's participation in Theophilos' bride show.[32] The courage, candour and wit she displays in the face of an emperor reflect her oeuvre, especially her epigrams.[33] Her assertion that Mary is the new Eve is not an isolated aside in a single homily but a theme recurring throughout the patristic tradition of Byzantium.[34] The account of the bride show portrays Kassia's gender in the same way as other Byzantine women were depicted. She is modest and a victim of the restricted range of social roles available to women in an empire where female status was largely derived from marriage or kinship.

At any rate, the scholarly debate over whether Kassia was also the woman whose beauty stole Theophilos' heart and whose wit left the emperor astonished has not been settled. The case against this relies on a fair deal of conjecture, and the case for this does not present unequivocal evidence. It is more prudent to reflect on the various uncertainties underpinning both arguments and acknowledge that a categorical resolution will be elusive. Ultimately, it is Kassia's literary output that affords posterity insights into one of the few women hymnographers of Byzantium. It is not

---

[28] See Lennart Rydén, 'The Bride-Shows at the Byzantine Court – History or Fiction?' *Eranos* 83 (1985): 175–91; Warren Treadgold, 'The Historicity of Imperial Bride-Shows', *JÖB* 54 (2004): 39–52.

[29] Marc D. Lauxtermann, 'Three Biographical Notes', *BZ* 91 (1998): 395.

[30] *Homily on the Annunciation of our Most Glorious Virgin Theotokos.* PG 50, 795.

[31] For the Greek text, see Fatouros, *Theodori Studitae epistulae*, 339–40, 501–2, 813–14. An English translation of the three epistles appears in Silvas, 'Kassia the Nun', 34–37.

[32] Anna Silvas, 'Kassia la Melode e il suo uso delle Scritture', in *Fra Oriente e Occidente: donne e Bibbia nell' alto Medioevo (secoli VI–XI): greci, latini, ebrei, arabi*, ed. Franca Ela Consolino and Judith Herrin (Trapani: Il Pozzo di Giacobbe, 2015), 55–60.

[33] Ilse Rochow, *Studien zu der Person, den Werken und dem Nachleben der Dichterin Kassia* (Berlin: Akademie-Verlag, 1967), 19.

[34] Meyendorff, *Byzantine Theology*, 147.

through biography that one can understand who Kassia was but through her hymns and what it meant to be a hymnographer.

Byzantine Hymnography and the *Sticheron Idiomelon*

Although it has often existed in the shadow of the *kontakion* and the *kanon*, the prevalence of the *sticheron* as a genre of Christian hymnography is apparent from its emergence in the ancient liturgy of Jerusalem until the end of Byzantium and beyond.[35] *Sticheron* is derived from the Greek word στίχος, which means 'verse' and refers to the singing of a hymn after a verse of a psalm during vespers or matins. More specifically, *stichera* were interpolated between verses of a psalm – Psalms 140, 141, 129 and 116 (in that order) during vespers, and Psalms 148–150 during matins. Whereas a *sticheron idiomelon* is sung to a unique melody, a *sticheron* could also be a contrafactum that borrows the metrical pattern and melody of a pre-existing hymn.[36]

The performance of this intercalation of psalmody and *stichera* varied according to the feast of the liturgical calendar that was celebrated. As few as four and as many as eight *stichera* that reflected on a biblical event or the life of a saint were chanted, though there were exceptions to this rule.[37] Whereas the text of various *stichera* can be found scattered throughout manuscripts of hymnals such as the *Triodion*, the *Sticherarion* was a dedicated collection of *stichera idiomela*, assembling the unique melodies of *stichera* sung throughout the liturgical year.[38]

Although the musical style of a *sticheron* is 'generally syllabic–neumatic', inasmuch as it employs one or two notes per syllable of text, it also boasts occasional melismatic flourishes, particularly in longer pieces.[39] These cadential melismas were usually on words or phrases that the composer wished to highlight, or they emphasised the liturgical context of the hymn, but they could also be a symptom of the *sticheron* being an *idiomelon*, which was more prone to melodic ornamentation.[40] This chapter will explore

---

[35] Although there is no monograph that traces the history of the *sticheron* (pl. *stichera*), see Wellesz, *A History of Byzantine Music*, 243–45; Lingas, 'Sunday Matins', 139–49; Frøyshov, 'The Georgian Witness', 227–67.

[36] Jeffreys, 'Sticheron', in *ODB*, 1956.   [37] Troelsgård, *Byzantine Neumes*, 81.

[38] Hundreds of *Sticheraria* from Byzantium are extant and several have been published as facsimile editions and transcriptions in the MMB Série Principale. See, for example, Carsten Høeg, H. J. W. Tillyard and Egon Wellesz, eds., *Sticherarium*, MMB Série Principale 1 (Copenhagen: Munksgaard, 1935). This is a reproduction of Codex Vindobonensis Theol. Graec. 181. Kassia's hymn appears in fols. 232v–233r.

[39] Troelsgård, *Byzantine Neumes*, 81–82.   [40] Lingas, 'Sunday Matins', 149.

Kassia's *sticheron idiomelon* for Holy Wednesday, which was a poetic and musical meditation on the woman who repented at Christ's feet, washing them with her tears and wiping them with her hair. While *Sticheraria* that contain music for Kassia's composition are extant, they are not from Kassia's lifetime but emerge a few centuries after her death. Some of these manuscripts, such as the late twelfth- early thirteenth-century *Sticherarion* EBE MS 883, designate Kassia as the composer of this hymn.[41] I will refer to this composition as Kassia's hymn *On the Sinful Woman*.

My analysis will briefly consider the musical dimension of this hymn through its genre rather than its appearance in musical manuscripts that emerge after Kassia's lifetime. Indeed, scholarship has begun to explore some of the melodic details of the hymn.[42] It is an important consideration since the genre of *On the Sinful Woman* sets it apart from Andrew of Crete's *Great Kanon* and Romanos' *kontakia* in two respects: textual economy and richness of melody. Whereas Romanos' hymns and Andrew's poem develop a narrative over multiple strophes, *On the Sinful Woman* is a monostrophic hymn. It is far shorter than a *kanon* or *kontakion* from a textual perspective but more elaborate in its melody. During its liturgical performance, sacred music and holy ritual sought to destabilise Christian personhood, inviting the faithful to contemplate the biblical narrative the hymn evoked and identify with the protagonist of the story.

Manuscripts, Editions and Translations

The manuscript tradition of Kassia's works begins as early as the tenth century with Sinai Graecus 734–735, fol. 159r–v, which contains her hymn *On the Sinful Woman* for Holy Wednesday and other compositions for the *Triodion*.[43] While this manuscript does not clearly attest her authorship, it is quite common for scribes to omit the literary origin of a hymn from such manuscripts and, in any case, 'ascriptions to hymn composers are in part notoriously untrustworthy'.[44] Nevertheless,

---

[41] Fol. 261v. See Diane Touliatos-Miles, *A Descriptive Catalogue of the Musical Manuscript Collection of the National Library of Greece: Byzantine Chant and Other Music Repertory Recovered* (Farnham: Ashgate, 2010), 27.

[42] See, for example, Jørgen Raasted, 'Voice and Verse in a Troparion of Cassia', in *Studies in Eastern Chant*, ed. Miloš Velimirović (London: Oxford University Press, 1973), 171–78. See also the transcription from the late twelfth- early thirteenth-century *Sticherarion* EBE MS 883, fol. 261v, by Diane Touliatos-Banker in James R. Briscoe, *Historical Anthology of Music by Women* (Bloomington, IN: Indiana University Press, 1986), 4–5.

[43] Krueger, *Liturgical Subjects*, 250.

[44] Frøyshov, 'The Georgian Witness', 237. See also Krueger, *Liturgical Subjects*, 157.

manuscripts ranging from the eleventh to the sixteenth century confer at least forty-nine hymns – twenty-three of which are not included in Byzantine liturgical books – and approximately 261 epigrams to Kassia.[45]

Rather than examining this extensive manuscript tradition, I focus on three of the earliest manuscripts of the *Triodion* containing Kassia's hymn *On the Sinful Woman*: Sinai Graecus 734–735, fol. 159r–v; Vaticanus Graecus 771, fol. 162v; and Grottaferrata Δβ I, fol. 161r. The hymn is also enshrined in the received tradition of the *Triodion* represented by the editions printed in Venice and Rome after the fall of Constantinople.[46] It also appears in a more recent collection of Kassia's hymns and epigrams.[47]

The text of the hymn in the early manuscripts of the *Triodion* is transmitted to the published editions of the *Triodion* with few variations. Three minor variations are of little consequence. First, whereas the early manuscripts have 'ὅτι νύξ με συνέχει' (for night contains me), modern editions have 'ὅτι νύξ μοι ὑπάρχει' (for night is upon me).[48] Second, 'τῇ ἀφράστῳ σου κενώσει' (by your inexpressible kenosis) is transmitted to modern editions as 'τῇ ἀφάτῳ σου κενώσει' (by your ineffable kenosis) – though 'ἀφράστῳ' can also be translated as 'ineffable'. Third, the ending of the hymn 'ὁ ἀμέτρητον ἔχων τὸ μέγα ἔλεος' (you who unmeasurably bear great mercy) is simply 'ὁ ἀμέτρητον ἔχων τὸ ἔλεος' (you who unmeasurably bear mercy) in modern editions. Notably, the edition printed in Rome in 1879 reflects the early manuscript tradition in all three cases. In addition to these three minor variations, there are some minor spelling errors in the Grottaferrata Δβ I manuscript: 'ζωφόδης' instead of 'ζοφώδης' (gloomy) and 'καινώσει' instead of 'κενώσει' (kenosis).

However, there are two more substantial variations that are worth considering briefly. First, whereas the *Triodion* printed in Rome in 1879 and other modern editions have: 'ἀποσμήξω τούτους δὲ πάλιν, τοῖς τῆς κεφαλῆς μου βοστρύχοις· ὧν ἐν τῷ Παραδείσῳ Εὔα τὸ δειλινόν κρότον τοῖς ὠσὶν ἠχηθεῖσα, τῷ φόβῳ ἐκρύβη' (I will tenderly kiss your undefiled feet and wipe them again with the tresses of my head; those feet at whose sound in the twilight of Paradise, resounding in her ears, Eve hid in fear), all three manuscripts differ in minor ways from this version.

[45] Silvas, 'Kassia la Melode', 59; Rochow, *Studien zu der Dichterin Kassia*, 32–58.
[46] See, for example, Τριῴδιον Κατανυκτικόν, 644–45.   [47] Tsironis, Κασσιανή, 41–42.
[48] Von Christ and Paranikas, *Anthologia graeca*, 104; Τριῴδιον Κατανυκτικόν [*Compunctious Triodion*] (Athens: Apostoliki Diakonia, 1960), 414; Tsironis, Κασσιανή, 41.

Sinai Graecus
734–735

ἀποσμίξω τούτους δὲ πάλιν τοῖς τῆς κεφαλῆς μου
βοστρύχοις. οὓς ἐν τῷ παραδείσῳ Εὔα τὸ δειλινὸν
κρότον τοῖς ὠσὶν ἠχηθεῖσα, τῷ φόβῳ ἐκρύβη.

Vaticanus
Graecus 771

ἀποσμήξω τούτους δὲ πάλιν. τοῖς τῆς κεφαλῆς μου
βοστρύχοις· οὓς ἐν τῷ παραδείσῳ Εὔα τὸ δειλινὸν·
κρότον τῶν ποδῶν ἠχηθεῖσα, τῷ φόβῳ ἐκρύβη.

Grottaferrata Δβ I

ἀποσμίξω τούτους δὲ πάλιν· τοῖς τῆς κεφαλῆς μου
βοστρίχοις· οὓς ἐν τῷ παραδείσῳ Εὔα τὸ δηλινὸν κρότῳ
τοῖς ποσῖν ἠχηθήσα τὸ φόβῳ ἐκρύβη.

This is the moment in the hymn when the protagonist wipes Christ's
feet with the tresses of her head, which is followed by an image of Eve
fleeing the sound of footsteps in the twilight of Paradise, referring to Eve's
encounter with God in the third chapter of Genesis. The use of the relative
pronoun (οὓς) in all three manuscripts is odd. This is also the case in the
manuscript of the eleventh-century *Sticherarion* Triodion Vatopedi
1488 and the fourteenth-century *Sticherarion* Codex Bibliothecae Ambrosianae A 139.[49] This may be a simple copying error, or it may be an attempt
to modify the syntax. If the latter is the case, it is a confusing alteration, as it
leaves 'κρότον' unconnected to 'πόδας'. The use of 'ὧν' connects naturally
with 'κρότον' as the expected possessive.[50] It also suggests that it was
Christ's feet walking through Eden, which caused Eve to hide in fear. This
point will be explored more closely later in this chapter.

The second noteworthy variation is the recurrence of the uncommon
word 'στημονίζων' instead of 'διεξάγων' in 'ὁ νεφέλαις διεξάγων τῆς
θαλάσσης τὸ ὕδωρ' (you who administer from the clouds the water of
the sea) in the early manuscript tradition of the *Triodion*.[51] This is not the
case in four manuscripts of Byzantine chant – the *Sticheraria* known as
Codex Vindobonensis Theol. Gr. 181, Triodion Vatopedi 1488, EBE MS
883 and Codex Bibliothecae Ambrosianae A 139 sup. – which have
'διεξάγων'.[52] Similarly, in the twelfth-century text from the Holy Sepulchre edited by Papadopoulos-Kerameus, the word 'διεξάγων' appears in

[49] Triodion Vatopedi 1488, fol. 79r; Ambr. gr. 139, fol. 230r–v. See Enrica Follieri and Oliver Strunk,
eds., *Triodium Athoum: Codex Monasterii Vatopedii 1488*, MMB Série Principale 9 (Copenhagen:
Munksgaard, 1975), 79; Lidia Perria and Jørgen Raasted, eds., *Sticherarium Ambrosianum*, MMB
Série Principale 11 (Copenhagen: Munksgaard, 1992).

[50] I thank Associate Professor John A. L. Lee for these insights.

[51] Sinai Graecus 734–735, Grottaferrata Δβ I and Vaticanus Graecus 771 all have the word
στημονίζων instead of διεξάγων.

[52] Vindobonensis Theol. Gr. 181, fol. 232v; Triodion Vatopedi 1488, fols. 78v–79r; EBE MS 883,
fol. 261v; Ambr. gr. 139, fol. 230r.

the hymn *On the Sinful Woman*.[53] The word 'στημονίζων' does not significantly change the meaning of the text, as it also underscores the omnipotence of the Logos, but it is a notable variation if only because the translation – 'you who weaves from the clouds the water of the sea'—is more elegant. It also solves the syntactical problem created by 'διεξάγων', which is a transitive verb that lacks a direct object. As the early manuscripts consistently contain the word στημονίζων, it may be the case that a copying error occurred at some point and became accepted in later manuscripts.[54] Modern editions of the text have favoured 'διεξάγων' over 'στημονίζων' on several occasions.[55] However, the *Triodion* printed in Rome in 1879 reflects the early manuscript tradition ('στημονίζων').[56] In the absence of a critical edition of Kassia's *On the Sinful Woman*, which systematically examines the manuscript tradition of the hymn, I follow the early manuscripts. Kassia's juxtaposition of images in this part of the hymn contrasts the humble tears of the protagonist with the magnificent depiction of the Logos weaving the sea from the threads of rain falling from the clouds. The hymnographer evokes a poignant image of how tears of compunction can move the all-powerful Creator to compassion.

There are a number of English translations of Kassia's works, including her hymn *On the Sinful Woman*. One of the earliest appears in the translation of the *Triodion* by Ware and Mother Mary.[57] Andrew Dyck, Antonia Tripolitis, Anna Silvas and other scholars have also translated this hymn into English.[58] The edition by Tripolitis is a bilingual collection of Kassia's various hymns and epigrams in Greek and English. Although I have considered these English translations, the translation that follows the Greek text below is my own. I quote the hymn in its entirety:

Κύριε, ἡ ἐν πολλαῖς ἁμαρτίαις περιπεσοῦσα γυνή, τὴν σὴν αἰσθομένη Θεότητα, μυροφόρου ἀναλαβοῦσα τάξιν, ὀδυρομένη μύρον σοι, πρὸ τοῦ ἐνταφιασμοῦ κομίζει. Οἴμοι! λέγουσα, ὅτι νύξ με συνέχει, οἶστρος ἀκολασίας, ζοφώδης τε καὶ ἀσέληνος, ἔρως τῆς ἁμαρτίας· δέξαι μου τὰς πηγὰς τῶν δακρύων, ὁ νεφέλαις στημονίζων τῆς θαλάσσης τὸ ὕδωρ· κάμφθητί μοι πρὸς τοὺς στεναγμοὺς τῆς καρδίας, ὁ κλίνας τοὺς οὐρανούς, τῇ ἀφράστῳ

53 Athanasios Papadopoulos-Kerameus, ed., Ἀνάλεκτα Ἱεροσολυμιτικῆς Σταχυολογίας, Vol. 2, 78.
54 Emmanuel Pantelakis, 'Τὰ Σιναϊτικὰ χειρόγραφα τῶν λειτουργικῶν βιβλίων τῆς Ὀρθοδόξου Ἐκκλησίας [The Sinaite Manuscripts of the Liturgical Books of the Orthodox Church]', Δελτίον Χριστιανικῆς Ἀρχαιολογικῆς Ἑταιρείας 2 (1933): 140–41.
55 Τριώδιον Κατανυκτικόν (1960 edition published in Athens), 414; von Christ and Paranikas, *Anthologia graeca*, 104; Tsironis, Κασσιανή, 41.
56 Τριώδιον Κατανυκτικόν, 645.   57 Ware and Mother Mary, *The Lenten Triodion*, 540–41.
58 Andrew R. Dyck, 'On Cassia, Κύριε ἡ ἐν πολλαῖς ...', *Byzantion* 56 (1986): 63–64; Tripolitis, *Kassia*, 76–79; Silvas, 'Kassia the Nun', 30.

σου κενώσει· καταφιλήσω τοὺς ἀχράντους σου πόδας, ἀποσμήξω τούτους
δὲ πάλιν, τοῖς τῆς κεφαλῆς μου βοστρύχοις, ὧν ἐν τῷ Παραδείσῳ Εὔα τὸ
δειλινόν, κρότον τοῖς ὠσὶν ἠχηθεῖσα, τῷ φόβῳ ἐκρύβη· ἁμαρτιῶν μου τὰ
πλήθη καὶ κριμάτων σου ἀβύσσους, τίς ἐξιχνιάσει ψυχοσῶστα Σωτήρ
μου; μή με τὴν σὴν δούλην παρίδῃς, ὁ ἀμέτρητον ἔχων τὸ μέγα ἔλεος.[59]

O Lord, the woman fallen into many sins, sensing your Divinity, takes up
the order of myrrhbearer, lamenting she brings you myrrh before your
entombment. 'Woe is me!' she says, 'for night contains me, the longing for
excess, gloomy and moonless, the eros of sinfulness. Accept my springs of
tears, you who weave from the clouds the water of the sea; bend down to
me, towards the groanings of my heart, you who bowed the heavens by
your ineffable kenosis. I will tenderly kiss your undefiled feet and wipe
them again with the tresses of my head; those feet at whose sound in the
twilight of Paradise, resounding in her ears, Eve hid in fear. Who can trace
out the multitude of my sins or the abyss of your mercy, O my soul-saving
Saviour? Do not cast me, your handmaid, aside, you who unmeasurably
bear great mercy.'

The Liturgical Context of Kassia's Hymn *On the Sinful Woman*

Kassia's hymn *On the Sinful Woman* was performed during Holy Wednesday, almost two weeks after the singing of Andrew of Crete's *Great Kanon*,
in close proximity to the liturgical celebration of Christ's Passion, and on
the same day as Romanos the Melodist's hymn *On the Harlot*. Although
Romanos' *kontakion* was performed during the *pannychis* (all-night vigil),
Kassia's hymn was sung during either vespers or matins. It is clear from the
three early manuscripts of the *Triodion* cited above that it formed part of
the collection of hymns for Holy Wednesday, though it is not entirely clear
whether it was sung during the evening or the morning. Although the
Typikon of the Great Church does not mention Kassia's hymn, according to
the *Synaxarion of the Monastery of the Theotokos Evergetis*, the *Typikon of the
Monastery of Christ the Saviour* at Messina, the *Typikon of the Anastasis* and
the *Typikon of St Sabas Monastery*, her hymn was assigned to vespers.[60]

[59] Τριώδιον Κατανυκτικόν, 644–45. Sinai Graecus 734–735, fol. 159r–v; Vaticanus Graecus 771,
fol. 162v; Grottaferrata ΔΒ I, fol. 161r.
[60] Jordan, *The Synaxarion of Theotokos Evergetis*, 466–67; Arranz, *Le Typicon du Saint-Sauveur*, 233.
The twelfth-century manuscript known as the *Typikon of the Anastasis* (Hagios Stavros Graecus 43),
which reflects liturgical practices from prior centuries, is edited by Athanasios Papadopoulos-
Kerameus in the second volume of Ἀνάλεκτα Ἱεροσολυμιτικῆς Σταχυολογίας, 77–78. For the
Sabaite milieu, see the twelfth-century manuscripts Sinai Graecus 1094 and Sinai Graecus 1096.
Although these manuscripts are vague about the order of service for Holy Wednesday, Kassia's
hymn appears in later redactions of these rubrics.

However, it would not have been unusual for singers to perform Kassia's hymn between psalm verses during the daybreak service, and she may have composed it for this purpose.[61] Indeed, in the received tradition of the *Triodion*, her hymn is performed during matins and vespers.[62] While acknowledging that Kassia's composition may have been performed during matins in Byzantium, it is clear that in certain monastic settings – Theotokos Evergetis, Christ the Saviour at Messina and possibly St Sabas – it was initially sung during evensong. As the previous chapter has already explored the daybreak service and its significance for the faithful, it is worth briefly examining the liturgical atmosphere of vespers as one of the contexts for the performance of Kassia's hymn.

Psalm 140 was 'the core of evensong in all traditions throughout Christendom' and it evoked a penitential mood.[63] The psalm begins with 'O Lord I have cried out to you, hear me' (Κύριε ἐκέκραξα πρός σέ, εἰσάκουσόν μου) and is performed as a song of imploration, in which the faithful ask:

> Κατευθυνθήτω ἡ προσευχή μου, ὡς θυμίαμα ἐνώπιόν σου,
> ἔπαρσις τῶν χειρῶν μου θυσία ἐσπερινή.[64]

> Let my prayer be set before you like incense,
> the lifting up of my hands as an evening sacrifice.

As early as the fourth century, patristic interpretations of this psalm as 'a salutary medicine and forgiveness of sins' pointed to the meaning of vespers as an act of compunction and repentance.[65] Unlike the sacrifices of old, prayer and entreaty became the act that sought forgiveness. The incense was not merely an abstract notion but an olfactory oblation that the faithful would have experienced through the incense burners carried by the clergy during this ritual.[66] This atmosphere of contrition was juxtaposed with the lighting of the lamps at sunset and the singing of one of the most ancient hymns of Christianity, *O Joyful Light*, which betokened a thanksgiving for the light that was embodied in the person of Christ who is 'the true light' that 'shines in the darkness' and upon everyone in the world.[67] Although

---

[61] Krueger, *Liturgical Subjects*, 155.   [62] Τριώδιον Κατανυκτικόν, 644–46.
[63] Robert F. Taft, '"Thanksgiving for the Light": Toward a Theology of Vespers', in *Beyond East and West: Problems in Liturgical Understanding* (Rome: Pontifical Oriental Institute, 1997), 169.
[64] Psalm 140:1–2.
[65] See the quotations from the writings of John Chrysostom and Basil the Great in Taft, '"Thanksgiving for the Light"', 170–71.
[66] Ibid., 180.
[67] John 1:5, 9. On the ancient evening hymn, Basil the Great remarked that not even he knew when it was first sung. *On the Holy Spirit* 29, 73, quoted in Taft, '"Thanksgiving for the Light"', 179.

the singing of this ancient hymn may have been omitted during Holy Week, its familiarity meant that its central message would not have been far from the mind of the worshipper.[68] Indeed, the first chapter of the Gospel of John would have been heard at the end of Holy Week as it was prescribed for the Sunday of Pascha, according to the *Typikon of the Great Church*.[69] This emotive juxtaposition of repentance and hope in the performance of evensong is reflected in Kassia's hymn and the experience of her protagonist.

Kassia's hymn echoes the biblical reading prescribed for Holy Wednesday. The *Typikon of the Great Church* assigns the Gospel passage from Matthew 26:6–16, the biblical narrative of the woman with the alabaster jar of myrrh, as part of the lectionary for that day.[70] Indeed, the other hymns appearing alongside Kassia's hymn *On the Sinful Woman* in the *Triodion* confirm that this scriptural figure and her repentance were the salient themes of the hymnody for Holy Wednesday. Moreover, Vaticanus Graecus 771 has a note in the left margin of Kassia's hymn that appears to prescribe the Gospel for the occasion as that of Luke 7:36–50.[71] This narrative is similar to but longer than the aforesaid passage from Matthew and was probably the scriptural foundation for the hymn, though there is 'some conflation with the anointing at Bethany' narrated in John 12:1–8.[72]

Reimagining the Performance of *On the Sinful Woman*

The first word of the hymn – Κύριε (Lord) – is an unadorned opening of a prayer yet it betokens the compunctious tone of the words that follow. Kassia continues her song by identifying her protagonist as a woman fallen into many sins and intimating how she is paradoxically able to perceive the divine nature of Christ. In a moment of compunction, the transformation of her protagonist begins. She rises from the depths of sin and becomes a myrrhbearer. As this happens, Kassia evokes the scene of the burial and resurrection of Christ, transporting the faithful away from the initial scene, which unfolds in Simon's house, to the moment when the myrrhbearers go to anoint Jesus' body in the tomb and become the first to learn he had

---

[68] The *Synaxarion of the Monastery of the Theotokos Evergetis*, the *Typikon of the Monastery of Christ the Saviour at Messina* and the *Typikon of St Sabas Monastery* are vague on this question. However, the Rome edition of the *Triodion* printed in 1879 clearly refers to the singing of this hymn during Holy Week. See Τριώδιον Κατανυκτικόν, 646.

[69] John 1:1–17. See Mateos, *Le Typicon de la Grande Église: Tome II*, 94.   [70] Ibid., 70.

[71] See fol. 162v.   [72] Silvas, 'Kassia the Nun', 30.

risen. Kassia's protagonist anoints Christ in anticipation of his death, blurring the two narratives.

The first word the woman utters – 'Οἴμοι!' (Woe is me!) – is reminiscent of the Homeric and Aristophanic literature of ancient Greece but is also the lament of Adam in the hymns for Cheese-Fare Sunday.[73] Several of the hymns sung on that day enact the exile of Adam and dramatise his cry – 'Οἴμοι!' – as he is estranged from the 'delight of Paradise' (Παραδείσου τῆς τρυφῆς).[74] But on Holy Wednesday, the exclamation of Adam becomes the lament of a woman who cries out with the paradisal nostalgia of the first-created human. Moreover, the performance of this hymn and the indeterminate personhood of the protagonist invite the faithful to sing her cry of woe as if this shout of repentance were their very own. The performance of the hymn liturgically fuses the singer's personhood with Kassia's protagonist.[75]

The hymn continues its recapitulation of the Lenten journey of exile, repentance and salvation by describing the concupiscence that has over-taken the woman as 'moonless' (ἀσέληνος). This striking metaphor is an hapax legomenon in Byzantine literature. Although the adjective itself is not entirely rare and is used to define the more common word 'σκοτομήνη' (dense darkness) as a 'moonless night' (νὺξ ἀσέληνος) in the tenth-century *Suda*, its metaphorical use by Kassia is not found elsewhere. In the hymn, the alienation of Kassia's protagonist from the divine is such that even the reflection of light is absent from her existence. But in the midst of night, without any natural light, the darkness gives way to a glimpse of the divine.

The woman's first petition mingles words with tears. She asks the Creator who weaves the waters of the sea from the rain falling from the clouds to accept her weeping. Although it could easily be a case of antithesis, contrasting her abjectness with the grandeur of the Lord's power, Kassia also appears to evoke the act of creation. She places her protagonist at the centre of a cosmic drama, where her fallenness and the groans of her heart ignite the divine eros of God, who leaves the summit of his omnipotence and is born as a helpless baby. The God who can bend the heavens to his will bends down to the compunction of a woman's heart. And as she kisses and caresses the feet of Christ, Kassia transports the faithful back to Eve's encounter with God in Eden, when she fled at the

---

[73] Dyck, 'On Cassia', 69; Topping, *Sacred Songs*, 213.
[74] See, for example, the *sticheron idiomelon* in Sinai Gr. 734–735, fol. 46r, Grottaferrata Δβ I, fol. 28v, and Τριῴδιον Κατανυκτικόν, 107–8, which begins: 'Οἴμοι! ὁ Ἀδάμ, ἐν θρήνῳ κέκραγεν' (Adam cried out in lament: 'Woe is me!').
[75] Krueger, *Liturgical Subjects*, 157.

sound of his footsteps after she had tasted the forbidden fruit. Yet, here, Kassia presents another antithesis: whereas Eve allowed her sin to alienate her from God, the woman in Kassia's hymn transcends her fallenness through repentance at the feet of the incarnate Logos.

The juxtaposition of the woman's manifold sins and the abyss of God's judgment echoes the imagery found in the wisdom literature of the Old Testament: Job 10:6; Wisdom of Solomon 9:16; Wisdom of Sirach 1:3.[76] And the hymn ends with a final apostrophe to Christ who is not only the saviour of the woman's soul but also the bearer of mercy that is unmeasurable. It is a plea that does not fall on deaf ears. In the days after the singing of Kassia's hymn, the faithful will follow the same feet that her protagonist kissed, wiped and anointed to Golgotha, where the crucifixion and death of the incarnate Logos will be liturgically enacted.

The protagonist's emergence from the utter darkness of sinfulness is enacted through tears, compunction and repentance. Kassia amplifies the biblical narrative, giving the sinful woman a voice and unveiling her interiority. Whereas the biblical figure that is the subject of the hymn is silent in the Gospel, her voice dominates Kassia's poem. After a brief, third-person prelude, the hymn becomes the first-person voice of the protagonist. The dramatic monologue offers an insight into the character's soul. However, even after guiding the faithful through the compunction and repentance of the woman who had fallen into many sins, Kassia leaves the question of her identity unresolved. The hymn also obscures the woman's harlotry by employing oblique references to the darkness of her eroticism, unlike Romanos' hymn *On the Harlot*, where there is no such ambiguity:

> ἴδε τὴν πόρνην ἣν βλέπεις   καθάπερ τὴν ἐκκλησίαν
> βοῶσαν· «Ἀποτάσσομαι,   ἐμφυσῶσα
> τῷ βορβόρῳ τῶν ἔργων μου».[77]

> Look at this harlot in front of you, as, like the Church,
> she cries out, 'I renounce and I blow upon
> *the filth of my deeds*'.

Although some scholars have suggested Kassia's hymn *On the Sinful Woman* is about the figure of Mary Magdalene, there is little evidence to support such a claim.[78] In the West, it was Gregory the Great who

---

[76] Topping, *Sacred Songs*, 216.   [77] Strophe 17.

[78] Whereas Alexander Kazhdan identifies the protagonist of the hymn with Mary Magdalene, Niki Tsironis refutes this claim. See Kazhdan, *A History of Byzantine Literature*, 318; Tsironis, 'The Body and the Senses in the Work of Cassia the Hymnographer: Literary Trends in the Iconoclastic Period', *Symmeikta* 16 (2003): 142–43.

'collapsed into one individual' – Mary Magdalene – three different women from the Gospel: the woman who washed Christ's feet with her tears; the Mary who was the sister of Martha and at whose beckoning Christ raised Lazarus; and the Mary Magdalene from whom Christ had expelled seven demons.[79] Gregory interpreted the seven demons driven from Mary Magdalene as a manifestation of her sinful life and unbridled sexuality – hence she became a repentant harlot. Gregory's Mary Magdalene was a polymorphic saint that 'ordained the agenda of Magdalen veneration for the entire Middle Ages and well beyond'.[80] However, Gregory's exegesis of the seven demons was not reflected in the East, which did not identify the anonymous figure of the sinful woman who tearfully repents at the feet of Christ with Mary Magdalene.[81] Kassia maintains the anonymity of this sinful woman, emphasising her compunction and repentance.

Feeling compunction is not simply a movement of the soul in the narrative of the hymn but also a physical and kinetic manifestation of interiority. Although Kassia does not explicitly refer to compunction in her hymn, it is portrayed using familiar motifs from the *kontakia* of Romanos the Melodist and Andrew of Crete's *Great Kanon*. Crying, anointing and wiping convey the emotion of compunction and a transformation of what was once erotic passion into a desire for Christ. Compunction is also presented as a blessed emotion that can activate one's spiritual senses, allowing the woman to sense Christ's divinity. While repentance is often portrayed as a change of mind, which is the etymology of the equivalent Greek word (μετάνοια), Kassia emphasises the role the body plays in this action.[82] She juxtaposes this relationship between interiority and exteriority with the historical figure of Christ, who is also the timeless Logos. The performance of the hymn blurs the distinctions between body and soul by meditating on the mystery of the Incarnation. Yet this is not without reason. The significance of the Logos becoming human extends beyond the moment the woman caresses the feet of Jesus to embrace the divine drama of salvation that begins with the exile from Eden and culminates in the crucifixion and resurrection of Christ.

---

[79] Katherine Ludwig Jansen, *The Making of the Magdalen: Preaching and Popular Devotion in the Later Middle Ages* (Princeton, NJ: Princeton University Press, 2000), 33.

[80] Ibid., 35.

[81] Vassiliki A. Foskolou, 'Mary Magdalene between East and West: Cult and Image, Relics and Politics in the Late Thirteenth-Century Eastern Mediterranean', *DOP* 65/66 (2011): 271.

[82] Tsironis, 'The Body and the Senses', 144.

Kassia's textual strategy differs from that of Romanos' *On the Harlot*: she subjectifies rather than objectifies, performing the compunction and repentance of a woman. However, Kassia also destabilises the identity of the protagonist. The woman who anoints Jesus is a porous figure of repentance who reminds the faithful of how Adam and Eve wept. Kassia's hymn enacts the fall and exile from paradise and, with the focus on Christ's imminent Passion, the text calls to mind Jesus' own tears in the garden of Gethsemane and the empty tomb the myrrhbearers encounter. The performance of Kassia's hymn becomes a 'chronotopos' insofar as it 'defies chronological linearity and spatial allocation' by collapsing the biblical past and future into the liturgical present.[83]

In touching Christ's feet, the woman's act of humiliation intersects with the site of divine humiliation. Out of the woman's yearning for salvation spring her tears, which betoken nostalgia for a lost paradise. At this moment in the hymn, the hymnographer invokes the scene in the book of Genesis where Eve fearfully flees the sound of God but reimagines the scriptural narrative in a profound way. The faithful would have been familiar with the story of the temptation, fall and exile of Adam and Eve, especially since the liturgical reading of Genesis was prescribed as part of the Lenten lectionary.[84] The text of Genesis 3:8, appearing in the *Prophetologion*, is as follows:

> Καὶ ἤκουσαν τῆς φωνῆς Κυρίου τοῦ Θεοῦ περιπατοῦντος ἐν τῷ παραδεί- σῳ τὸ δειλινόν, καὶ ἐκρύβησαν ὅ τε Ἀδὰμ καὶ ἡ γυνὴ αὐτοῦ ἀπὸ προσώπου Κυρίου τοῦ Θεοῦ ἐν μέσῳ τοῦ ξύλου τοῦ παραδείσου.[85]

> And they heard the voice of the Lord God walking in paradise in the twilight; and both Adam and his wife hid themselves from the face of the Lord God in the midst of the trees of paradise.[86]

Although the faithful would not have been surprised by the notion of God walking through Eden, Kassia's hymn suggests it was the very feet of Christ that were perambulating the garden. The relevant line of the hymn – 'at whose sound in the twilight of Paradise breaking on Eve's ears'[87] – identifies the feet the protagonist washes with her tears with the feet of God, who appeared to Adam and Eve in Eden. This textual synchronicity

[83] Alexander Riehle, 'Authorship and Gender (and) Identity. Women's Writing in the Middle Byzantine Period', in Pizzone, ed., *The Author in Middle Byzantine Literature*, 248.

[84] See the reading of Genesis 2:20–3:20 from the *Prophetologion* prescribed for the Friday in the first week of Lent. Høeg, Zuntz and Engberg, *Prophetologium*, 150–55.

[85] Ibid., 152–53.   [86] The English translation is my own.   [87] Τριῴδιον Κατανυκτικόν, 645.

between the Old Testament and the Gospel weaves a fascinating dialogue between a prelapsarian world and the new creation inaugurated by the Incarnation. Kassia's hymn engendered liturgical time through sacred song and holy ritual, interweaving biblical figures and events from the past and the future into the liturgical moment of performance.

On the Sinful Woman concludes with the confession and prayer of the protagonist, juxtaposing the multitude of her sins with the abyss of Christ's mercy. Her desire to experience the mercy of her 'soul-saving Saviour' and her petition not to be cast aside, leads the faithful to the same crossroads of repentance and hope. The singer takes on the role of Kassia's protagonist, who becomes a model for the Christian and a paradigm of compunction.[88] Although Kassia probably composed this hymn for the nuns of her monastery, the *Triodion* did not edit the explicitly feminine ending of the poem – 'do not cast me, your handmaid, aside' – suggesting that a liminal experience of gender and a desire to live above gender emerged in the performance of this hymn.

The ritual performance of various hymns, Scripture and homilies devoted to the theme of the harlot as a paradigm of repentance during Holy Wednesday shows how this figure 'became a canonical type for all Byzantine Christians'.[89] Stories of harlots who transformed their lives and transfigured their eros were powerful images of conversion that were far more efficacious than any moralising discourse.[90] According to the rubrics for the monasteries of Evergetis near Constantinople and Christ Saviour in Messina, during Holy Wednesday the homilies of John Chrysostom and Ephrem the Syrian on the theme of the repentant harlot were read to the faithful.[91] As we have seen, the image of the repentant harlot also features prominently in the poetry of Romanos the Melodist and Andrew of Crete. Moreover, the image of the sinful woman who repents at Christ's feet often became the subject of dialogue hymns in Syriac by Ephrem and Jacob of Serug.[92] Kassia taps this rich tradition as she evokes the compunction of a woman whose tears and voice become the emotion and exclamation of the faithful.

---

[88] Krueger, *Liturgical Subjects*, 157.   [89] Ibid., 152.

[90] Benedicta Ward, *Harlots of the Desert: A Study of Repentance in Early Monastic Sources* (Kalamazoo, MI: Cisternian Publications, 1987), 7–8.

[91] Jordan, *The Synaxarion of the Monastery of the Theotokos Evergetis*, 468–69; Arranz, *Le Typicon du monastère du Saint-Sauveur*, 232.

[92] Susan Ashbrook Harvey, 'Why the Perfume Mattered: The Sinful Woman in Syriac Exegetical Tradition', in *In Dominico Eloquio/In Lordly Eloquence: Essays on Patristic Exegesis in Honour of Robert Louis Wilken*, ed. Paul M. Blowers (Grand Rapids, MI: Eerdmans, 2002), 69–89.

A Harlot's Tears

The tears of the woman who had fallen into many sins in Kassia's hymn betoken the experience of compunction in Byzantium. Although William Blake will tell us that 'a tear is an intellectual thing', insofar as we cry because we think, the spiritual valency of tears for Eastern Christianity is profound.[93] According to Isaac the Syrian, tears could dissolve the boundary between the body and the spirit and circumscribe 'the path that leads towards the new age'.[94] This eschatological transition is portrayed as a rebirth into the life of the age to come and yet as a return to the paradisal bliss of old: 'I do not have a sorrowful heart to search for you, I do not have repentance, I do not have compunction nor tears which return children to their homeland'.[95] A tension between the eschaton and paradisal nostalgia in Kassia's hymn is palpable. The tears of compunction that her song enacted show how religious crying was not simply a natural phenomenon but a gift or a way. As John Klimakos remarked:

Ἐγὼ δὲ καὶ αὐτὴν τὴν τῆς κατανύξεως ποιότητα ἐννοῶν ἐξίσταμαι· πῶς δὲ πένθος, καὶ λύπη λεγομένη τὴν χαρὰν καὶ τὴν εὐφροσύνην ἔνδοθεν ὥσπερ μελικηρίῳ συμπεπλεγμένην κέκτηται. Τί δὲ ἐκ τούτου μανθάνομεν; Ὅτι κυρίως Κυρίου δῶρον ἡ τοιαύτη κατάνυξις καθέστηκεν· οὐκ ἔστιν ἐν τῇ ψυχῇ τότε ἀνήδονος ἡδονή, τοῦ Θεοῦ λεληθότως παρακαλοῦντος τοὺς συντεθλασμένους τῇ καρδίᾳ.[96]

As I ponder the quality of compunction, I am amazed. How does grief and so-called sadness, joy and gladness, mingle inside us like honeycomb? What can we learn from this? That this compunction has been properly ordained a gift of God. Then there is no disagreeable pleasure in the soul, since God secretly brings consolation to those who are contrite in heart.[97]

Tears could trace a pathway to the divine, deconstructing the dichotomy of interiority versus exteriority and mediating the liminal space between God and the faithful. Not unlike how the earthly and heavenly realms were portrayed as converging in the mystagogy of liturgy, tears of compunction could emerge in the liminality of sacred space, amidst the liturgical world of hymnody, suspended between paradisal nostalgia and the eschaton.

---

[93] Jerome Neu, *A Tear Is an Intellectual Thing: The Meanings of Emotion* (New York, NY: Oxford University Press, 2000), 2.
[94] Homilies 35 [37] and 14. Quoted in Ware, 'The Mystery of Tears', 250.
[95] Isaac the Syrian, *Discourses* 2, 'Concerning Renunciation of the World'. Quoted in Archbishop Stylianos Harkianakis, *On Prayer* (Athens: Armos, 1999), 96.
[96] *Ladder of Divine Ascent*, PG 88, 812A.   [97] The English translation is my own.

There is a familiar texture in Kassia's image of 'springs of tears' (τὰς πηγὰς τῶν δακρύων) that marks the poignant entreaty in the dramatic monologue of her protagonist. It is reminiscent of a trope that John Chrysostom uses to speak about compunction in his letter *To Demetrius, On Compunction*. Chrysostom's letters *To Demetrius* and *To Stelechius, On Compunction*,[98] evoke the 'fire [of compunction]'[99] and the 'fountains of tears' (αἱ τῶν δακρύων πηγαί)[100] of his addressees. The prophet Jeremiah is known for his lamentations, one of which is echoed in Kassia's hymn.[101] As we saw in Chapter 3, the phrase 'speak in your hearts and feel compunction on your beds'[102] would have been familiar to the congregation:

> For in death no one remembers you, and in Hades who will give you thanks? I was weary with my groaning; I shall bathe my bed every night; I will drench my couch with my tears.[103]

The lachrymose image Kassia employs would have been an evocative one for the faithful participating in the sacred rituals and immersed in the auditory culture of Byzantium. Hymns exemplify how the 'oral delivery and aural reception of the Christian message' constructed through performance a liturgical world of images and created an affective space where blessed emotions could be perceived and felt.[104]

The portrayal of Kassia's protagonist is that of a person who experiences compunction at the nadir of sinfulness. But she does not allow her fallenness to become a 'gloomy and moonless' prison. She tears down the defences she has built around her, is wounded by compunction, and is able to sense the divinity of Christ. This is in stark contrast to the image John Chrysostom evokes of a person who resists any stimulation that may lead to a contrite heart:

> ὅθεν οὐδὲ μικρὰν παρείσδυσιν ἡ κατάνυξις εὑρεῖν δυνήσεται, τοσούτοις εἰργομένη τειχίσμασιν· ἀγαπητὸν γὰρ καὶ πάντων τούτων ἀπηλλαγμένην δυνηθῆναι ἐν αὐτῇ τοῦτο φυτεῦσαι τὸ καλόν.[105]

---

[98] PG 47, 393–422.   [99] *To Stelechius*, chapter 1, PG 47, 411.

[100] *To Demetrius*, chapter 1, PG 47, 394.

[101] 'Who will give my head water and my eyes a fountain of tears so that I might weep for my people day and night . . .?' Jeremiah 9:1.

[102] Psalm 4:5.

[103] Psalm 6:6–7. Chrysostom had elsewhere preached about the power of tears as 'a laver that cleanses away sins'. See John Chrysostom, 'On Repentance and Compunction', in *St John Chrysostom: On Repentance and Almsgiving*, trans. Gus George Christo (Washington, DC: The Catholic University of America Press, 1998), 101.

[104] Harrison, *The Art of Listening*, 62.   [105] *To Stelechius*, chapter 3. PG 47, 414.

therefore, compunction is unable to find even a small opening to enter, being inhibited by so many fortifications; it loves being able to overthrow all these obstacles and implant such goodness within the soul.

Compunction in Kassia's hymn – and the repentance it heralded – emerged as an act of extreme vulnerability. It was dramatised as a tearing down of the fortifications that protected the faithful from experiencing the assault of divine passion and as a recognition of human powerlessness.

Although for Eastern Christianity 'outward and visible weeping' was for the most part not 'considered weak and unmanly' and was not the exclusive domain of women – men did cry in antiquity and in Byzantium[106] – the gender of Kassia's protagonist and the intimacy of her repentance cannot be ignored.[107] Medieval women had 'a limited number of outlets through which they might express their holiness' and 'tears were one way of communicating this holiness' and making it visible.[108] The physical intimacy of the woman's repentance is manifest in *On the Sinful Woman*. The protagonist does not simply weep. She touches Christ's feet, washes them with her 'springs of tears' and wipes them with her hair. It is a vivid and somatic image of compunction – arguably the most sensual in the New Testament and in Byzantine hymnography. Although Peter and the prodigal son wept, the portrayal of their repentance in Scripture and in hymns does not match the intimacy of the woman's actions in Kassia's hymn. Peter's repentance culminated in a dialogue with Christ. While the father embraces the prodigal son in the biblical parable, hymnody does not contemplate this corporeal image of compunction and forgiveness.

The other conspicuous gendering in Kassia's hymn is the spiritual awareness of her protagonist. She perceives Christ's divinity when so many others could not see his true nature. Throughout the entire text of the Gospel, it is difficult to find an occasion where someone senses the true nature of Jesus. It is usually demon-possessed figures that are able to see beyond the human nature and perceive the divine nature.[109] Unlike the proud law-keeper known as Simon, who invites Jesus to eat in his house but does not perceive his divinity, the sinful woman senses his divine nature and humbly seeks forgiveness. Kassia's hymn amplifies the biblical

---

[106] See Ann Suter, 'Tragic Tears and Gender', in *Tears in the Graeco-Roman World*, ed. Thorsten Fögen (Berlin: De Gruyter, 2009), 59–83; Ilaria Ramelli, 'Tears of Pathos', 367–96.

[107] Ware, 'The Mystery of Tears', 245.

[108] Kimberley-Joy Knight, '*Si puose calcina a' propi occhi*: The Importance of the Gift of Tears for Thirteenth-Century Religious Women and Their Hagiographers', in Gertsman, ed., *Crying in the Middle Ages*, 139.

[109] Luke 8:26–39.

tale of repentance and forgiveness, showing the faithful a woman's vision of the Logos and evoking the mystery of the Incarnation. Her compunction and restoration invoke the salvific power of Christ's crucifixion and resurrection, and they render her a paragon of repentance for the faithful.

The gender of Eve is also intriguing. In recalling the fall of Adam and Eve, Kassia does not mention Adam, but only the experience of Eve as she hides in fear once she hears the footsteps of God. By focusing on Eve, Kassia calls to mind a woman who is curiously absent from the hymn but implicitly present as the second Eve – Mary, the Theotokos. From the early Christian period, to the fifth-century Proclus of Constantinople and beyond, Christian tradition established a parallel between the Eve of Genesis and the Mary of the Lukan Gospel.[110] The disobedience of Eve and the obedience of Mary represented the dialectic of human freedom in history. And Byzantine hymns often allegorised the Theotokos as the 'spiritual paradise' from which 'Christ the new Adam' blossoms.[111] Similarly, church fathers such as Gregory of Nyssa contrasted the first Adam with Christ – the second Adam:

τότε λαβὼν χοῦν ἀπὸ τῆς γῆς τὸν ἄνθρωπον ἔπλασε, πάλιν λαβὼν τὸν ἐκ τῆς παρθενίας χοῦν οὐχ ἁπλῶς τὸν ἄνθρωπον ἔπλασεν, ἀλλ᾽ ἑαυτῷ περιέπλασε·[112]

Once [God the Logos] took dust from the ground and shaped man, then he took the dust from the Virgin and did not simply shape man, but shaped him round Himself.[113]

But Kassia juxtaposes the first Eve with the second Adam to show how the Logos assumed human nature through the Theotokos and bridged the chasm between Creator and creation of his own desire but not without the willing participation of Mary. Whereas Adam and Eve closed the gates of Eden, Christ and Mary open the doors of repentance and invite the woman who had fallen into many sins – and indeed the congregation – to

---

[110] Meyendorff, *Byzantine Theology*, 146–49; Jaroslav Pelikan, *Mary through the Centuries: Her Place in the History of Culture* (New Haven, CT: Yale University Press, 1996), 39–54.

[111] Christian Hannick, 'The Theotokos in Byzantine Hymnography: Typology and Allegory', in *Images of the Mother of God: Perceptions of the Theotokos in Byzantium*, ed. Maria Vassilaki (Aldershot: Ashgate, 2005), 75. See also 1 Corinthians 15:45.

[112] *Against Eunomius*, book 3, chapter 2. *Contra Eunomium Libri. Liber III*, ed. Wernerus Jaeger. GNO 2 (Leiden: Brill, 1960), 70. (PG 45, 637A–B.)

[113] My translation is based on the one by Stuart G. Hall in *Gregory of Nyssa. Contra Eunomium III. An English Translation with Commentary and Supporting Studies*, eds. Johan Leemans and Matthieu Cassin (Leiden: Brill, 2014), 82. This passage is also quoted in Pelikan, *Mary through the Centuries*, 51.

experience the mercy of God.[114] The mystical communion between the flesh of Mary and the flesh of Christ is reflected in the mystical marriage between God and creation.[115] The Incarnation, as a personal and cosmic event, echoes throughout Kassia's hymn, wherein the juxtaposition of the omnipotence of the Logos and the contingency of his creation is a recurring theme.

The evocative exclamation of Kassia's protagonist – 'Woe is me!' – also calls to mind the hymn *On the First-Created Humans*, which the faithful sang at the beginning of Lent.[116] This hymn is a *kanon* sung in the plagal second mode of Byzantine music on Cheese-Fare Sunday, the last Sunday before Great Lent. The exile of Adam and Eve from the delight of Eden frames the present-day experience of the singer's soul in the hymn *On the First-Created Humans*:

Δεῦρο ψυχή μου ἀθλία, κλαῦσον τὰ σοί, πεπραγμένα σήμερον, μνημονεύουσα τῆς πρίν, ἐν Ἐδὲμ γυμνώσεως, δι᾿ ἧς, ἐξεβλήθης τῆς τρυφῆς, καὶ τῆς ἀλήκτου χαρᾶς.[117]

Come my wretched soul; weep over your deeds committed today, remembering how once you were stripped naked in Eden and cast out from delight and unending joy.

The estrangement of the faithful from, and their desire for, paradise is often enunciated using the same exclamation that Kassia's protagonist employs:

Θρηνῶ, στενάζω, καὶ ἀποδύρομαι, τὰ Χερουβὶμ φλογίνη τῇ ῥομφαίᾳ θεώμενος, τῆς εἴσοδον φυλάττειν ταχθέν, πᾶσι τοῖς Ἐδὲμ τὴν παραβάταις, οἴμοι! ἀπρόσιτον, εἰμὴ σὺ ἀκώλυτον Σωτήρ, ταύτην ποιήσεις μοι.[118]

Seeing the Cherubim with the flaming sword set to guard the entrance of Eden against all transgressors, I weep, I groan and I lament. Woe is me! It is unapproachable, O Saviour, unless you allow me to pass unhindered.

---

[114] See Behr, *Irenaeus of Lyons*, 91–93.

[115] Panayiotis Nellas, 'The Mother of God and Theocentric Humanism', in *Synaxis. Volume I: Anthropology, Environment, Creation*, ed. John Hadjinicolaou (Montreal: Alexander Press, 2006), 135. Although Nellas was a twentieth-century theologian, he, Georges Florovsky, Vladimir Lossky and others formed part of the Orthodox neopatristic movement, which analysed Western influences on Orthodox theology and held that the Christian Hellenism of the past was 'the norm by which all modern theological proposals were to be judged'. See Paul L. Gavrilyuk, 'Florovsky's Neopatristic Synthesis and the Future Ways of Orthodox Theology', in *Orthodox Constructions of the West*, eds. George E. Demacopoulos and Aristotle Papanikolaou (New York, NY: Fordham University Press, 2013), 102.

[116] The title 'On the First-Created Humans' (Κανών εἰς πρωτόπλαστας) appears in Grottaferrata Δβ I, fol. 29r. The hymn also appears in Sinai Graecus 734–735, fols. 46v–49r. See also Τριώδιον Κατανυκτικόν, 102–7. The English translations that follow are my own.

[117] First ode, first strophe.   [118] Ninth ode, third strophe.

Indeed, the remorseful cry of 'woe is me' is uttered nine times throughout the hymn *On the First-Created Humans*. However, the final strophe at the end of every ode in the hymn entreats the 'Holy Lady' who 'opened to all the faithful the gates of Paradise'[119] and who 'covered fallen Adam's nakedness'[120] to call the faithful out of exile, back again to Eden:

> Νυμφῶνα δόξης σε μυστικόν, πάντες καταγγέλλομεν πιστοί, Θεοκυῆτορ, πανάμωμε· ὅθεν δυσωπῶ σε Ἁγνὴ πεσόντα με, νυμφῶνος Παραδείσου, οἰκεῖον ποίησον.[121]

> We, all the faithful, proclaim you as the mystical bridal chamber of glory, O all-blameless Mother of God. Wherefore, I who have fallen beseech you, O Pure One, make the bridal chamber of Paradise my home.

The faithful cry out to the Theotokos as the bridal chamber of the Logos and the one who paves the way to a heavenly abode. The actions and words of Kassia's protagonist reveal how she has heard this call to return to paradise and so embraces the Logos who was incarnate of the Virgin Mary.

In Kassia's hymn *On the Sinful Woman*, the woman's tears of compunction, her elevation to the order of myrrhbearer, indeed the mystery of salvation itself, are played out in the sacred drama of liturgical performance. Images of crying, bending, kissing and wiping portray compunction as unfolding in the human heart as an embodied experience. Yet in this sacred drama there are no spectators, only actors. Unlike Romanos' hymn *On the Harlot*, there is no dramatic dialogue between characters, but a short third-person narrative followed by a first-person speech. Although there are no counter-ideals that appear beside the exemplar of repentance in Kassia's hymn, the other hymns that were sung alongside *On the Sinful Woman* briefly allude to Judas as a paradigm of unrepentance.[122] In liturgical performance, gender does not become a stumbling block for the congregation; it does not represent the sinful woman as limited by society and culture. For Kassia, the woman's tears are the lament of the entire world yearning for salvation. She is not simply a male or female protagonist, but a universal figure that undoes stereotypes and lives above gender.

The Sacred Music of Kassia's Hymn *On the Sinful Woman*

The performance of Kassia's hymn opened a liminal space, where personal contemplation and the collective song of the faithful converged. Singing

---

[119] Fourth ode, fifth strophe.   [120] Second ode, fourth strophe.   [121] Fifth ode, fourth strophe.
[122] See Sinai Graecus 734–735, fols. 158v–159v, Vaticanus Graecus 771, fol. 162r–v, Grottaferrata Δβ I, fols. 160v–161r.

the hymn became a liturgical act that could mirror and transform the emotions of the singer's soul. Words and melody invited the faithful to contemplate the striking paradox of how, in the depths of darkness, amidst the eros of sinfulness, Kassia's protagonist senses the divinity of the Logos and feels compunction. The melody of Kassia's hymn is in the same mode of Byzantine music as Romanos' hymn *On the Harlot* – plagal fourth mode[123] – which suggests the faithful could have used this common musical thread linking Kassia's hymn with Romanos' to reflect on how the paradigm of the repentant harlot evolved during the liturgical events of Holy Wednesday. The melody of the plagal fourth mode of Byzantine music is described in the following poem:

> Ἤχων σφραγὶς, Τέταρτε, σὺ τῶν πλαγίων,
> Ὡς ἐν σεαυτῷ πᾶν καλὸν μέλος φέρων.
> Ἀνευρύνεις σὺ τοὺς κρότους τῶν ἀσμάτων,
> Ἤχων κορωνὶς, ὡς ὑπάρχων καὶ τέλος.
> Ὡς ἄκρον ἐν φθόγγοις τε καὶ φωνῶν στάσει,
> Ἄκρον σε φωνῆς δίς σε καλῶ καὶ τέλος.[124]

> O Plagal Fourth, you are the seal of the plagal modes,
> For in yourself you carry every beautiful melody.
> You broaden the striking sounds of songs.
> You are the peak and finale of all modes,
> As the pinnacle in both sounds and pitch of voices,
> Twice I call you, zenith and fulfilment of voice.

This poetic description is rich and evocative but somewhat mysterious. Although it suggests that this mode was the crowning glory of the eight modes of Byzantine music, it is not a meaningful elaboration of the music of Kassia's hymn. As was the case in previous chapters, it is more fruitful to explore how the hymn was set within its genre.

Kassia's hymn does not exhibit the characteristics of the *kanon* nor is it in the style of a sung sermon with a refrain like the *kontakion*. Being a *sticheron idiomelon*, Kassia's hymn has a unique melody characterised by melismatic flourishes during its performance.[125] It amplified the story of the hymn, allowing melody to explore textuality and encouraging the faithful to meditate on the divine drama unfolding before them. The performance of this *sticheron idiomelon* during Holy Wednesday embodied

---

[123] The plagal fourth mode of Byzantine sacred music belonged to the diatonic genus.

[124] *Grottaferrata Heirmologion* II – quoted in Desby, 'The Modes and Tunings', 27–28. I have modified Desby's translation.

[125] Raasted, 'Voice and Verse', 171–78; Wellesz, *A History of Byzantine Music*, 395–97.

the feeling of compunction within a meaningful practice, inviting the faithful to enter its poetic and musical universe, and internalise the repentance it enacted. For the faithful, the sacred drama that unfolded in the performance of Kassia's hymn *On the Sinful Woman* and the other hymns for Holy Wednesday invited human feelings to become liturgical emotions. These hymns portrayed blessed emotions such as compunction as a movement of the soul that enkindled body and mind. The compunction of the harlot entailed a turning of the mind, an outpouring of tears and a metamorphosis of passion. At the centre of Kassia's hymn was a universal figure of repentance, a person who rose above sinfulness, who became wise and a myrrhbearer, and who lived above gender.

Concluding Remarks

Kassia's hymn became a collective space of liturgical action that sought to draw in the faithful who yearned to experience the sacred drama that unfolded during Holy Week in Constantinople. The congregation could follow the footsteps of and identify with the woman who had fallen into many sins as she journeyed toward repentance. In entering this sacred narrative, they did not remain in one point of time but followed the protagonist as she travelled with Christ to the exile of Adam and Eve from Eden and then to his crucifixion, death and resurrection. The passage of time collapsed into different moments in the history of salvation, placing the individual at the centre of a cosmic drama and generating a sense of helplessness. *On the Sinful Woman* was chanted a few days before Christ's Passion, evoking the existential abyss created by the absence of the divine from the life of the faithful and unveiling how tears of compunction could bridge this chasm.

In Kassia's hymn, compunction overcomes the limitations that gender and historical conditioning perpetuate. Not unlike the author's life of monasticism and renunciation of secular ambition, the protagonist of her hymn rises above her gender and social standing. Compunction suspends the determinism associated with gender and shows the uniqueness of the person who is aware of her limitations. Her story is a universal song of repentance that can be sung by those who wish to feel compunction and paradisal nostalgia. Kassia inflected a variety of sacred narratives through the lens of hymnography. Retelling and interweaving the biblical stories of the woman who anoints Christ, the woman who was cast out from paradise and the woman who reopened the gates of Eden, Kassia energised the emotion underlying the narrative and unlocked its personal significance for the faithful. She recreated within the sacred space of liturgy the experience of personalising religious narratives, not doctrinal proclamations.

The performance of the hymn sought to arouse the emotion of compunction in the faithful and shape a liturgical and emotional community through a shared aesthetic experience. The sacred melody, with its occasional cadential melismas represented the ladder of tears that link God and the world, allowing music to become a medium of transfiguration. In Kassia's hymn *On the Sinful Woman*, tears of compunction elicited an intimacy between God and humanity. This is reflected in the unique form of her hymn, which is not a *kontakion*, nor a *kanon*, but a *sticheron idiomelon*. It was chanted with a unique and florid melody, which amplified the salvific significance of the narrative and heightened the tenderness of the image of the woman repenting at the feet of God. The powerful musicality and linguistic economy sought to disassemble logic and provoke introspection through an emotive performance of the divine drama of salvation. Indeed, the ritual performance of Kassia's liturgical hymn embodied what compunction signified for Byzantine Christianity – a blessed emotion that could traverse social and cultural lines.

Conclusion

At the end of the Lenten journey, at the conclusion of Holy Week, the faithful came to a table laden with the 'wine of compunction'[1] and the ending became the beginning of all things. 'It was dark but love lighted the way' to the tomb of Christ.[2] Like the maiden who was filled with 'ardent longing and the fire of love', they mingled 'joy with fear and happiness with grief' as the day of Pascha dawned.[3] The joyful sorrow of the Passion mediated a crucified love that they beheld through eyes that had wept tears of compunction. And it is here that they remembered how the story began, all its twists and turns, even how it would end, through the words of the eucharistic prayer: 'You brought us out of non-existence into being, and when we had fallen you raised us up again, and left nothing undone until you had brought us up to heaven and had granted us your Kingdom that is to come'.[4]

This book has grappled with the intricate symbiosis of poetry, song and theology in hymns by Romanos the Melodist, Andrew of Crete and Kassia. It has explored how these hymns enkindled and enacted compunction by bringing them into dialogue with the history of emotions and reimagining their liturgical performance in Byzantium. By reimagining the performance of hymnography, I have sought to pave the way to liturgical emotions and how they came to life in the sacred rituals of Constantinople. Three of the earliest extant manuscripts of the *Triodion* have proven indispensable in this regard. And by carefully considering what emotions and performance meant for the Byzantines, I have sought to avoid the perils of retrofitting a second-order discourse of emotion or performativity on Byzantium.

---

[1] Psalm 59:5.
[2] Romanos the Melodist, *On the Resurrection*, strophe 3 in Lash, *On the Life of Christ*, 168.
[3] Ibid., 172, 177 (strophes 11 and 22).   [4] *The Divine Liturgy*, 31.

The mystical and performative significance of hymnody for Christianity has been my refrain as I explored liturgical emotions in Byzantium. Performativity is not an anachronistic concept for Byzantine hymnody when it is viewed though the lenses of theology and liturgy. Hymns by Romanos, Andrew and Kassia evoke a theology of performance, where sacred drama dissolves the limits of history, breaks the bounds of Scripture and suspends the divide between the congregation and the poetic universe of hymnody. The performativity of hymnody could open a liminal space where the faithful could behold a polytemporal vision of the Creation, the Fall, the Incarnation and the Passion, and become protagonists in this mystery unfolding before them.

By exploring the performance of hymns and unearthing their liturgical context over a period of nearly four centuries in Constantinople, I have investigated how the texts by Romanos the Melodist, Andrew of Crete and Kassia were emotionally meaningful for the Byzantine faithful during the Lenten journey to Pascha. After all, the words of hymns were not read in silence but were performed in sacred space as divine song. They interacted with other liturgical arts and were grounded in church ritual. It is when all these facets came together that a rich image of meaning for the worshipping faithful crystallised. For the Byzantines, the performance of hymns became an aural image amidst the mystagogy of liturgical events. The melodic contour and imagerial quality of the hymns came to life as the faithful experienced these texts in a multisensory environment that entailed singing, seeing, hearing, smelling, touching and tasting during their performance. Alongside these hymns, sacred space was portrayed as the *habitus* of compunction, as the liturgical world where heaven and earth converged in the hearts of the faithful and the affective field where they could feel blessed emotions.

Hymnographers invited the congregations of Constantinople to enter the story song of their hymns, asking them to become part of the divine economy of salvation and to feel the emotions of biblical characters. The scriptural narrative of this divine economy and the actions of God's people came together in a liturgical panorama. Hymnody envisioned a communion of saints and embodied a mystical harmony between humanity and creation. Sacred ritual opened a liminal space where personal contemplation and the collective song of the faithful dovetailed in the mystical body of Christ. Singing hymns was portrayed as a liturgical act that mirrored and shaped the emotions of the singer's soul. Hymnody embodied and enacted a mystical vision where liturgical emotions could be perceived and felt in the singer's encounter with the Divine.

In Romanos' compositions, hymns became liturgical scripts through which the faithful besought tears of compunction and God's compassionate mercy. Biblical exemplars, such as the prodigal and the harlot, underscored the link between compunction and repentance. And the eschaton was a call to cultivate compunction, not simply as a preparation for future death and judgment, but as an interaction with a reality that was proleptically and liturgically internalised in the hearts of the faithful. Andrew of Crete's *Great Kanon* also sought to immerse the faithful in the biblical narrative of salvation, taking them on a liturgical journey through Scripture and conjuring a host of repentant exemplars as companions. But in singing the story of salvation this hymn dramatised, and in praying for tears of compunction, the faithful could transform these words into *their* story of salvation and *their* remorseful weeping. Sacred song mediated feelings that were collective yet personal. This interplay between personal and collective feeling is also evident in the tears that are poignantly and intimately enacted in Kassia's hymn *On the Sinful Woman*. Her protagonist's desire to experience the mercy she senses in Christ's divinity leads the faithful to the same crossroads of repentance and hope. Yet her compunction is also an icon of the entire world longing for salvation.

In the corpora of Romanos, Andrew and Kassia – and in the *Triodion* more broadly – repentance and salvation are the ultimate yet perennial goal of compunction. Repentance is not a point on a continuum, and salvation is not the destination; they are the very journey of the faithful desiring compunction. Hymnody embodied this journey and invited the faithful to experience it in the mystagogy of liturgy. While the ways that Romanos, Andrew and Kassia nuanced compunction in their hymns emerged during distinct periods in the history of Byzantium, these hymns converged within the liturgical framework of the *Triodion*. Following the liturgical reforms of the Monastery of Saint John the Forerunner at Stoudios in Constantinople in the early ninth century, the faithful could experience these subtle variations in expression and feeling. The performance of these hymns was framed by the journey to Pascha, and each song was an aspect of an intricate liturgical mosaic. Indeed, the textual, musical and imagerial interrelationships that emerge in liturgical performance and sacred ritual have afforded us a richer glimpse into what compunction signified for the faithful.

The performance of compunction was also coloured by the genre of hymnography (*kontakion*, *kanon* and *sticheron idiomelon*) and shaped by liturgical ritual (*pannychis*, *orthros* and vespers). Each genre and ritual unveiled subtle shades of compunction and aroused other liturgical emotions in an ecosystem of affective mystagogy. Compunction was a comforter during the darkness of the *pannychis*, the companion of hope during evensong and the harbinger of delight at *orthros*. The melody of compunction could be a lively dance, a wonderful reverie or a contemplative melisma. Although music arouses emotions in a mysterious way, an intriguing insight that has emerged is that the plagal modes of Byzantine hymnody were more suited to compunction, while the authentic modes were more fitting for hymns of praise.

The mystical and theological dimensions of liturgical feeling have fascinating implications for the history of emotions in Byzantium, disrupting the modern stalemate between arguments for emotions as either biological, therefore universal, and emotions as socially constructed. Feeling liturgically entailed participation in the mystery and otherness of the Divine. As members of Christ's body, as an emotional and liturgical community that was taught to feel things beyond its nature, the faithful were invited to experience godly emotions. These emotions were constructed within a liturgical event, in the affective mystagogy of hymnody and ritual. While the social and cultural milieu where these emotions emerged cannot be discounted, liturgical emotions became a prism through which the faithful might have seen their world and made judgments in the course of everyday life. Liturgical emotions are, in some respects, transhistorical and transcultural phenomena.

Compunction was one emotion in a constellation of emotions that emerged during the journey to Pascha. It was not the only emotion that sacred song invited the faithful to feel. The hymns of the *Triodion* formed part of a sumptuous liturgical calendar of feasts, fasts and celebrations that the faithful navigated. While there were many beginnings and endings in these sacred rituals and liturgical cycles, they ultimately formed a mystical vision of the adventure of human freedom, where the mystery of the human heart and the sacred drama of salvation converged. Hymnody brought the faithful to the precipice of the eschaton, giving them a glimpse of a new heaven and a new earth, where God wipes away every tear from their eyes.[5] Tears of compunction paradoxically became meaningful amidst the joy of Pascha and the paradisal bliss that awaited in the life of the age to come, which began in the liturgical now.

---

[5] Revelation 21:1, 4.

Glossary

AMBO (ἄμβων). A platform in the nave of a church that was a liturgical focal point during Byzantine worship. Processions from the part of the church containing the altar would converge on the ambo, from which the Gospel was proclaimed, deacons intoned litanies, choirs sang hymns and sermons were delivered.

BYZANTIUM (Βυζάντιο). The conventional name of the eastern Roman Empire that existed from the fourth century until the fall of Constantinople on 29 May 1453.

CHEROUBIKON (χερουβικόν). The cherubic hymn composed in the sixth century to accompany the Great Entrance. Its name derives from its opening words, in which the singers identify with the cherubim of God.

COMPUNCTION (κατάνυξις). A feeling of remorse, often accompanied by tears, that arises from the consciousness of one's own sinfulness and engenders a desire for repentance.

CONTRAFACTUM (προσόμοιον). A style of hymn sung according to a pre-existing melody and metric pattern of an older *troparion*.

EMOTION (πάθος). In a spiritual context, a movement of the soul that was, for some Byzantine theologians and ascetics, a natural aspect of human nature and part of the original formation of the human being.

GREAT ENTRANCE (μεγάλη εἴσοδος). The ritual procession of the bread and wine for the Eucharist through the nave of the church to the altar.

HYMN (ὕμνος). A liturgical poem composed and sung according to the tradition of Byzantine sacred music. In early Christianity, a hymn was any form of devotional chant. However, it later came to mean new poems that were different from the biblical psalms and canticles.

HYMNODY (ὑμνωδία). The singing of hymns.

HYMNOGRAPHY (ὑμνογραφία). The composition of Byzantine hymns but also, more generally, the body of literature that was an intrinsic part of Byzantine worship.

HYMNOLOGY (ὑμνολογία). The study of hymnody and hymnography. However, hymnology can also refer to sacred songs and the singing of these songs.

KANON (κανών). The *kanon* is a genre of hymnography that gradually replaced the nine biblical canticles previously chanted during the *orthros*.

KONTAKARION (κοντακάριον). A liturgical book containing a collection of *kontakia* (sing. *kontakion*) that were performed during the Byzantine rite.

KONTAKION (κοντάκιον). A hymn consisting of a short prelude and numerous strophes that was chanted during the *pannychis*, and which usually celebrated a liturgical feast by amplifying and contemplating the biblical narrative of the day.

LITURGY (λειτουργία). Specifically, the celebration of the Eucharist. More generally, the term can be applied to other liturgical rites and services, such as baptism or vespers.

MENOLOGION (μηνολόγιον). A collection of vitae arranged according to the celebration of the feast of each saint in the liturgical calendar of Byzantium.

MODE (ἦχος) of Byzantine chant. Each of the eight melodic formulae for Byzantine chant is known as a mode. Each mode of Byzantine chant has a unique melody peculiar to it that can be executed in different ways. The eight modes are divided into two groups: four described as 'authentic' (first mode, second mode, third mode, fourth mode) and four designated as 'plagal' (plagal first mode, plagal second mode, grave mode, plagal fourth mode). The modes are divided according to three types of basic scales: the enharmonic ('harmonious') genus, the chromatic ('coloured') genus, and the diatonic ('through-toned') genus.

OKTOECHOS (ὀκτώηχος). A liturgical book containing hymns for the daily liturgical cycle (except for Lent, Easter and Pentecost). It is framed by the eight modes of Byzantine chant. *Oktoechos* can also denote these eight modes.

ORTHROS (ὄρθρος). Byzantine matins. A daybreak service comprised of psalms, canticles and other hymns.

PANNYCHIS (παννυχίς). A nocturnal liturgical vigil, usually on the eve of a feast.

PENTEKOSTARION (πεντηκοστάριον). The liturgical hymnal for the paschal season and the cycle of Pentecost. Originally, the *Triodion* included hymns for this liturgical period in a single tome. However, the *Pentekostarion* later emerged as a separate hymnbook.

PERFORM (τελειόω). To execute Byzantine liturgical acts, such as the singing of hymns, the consecration of the Eucharist and the consummation of other sacraments, which sought to initiate the faithful into the divine mystery of God.

PERFORMATIVITY. In performance theory, the notion that certain words do not simply describe phenomena – they perform an action and perhaps even engender a new reality. In the context of Byzantine hymnody, the liturgical and mystical qualities of hymns, which were performed by the choir and the faithful during worship as sacred songs.

PROPHETOLOGION (προφητολόγιον). The Old Testament lectionary of Constantinople.

PSALMODY (ψαλμωδία). The liturgical singing of the biblical psalms.

PSALTIKON (ψαλτικόν). The liturgical book containing the soloist's chants for the cathedral rite of Constantinople.

STICHERARION (στιχηράριον). A notated chantbook containing *stichera* (sing., *sticheron*) for the Byzantine rite.

STICHERON (στιχηρόν). A hymn sung after a verse of a psalm.

STICHERON IDIOMELON (στιχηρόν ἰδιόμελον). A hymn sung after a verse of a psalm and characterised by a unique melody.

SYNAXARION (συναξάριον). Often a church calendar of fixed feasts with the relevant lections indicated for each one. However, this term can also refer to a specific collection of hagiographical notices.

THEOTOKOS (Θεοτόκος). Mother of God. A title of the Virgin Mary in Byzantine theology and hymnography.

TRIODION (τριώδιον). The liturgical hymnbook for the Lenten cycle that contains the hymnography for the pre-Lenten period, Great Lent and Holy Week. Often entitled Τριώδιον Κατανυκτικόν in Greek editions, which literally means *Compunctious Triodion*, though it is usually called the *Lenten Triodion* in English translations, or simply *Triodion*.

TRISAGION (τρισάγιον). Byzantine sanctus: 'Holy God, holy mighty, holy immortal! Have mercy on us!'

TROPARION (τροπάριον). The earliest and most basic form of the Byzantine hymn, which began as a short prayer sung after each verse of the psalms but later became a musical meditation on liturgical feasts (pl. *troparia*).

TROPOLOGION (τροπολόγιον). A liturgical book containing *troparia* and *stichera*.

TYPIKON (τυπικόν). A book containing the rubrics for liturgical services. However, in Byzantium, *typikon* could refer to the document governing a monastic foundation.

VESPERS (ἑσπερινός). Byzantine evensong celebrated at the lighting of the lamps, which served as a symbol of Christ, the light of the world.

Bibliography

Manuscripts

Grottaferrata Δβ I (eleventh to twelfth centuries).
Patmos 266 (early tenth century).
Sinai Graecus 734–735 (tenth century).
Sinai Graecus 1094 (twelfth century).
Sinai Graecus 1096 (twelfth century).
Vaticanus Graecus 771 (eleventh century).

Primary Sources

Anastasios of Sinai. *Questions and Answers. Quaestiones et Responsiones.* Edited by Marcel Richard and Joseph A. Munitiz. CCSG 59. Turnhout: Brepols, 2006.

Andrew of Crete. *Great Kanon.* PG 97, 1329–85.
   St Andrew of Crete. The Great Kanon. The Life of St Mary of Egypt. Translated by Sister Katherine and Sister Thekla. Whitby: The Greek Orthodox Monastery of the Assumption, 1980.

Aristides Quintilianus. *On Music.* Translated by Thomas J. Mathiesen, *Aristides Quintilianus: On Music, In Three Books.* New Haven, CT and London: Yale University Press, 1983.

Athanasius of Alexandria. *Letter to Marcellinus on the Interpretation of the Psalms.* PG 27, 12–46.
   The Life of Antony and the Letter to Marcellinus. Translated by Robert C. Gregg. New York, NY: Paulist Press, 1980.
   On Sickness and Health. In *Analecta Patristica,* 5–8. Edited by F. Diekamp. OCA 117. Rome: Pontificium Institutum Orientalium Studiorum, 1938.

Augustine, *De musica,* ed. Martin Jacobsson, Corpus Scriptorum Ecclesiasticorum Latinorum 102. Berlin: De Gruyter, 2017.
   On Music. Translated by Robert Catesby Taliafero in *The Fathers of the Church* 4. Washington, DC: Catholic University of America Press, 2002.

Barsanuphios and John. *Barsanuphe et Jean de Gaza: Correspondance.* Edited by François Neyt and Paula de Angelis-Noah. 5 vols. SC 426–27, 450–51, 468. Paris: Éditions du Cerf, 1997–2002.

Letters. Translated by John Chryssavgis. 2 vols. Washington, DC: Catholic University of America Press, 2006–07.

Basil the Great. *Address to Youth.* PG 31, 564–89.

   Address to Youth: On How They Might Benefit from Classical Greek Literature. Translated by Dimitri Kepreotes. Sydney: St Andrew's Orthodox Press, 2011.

   Asketikon: The Shorter Responses. PG 31, 1052–320.

   The Asketikon of St Basil the Great. Translated by Anna M. Silvas. Oxford: Oxford University Press, 2005.

   Exegetical Homilies. Translated by Sister Agnes Clare Way. Washington, DC: Catholic University of America Press, 1963. *On the Holy Spirit.* PG 32, 67–217.

   On the Holy Spirit. Translated by Stephen M. Hildebrand. Crestwood, NY: St Vladimir's Seminary Press, 2011.

   Homilies on the Psalms. PG 29, 209–494.

Bekker, I., ed. *Georgius Cedrenus, Ioannis Scylitzae Ope.* Bonn: Weber, 1838.

Chronicon Paschale 284–628 AD. Translated by Michael Whitby and Mary Whitby. Liverpool: Liverpool University Press, 1989.

Clement of Alexandria. *The Exhortation to the Greeks, the Rich Man's Salvation, and the Fragment of an Address Entitled to the Newly Baptised.* Edited and translated by G. W. Butterworth. Loeb Classical Library 92. Cambridge, MA: Harvard University Press, 1960.

Contacarium Ashburnhamense: Codex Bibl. Laurentianae Ashburnhamensis 64 photo-typice depictus. Edited by Carsten Høeg. MMB Série Principale 4. Copen-hagen: Ejnar Munksgaard, 1956.

Cunningham, Mary B., trans. *Wider than Heaven: Eighth-Century Homilies on the Mother of God.* Crestwood, NY: St Vladimir's Seminary Press, 2008.

Cyril of Alexandria. *Commentary on the Gospel of John, 7–8.* PG 74, 9–104. Translated by Norman Russell in *Cyril of Alexandria,* 96–129. London: Routledge, 2000.

   Explanation of the Twelve Chapters. PG 76, 293–312. Translated by Norman Russell in *Cyril of Alexandria,* 175–89. London: Routledge, 2000.

Dionysius the Areopagite. *Corpus Dionysiacum II: Pseudo-Dionysius Areopagita. De coelesti hierarchia, De ecclesiastica hierarchia, De mystica theologia, Epistulae.* Edited by Günter Heil and Adolf Martin Ritter. Patristische Texte und Studien. Berlin: De Gruyter, 2012.

   Pseudo-Dionysius: The Complete Works. Translated by Colm Luibhéid and Paul Rorem. New York, NY: Paulist Press, 1987.

The Divine Liturgy of Our Father among the Saints, John Chrysostom. Translated by Ephrem Lash et al. Oxford: Oxford University Press, 1995.

Egeria. *Travels.* Translated by John Wilkinson, *Egeria's Travels.* Warminster: Aris & Phillips, 2002.

Ephrem the Syrian [Ephrem Graecus]. *On Psalmody.* In Ὁσίου Ἐφραίμ τοῦ Σύρου ἔργα [*The Works of St Ephrem the Syrian*]. Vol. 5. Edited by K. G. Phrantzoles, 129–32. Thessaloniki: To Perivoli tes Panagias, 1994.

L'Eucologio Barberini Gr. 336. Edited by Stefano Parenti and Elena Velkovska. Rome: Edizioni Liturgiche, 1995.

L'Eucologio Cryptense Γβ VII. Edited by Gaetano Passarelli. Thessaloniki: Patriarchal Institute for Patristic Studies, 1982.

George Pachymeres. *Syntagma. Quadrivium de Georges Pachymère.* Edited by Paul Tannery. Vatican City: Biblioteca Apostolica Vaticana, 1940.

Germanos of Constantinople. *Ecclesiastical History and Mystical Contemplation. St Germanus of Constantinople on the Divine Liturgy.* Edited and translated by Paul Meyendorff. Crestwood, NY: St Vladimir's Seminary Press, 1984.

Gregory of Nazianzus. *Against Anger.* PG 37, 813–51.

On His Own Verses. PG 37, 1329–36.

Oration on Theophany. In *Grégoire de Nazianze: Discours 38–41.* Edited by Claudio Moreschini. SC 358. Paris: Éditions du Cerf, 1990.

Gregory of Nazianzus: Autobiographical Poems. Translated and edited by Carolinne White. Cambridge: Cambridge University Press, 1996.

Gregory of Nazianzus. Translated by Brian E. Daley. London: Routledge, 2006.

Poems on Scripture. Translated by Brian Dunkle. New York, NY: St Vladimir's Seminary Press, 2012.

Gregory of Nyssa. *Against Eunomius, 3. Contra Eunomium Libri. Liber III.* Edited by Wernerus Jaeger. GNO 2. Leiden: Brill, 1960. Translated by Stuart G. Hall in *Gregory of Nyssa. Contra Eunomium III. An English Translation with Commentary and Supporting Studies,* 42–233. Edited by Johan Leemans and Matthieu Cassin. Leiden: Brill, 2014.

On the Formation of the Human Being. PG 44, 124–256.

Funeral Oration on the Empress Flacilla. PG 46, 877–92.

Gregorii Nysseni. De anima et resurrectione: opera dogmatica minora, pars III. Edited by Andreas Spira. GNO 3. Leiden: Brill, 2014.

Homilies on the Song of Songs. Edited and translated by Richard A. Norris, Jr. Atlanta, GA: Society of Biblical Literature, 2012.

Gregorii Nysseni. In inscriptiones Psalmorum: In sextum Psalmum: In ecclesiasten homiliae. Edited by J. McDonough and P. Alexander. GNO 5. Leiden: Brill, 1986.

Gregory of Nyssa's Treatise on the Inscriptions of the Psalms. Translated by Ronald E. Heine. Oxford: Oxford University Press, 1995.

On the Soul and the Resurrection. Translated by Catharine P. Roth. Crestwood, NY: St Vladimir's Seminary Press, 1993.

Gregory Palamas. *Triads in Defence of the Holy Hesychasts.* Translated by John Meyendorff in *Gregory Palamas: The Triads.* New York, NY: Paulist Press, 1983.

The Hypotyposis of the Monastery of the Theotokos Evergetis, Constantinople (11th–12th Centuries): Introduction, Translation and Commentary. Translated by Robert H. Jordan and Rosemary Morris. Farnham: Ashgate, 2012.

Isaac the Syrian. *The Ascetical Homilies.* Translated by Dana Miller. Boston, MA: Holy Transfiguration Monastery, 1984.

John Chrysostom. *To Demetrius, On Compunction* and *To Stelechius, On Compunction*. PG 47, 393–422.

A Companion for the Sincere Penitent: Or, a Treatise on the Compunction of the Heart. In Two Books. Translated by John Veneer. London: Judge's-Head, St Dunstan's Church, 1728.

Homilies on the Epistles to the Corinthians. PG 61, 9–610. Translated by Philip Schaff in *Saint Chrysostom: Homilies on the Epistles of Paul to the Corinthians*, 7–741. New York, NY: Christian Literature Company, 1899.

Homilies on Matthew, 55. PG 58, 539–50. Translated in *St John Chrysostom. The Homilies of S. John Chrysostom, Archbishop of Constantinople, on the Gospel of St Matthew. Part 2. Hom. 26–58*. Oxford: John Henry Parker, 1844.

Homilies on the Statues. PG 49, 15–222.

Homily on the Annunciation of Our Most Glorious Virgin Theotokos. PG 50, 791–96.

Homily on the Apostolic Saying That States: But Know This, That in the Last Days Perilous Times Will Come. PG 56, 271–80.

Homily on Repentance and Compunction. PG 49, 323–36. Translated by Gus George Christo in *St John Chrysostom: On Repentance and Almsgiving*, 86–110. Washington, DC: The Catholic University of America Press, 1998.

John Chrysostom. Translated by Wendy Mayer and Pauline Allen. New York, NY: Routledge, 2000.

On Eutropius. PG 52, 391–96.

On the Second Epistle to the Corinthians. PG 61, 381–610.

John of Damascus. *Apologetic Orations on the Holy Icons*. Edited by Bonifatius Kotter, *Die Schriften des Johannes von Damaskos III. Contra imaginum calumniatores orationes tres*. Berlin: De Gruyter, 1975.

Exposition on the Orthodox Faith. Edited by Bonifatius Kotter, *Die Schriften des Johannes von Damaskos II. Expositio fidei*. Berlin: De Gruyter, 1973.

Kanon for the Sunday of Pascha. PG 96, 840–44.

Three Treatises on the Divine Images. Translated by Andrew Louth. Crestwood, NY: St Vladimir's Seminary Press, 2003.

John Klimakos. *Ladder of Divine Ascent*. PG 88, 631–1161. Translated by Colm Luibhéid and Norman Russell. New York, NY: Paulist Press, 1982.

Justinian. *Corpus iuris civilis, 3. Novellae*. Edited by Rudolf Schöll and Wilhelm Kroll. Berlin: Apud Weidmannos, 1954.

Kassia. *On the Sinful Woman*. In Sinai Graecus 734–735, folio 159r–v; Vaticanus Graecus 771, folio 162v; Grottaferrata Δβ I, folio 161r.

Edited by Athanasios Papadopoulos-Kerameus. In Ἀνάλεκτα Ἱεροσολυμιτικῆς Σταχυολογίας, Vol. 2, 78. St Petersburg: Kirschbaum, 1894.

Edited by Niki Tsironis. In Κασσιανή ἡ ὑμνωδός, 41–42. Athens: Phoinika, 2002.

Lactantius. *Divine Institutes*. Translated by Anthony Bowen and Peter Garnsey Liverpool: Liverpool University Press, 2003.

Life of St Andrew of Crete. Edited by Panagiotes Skaltses. Βίος τοῦ ἐν ἁγίοις Πατρὸς ἡμῶν Ἀνδρέου τοῦ Ἱεροσολυμίτου, ἀρχιεπισκόπου Κρήτης [Life of our Father among the Saints Andrew of Jerusalem, Archbishop of Crete].' In Ὁ Ἅγιος Ἀνδρέας Ἀρχιεπίσκοπος Κρήτης ὁ Ἱεροσολυμίτης, Πολιοῦχος Ἐρεσοῦ Λέσβου. Πρακτικά Ἐπιστημονικοῦ Συνεδρίου (1–4 Ἰουλίου 2003). Mytilene: Holy Metropolis of Mytilene, 2005.

Edited by Athanasios Papadopoulos-Kerameus. 'Life of St Andrew of Crete.' In Ἀνάλεκτα Ἱεροσολυμιτικῆς Σταχυολογίας, Vol. 5, 169–79. St Petersburg: Kirschbaum, 1898.

Life of St Mary of Egypt. PG 87, 3697–726.

Translated by Maria Kouli. In *Holy Women of Byzantium: Ten Saints' Lives in English Translation*, edited by Alice-Mary Talbot, 65–93. Washington, DC: Dumbarton Oaks, 1996.

Mango, Cyril. *The Art of the Byzantine Empire, 312–1453: Sources and Documents.* Toronto: University of Toronto Press, 1986.

Manuel Bryennius. *Harmonics. The Harmonics of Manuel Bryennius.* Edited by G. H. Jonker. Gröningen: Wolters-Noordhoff, 1970.

Maximus the Confessor. *Centuries on Love. Capitoli sulla carità.* Edited by Aldo Ceresa-Gastaldo. Rome: Editrice Studium, 1963.

Maximi Confessoris Mystagogia. Edited by Christian Boudignon. CCSG 69. Turnhout: Brepols, 2011.

Maximus Confessor: Selected Writings. Translated by George C. Berthold. New York, NY: Paulist Press, 1985.

To Thalassius. PG 90, 241–786.

The Miracles of St Artemios: A Collection of Miracle Stories by an Anonymous Author of Seventh-Century Byzantium. Edited and translated by Virgil S. Crisafulli and John W. Nesbitt. Leiden: Brill, 1997.

New Testament. *The Greek New Testament. Fourth Revised Edition.* Edited by Barbara Aland, Kurt Aland, Johannes Karavidopoulos, Carlo M. Martini and Bruce M. Metzger. Stuttgart: Deutsche Bibelgesellschaft, 1994.

Nicholas Cabasilas. *Commentary on the Divine Liturgy. Nicolas Cabasilas: Explication de la Divine Liturgie.* Edited by René Bornert, Jean Gouillard, Pierre Périchon and Sévérien Salaville. SC 4. Paris: Éditions du Cerf, 1967.

A Commentary on the Divine Liturgy. Translated by J. M. Hussey and P. A. McNulty. London: SPCK, 1977.

On the Lament of Adam. In Paul Mass, ed., *Frühbyzantinische Kirchenpoesie: I. Anonyme Hymnen des v–vi Jahrhunderts*, 16–20. Berlin: De Gruyter, 1931.

Nikephoros of Constantinople. *Treatise on Our Immaculate, Pure and Unmixed Christian Faith and against Those Who Glorify and Worship Idols.* PG 100, 533–849.

Origen. *Commentary on the Song of Songs.* PG 17, 253–88.

The Song of Songs: Commentary and Homilies. Translated by R. P. Lawson. New York, NY: The Newman Press, 1957.

The Orthodox Study Bible. Nashville, TN: Thomas Nelson, 2008.

Paul the Silentiary. *Ekphrasis of Hagia Sophia.* In *Prokop: Werke.* Vol. 5. Edited by Otto Veh, 306–57. Munich: Heimeran, 1977.

Ekphrasis of the Ambo. In *Prokop: Werke*. Vol. 5. Edited by Otto Veh, 358–75. Munich: Heimeran, 1977.

Philokalia. Translated by G. E. H. Palmer, Philip Sherrard and Kallistos Ware. *The Philokalia: The Complete Text*. 4 vols. London: Faber and Faber, 1979–95.

Photios. *Homilies*. Φωτίου Ομιλίαι. Edited by Vasileios Laourdas. Thessaloniki: Centre for Macedonian Studies, 1959.

The Homilies of Photius Patriarch of Constantinople. Translated by Cyril Mango. Cambridge, MA: Harvard University Press, 1958.

Prokopios. *Buildings*. In *Prokop: Werke*. Vol. 5. Edited by Otto Veh, 16–305. Munich: Heimeran, 1977.

Prophetologium. Edited by Carsten Høeg, Günther Zuntz and Gudrun Engberg. MMB Série Lectionaria 1. Copenhagen: Ejnar Munksgaard, 1939–81.

Romanos the Melodist. *Romanos le Mélode*. *Hymnes*. Edited by José Grosdidier de Matons. 5 vols. SC 99, 110, 114, 128, 283. Paris: Éditions du Cerf, 1964–81.

Kontakia of Romanos, Byzantine Melodist. Translated by Marjorie Carpenter. 2 vols. Columbia, MO: University of Missouri Press, 1970–73.

Sancti Romani melodi cantica: cantica dubia. Edited by Paul Maas and C. A. Trypanis Berlin: De Gruyter, 1970.

Sancti Romani melodi cantica: cantica genuina. Edited by Paul Maas and C. A. Trypanis Oxford: Clarendon Press, 1963.

On the Life of Christ: Chanted Sermons by the Great Sixth-Century Poet and Singer St Romanos. Translated by Ephrem Lash. Sacred Literature Series. Lanham, MD: AltaMira Press, 1998.

Sacred Song from the Byzantine Pulpit: Romanos the Melodist. Translated by R. J. Schork. Gainesville, FL: University Press of Florida, 1995.

The Russian Primary Chronicle: Laurentian Text. Translated and edited by Samuel Hazard Cross and Olgerd P. Sherbowitz-Wetzor. Cambridge, MA: Harvard University Press, 1973.

Sarapion of Thmuis. *Against the Manicheans*. Edited by R. P. Casey, *Serapion of Thmuis against the Manichees*. Cambridge, MA: Harvard University Press, 1931. Translated by Oliver Herbel in *Sarapion of Thmuis:* Against the Manicheans *and* Pastoral Letters, 81–134. Early Christian Studies 14. Strathfield: St Paul's Publications, 2011.

Sayings of the Desert Fathers: The Alphabetical Collection. Translated by Benedicta Ward. Kalamazoo, MI: Cistercian Publications, 1975.

Septuagint. *Septuaginta: Id est Vetus Testamentum Graece iuxta LXX interpretes*. Edited by Alfred Rahlfs. Stuttgart: Privilegierte Württembergische Bibelanstalt, 1935.

A New English Translation of the Septuagint. Translated by Albert Pietersma and Benjamin G. Wright. New York, NY: Oxford University Press, 2007.

Sticherarium. Edited by Carsten Høeg, H. J. W. Tillyard and Egon Wellesz. MMB Série Principale 1. Copenhagen: Munksgaard, 1935.

Sticherarium Ambrosianum. Edited by Lidia Perria and Jørgen Raasted. MMB Série Principale 11. Copenhagen: Munksgaard, 1992.

Suda Lexicon. Edited by Ada Adler. *Suidae Lexicon.* 5 vols. Leipzig: Teubner, 1928–38.

Symeon the Logothete. *Chronikon.* In *Symeonis Magistri et Logothetae Chronicon.* Edited by Staffan Wahlgren. Berlin: De Gruyter, 2006.

The Synaxarion of the Monastery of the Theotokos Evergetis: March–August, the Movable Cycle. Translated by Robert H. Jordan. Belfast: Belfast Byzantine Enterprises, 2005.

Theodore the Stoudite. *Letters. Theodori Studitae epistulae.* Edited by George Fatouros. Vol. 2. Berlin: De Gruyter, 1992.

    Oration on the Veneration of the Precious and Life-Giving Cross in Mid-Lent. PG 99, 692–700.

    Small Catechesis. Sancti patris nostri et confessoris Theodori Studitis praepositi Parva catechesis. Edited by Emmanuel Auvray. Paris: Apud Victorem Lecoffre, 1891.

Theophanes the Confessor. *Chronographia. Theophanis Chronographia.* Edited by Carolus de Boor. Leipzig: Teubner, 1893.

    The Chronicle of Theophanes the Confessor: Byzantine and Near East History AD *284–813.* Translated by Cyril Mango and Roger Scott. Oxford: Clarendon Press, 1997.

Triodium Athoum: Codex Monasterii Vatopedii 1488. Edited by Enrica Follieri and Oliver Strunk. MMB Série Principale 9. Copenhagen: Munksgaard, 1975.

Triodion Katanyktikon. MSS Sinai Gr. 734–735, Vat. Gr. 771, Grottaferrata Δβ I. Τριώδιον. Edited by Andrea Cunadi. Venice: de Sabio, 1522.

    Τριώδιον Κατανυκτικόν, περιέχον ἅπασαν τὴν ἀνήκουσαν αὐτῷ ἀκολουθίαν τῆς ἁγίας καὶ μεγάλης Τεσσαρακοστῆς. Rome: [n.p.], 1879.

    Τριώδιον Κατανυκτικόν. Athens: Apostoliki Diakonia, 1960.

    The Lenten Triodion. Translated by Kallistos Ware and Mother Mary, Boston, MA: Faber, 1978.

Trypanis, Constantine A. *Fourteen Early Byzantine Cantica.* Vienna: Böhlau in Kommission, 1968.

Le Typicon de la Grande Église. Edited by Juan Mateos. 2 vols. OCA 165, 166. Rome: Pontificium Institutum Orientalium Studiorum, 1962–63.

Le Typicon du monastère du Saint-Sauveur à Messine. Edited by M. Arranz. OCA 185. Rome: Pontificium Institutum Orientalium Studiorum, 1969.

Typikon of St Sabas Monastery. Edited by André Lossky in 'Le Typikon byzantin: Édition d'une version grecque partiellement ineditée: Analyse de la partie liturgique.' ThD dissertation, St Sergius Institute, 1987.

Von Christ, Wilhelm, and Matthaios Paranikas. *Anthologia graeca carminum christianorum.* Leipzig: Teubner, 1963.

Ware, Kallistos, and Mother Mary. *The Festal Menaion.* London: Faber, 1969.

Secondary Sources

Andreopoulos, Andreas. 'Mystical and Apophatic, Beyond Philosophical: A Defence of the Liturgical Reading of the Corpus Areopagiticum.' Paper presented at the Seventeenth International Conference on Patristic Studies. Oxford, 2015.

Andreou, Georgios. 'Il *Praxapostolos* bizantino dell'XI secolo: Vladimir 21/Savva 4 del Museo Storico di Mosca: edizione e commento.' PhD dissertation, Pontifical Oriental Institute, 2008.

Angold, Michael. 'The Autobiographical Impulse in Byzantium.' *DOP* 52 (1998): 52–73.

Archimandrite Vasileios. *Hymn of Entry: Liturgy and Life in the Orthodox Church.* Translated by Elizabeth Briere. New York, NY: St Vladimir's Seminary Press, 1984.

Arentzen, Thomas. *The Virgin in Song: Mary and the Poetry of Romanos the Melodist.* Philadelphia, PA: University of Pennsylvania Press, 2017.

———. 'Voices Interwoven: Refrains and Vocal Participation in the Kontakia.' *JÖB* 66 (2017): 1–10.

Arranz, Miguel. 'N. D. Uspensky: The Office of the All-Night Vigil in the Greek Church and in the Russian Church.' *St Vladimir's Theological Quarterly* 24 (1980): 83–113, 69–95.

Austin, J. L. *How to Do Things with Words.* Oxford: Clarendon Press, 1975.

Auzépy, Marie-France. 'La carrière d'André de Crète.' *BZ* 88 (1995): 1–12.

Babiniotis, George D. Λεξικό της Νέας Ελληνικής Γλώσσας [*Dictionary of the Modern Greek Language*]. Athens: Centre of Lexicology, 1998.

Baghos, Mario. 'St Basil's Eschatological Vision: Aspects of the Recapitulation of History and the Eighth Day.' *Phronema* 25 (2010): 85–103.

Bailey, Merridee L., and Katie Barclay, eds. *Emotion, Ritual and Power in Europe, 1200–1920: Family, State and Church.* Basingstoke: Palgrave, 2017.

Bakker, Michael. 'Maximus and Modern Psychology.' In *The Oxford Handbook of Maximus the Confessor*, edited by Pauline Allen and Bronwen Neil, 533–47. Oxford: Oxford University Press, 2015.

Baldovin, John F. *The Urban Character of Christian Worship: The Origins, Development and Meaning of Stational Liturgy.* OCA 228. Rome: Pontificium Institutum Studiorum Orientalium, 1987.

Balthasar, Hans Urs von. *Theo-Drama: Theological Dramatic Theory, Vol. 1: Prolegomena.* Translated by Graham Harrison. San Francisco, CA: Ignatius Press, 1988.

Bathrellos, Demetrios. 'Passions, Ascesis and the Virtues.' In *The Oxford Handbook of Maximus the Confessor*, edited by Pauline Allen and Bronwen Neil, 287–306. Oxford: Oxford University Press, 2015.

Baumstark, Anton. 'Das Typikon der Patmos-Handschrift 266 und die Altkonstantinopolitanische Gottesdienstordnung.' *Jahrbuch für Liturgiewissenschaft* 6 (1926): 98–111.

Behr, John. *Irenaeus of Lyons: Identifying Christianity.* Oxford: Oxford University Press, 2013.

———. *The Mystery of Christ: Life in Death.* Crestwood, NY: St Vladimir's Seminary Press, 2006.

Bertonière, Gabriel. *The Sundays of Lent in the Triodion: The Sundays without a Commemoration.* OCA 253. Rome: Pontificio Istituto Orientale, 1997.

Betancourt, Roland. 'Tempted to Touch: Tactility, Ritual, and Mediation in Byzantine Visuality.' *Speculum* 91, no. 3 (2016): 660–89.

Bitton-Ashkelony, Brouria. 'Penitence in Late Antique Monastic Literature.' In *Transformations of the Inner Self in Ancient Religions,* edited by Jan Assmann and Guy G. Stroumsa, 179–94. Leiden: Brill, 1999.

Blowers, Paul M. *Drama of the Divine Economy: Creator and Creation in Early Christian Theology and Piety.* Oxford: Oxford University Press, 2012.

'Gentiles of the Soul: Maximus the Confessor on the Substructure and Transformation of Human Passions.' *JECS* 4, no. 1 (1996): 57–85.

'Hope for the Possible Self: The Use and Transformation of the Human Passions in the Fathers of the *Philokalia*.' In *The Philokalia: A Classic Text of Orthodox Spirituality,* edited by Brock Bingaman and Bradley Nassif, 216–29. New York, NY: Oxford University Press, 2012.

Maximus the Confessor: Jesus Christ and the Transfiguration of the World. Oxford: Oxford University Press, 2016.

Bornert, René. *Les commentaires byzantins de la Divine Liturgie du VIIe au XVe siècle.* Paris: Institut Français d'Études Byzantines, 1966.

Bradshaw, David. *Aristotle East and West: Metaphysics and the Division of Christendom.* Cambridge: Cambridge University Press, 2004.

'The Mind and the Heart in the Christian East and West.' *Faith and Philosophy* 26, no. 5 (2009): 576–98.

Bradshaw, Paul F., and Maxwell E. Johnson. *The Origins of Feasts, Fasts and Seasons in Early Christianity.* Collegeville, MN: Liturgical Press, 2011.

Breck, John. *The Power of the Word: In the Worshiping Church.* Crestwood, NY: St Vladimir's Seminary Press, 1986.

Briscoe, James R. *Historical Anthology of Music by Women.* Bloomington, IN: Indiana University Press, 1986.

Brottier, Laurence. *Propos sur la contrition de Jean Chrysostome: le destin d'écrits de jeunesse méconnus.* Paris: Éditions du Cerf, 2010.

Brubaker, Leslie, ed. *Byzantium in the Ninth Century: Dead or Alive? Papers from the Thirtieth Spring Symposium of Byzantine Studies, Birmingham, March 1996.* Aldershot: Ashgate, 1998.

'Icons before Iconoclasm?' *Settimane di Studio del Centro Italiano di Studi sull'Alto Medioevo* 45, no. 2 (1998): 1215–54.

Brubaker, Leslie, and John Haldon. *Byzantium in the Iconoclast Era, c. 680–850: A History.* Cambridge: Cambridge University Press, 2011.

Bucur, Bogdan G. 'Exegesis of Biblical Theophanies in Byzantine Hymnography: Rewritten Bible?' *Theological Studies* 68, no. 1 (2007): 92–112.

Butler, Judith. *Gender Trouble: Feminism and the Subversion of Identity.* New York, NY: Routledge, 1990.

Bynum, Caroline Walker. *Fragmentation and Redemption: Essays on Gender and the Human Body in Medieval Religion.* New York, NY: Zone Books, 1991.

Cameron, Averil. 'Disputations, Polemical Literature and the Formation of Opinion in the Early Byzantine Period.' In *Dispute Poems and Dialogues in the Ancient and Mediaeval Near East: Forms and Types of Literary Debates in Semitic and Related Literatures*, edited by G. J. Reinink and H. L. J. Vanstiphout, 91–108. Leuven: Departement Oriëntalistiek, 1991.

Caseau, Béatrice. 'Euodia: The Use and Meaning of Fragrances in the Ancient World and their Christianization (100–900 AD).' PhD dissertation, Princeton University, 1994.

'Experiencing the Sacred.' In *Experiencing Byzantium: Papers from the 44th Spring Symposium of Byzantine Studies, Newcastle and Durham, April 2011*, edited by Claire Nesbitt and Mark Jackson, 59–77. Farnham: Ashgate, 2013.

'The Senses in Religion: Liturgy, Devotion, and Deprivation.' In *A Cultural History of the Senses in the Middle Ages, 500–1450*, edited by Richard G. Newhauser, 89–110. London: Berg Publishers, 2014.

Cholij, Roman. *Theodore the Stoudite: The Ordering of Holiness*. Oxford: Oxford University Press, 2002.

Chryssavgis, John. *Ascent to Heaven. The Theology of the Human Person according to Saint John of the Ladder*. Brookline, MA: Holy Cross Orthodox Press, 1989.

John Climacus: From the Egyptian Desert to the Sinaite Mountain. Aldershot: Ashgate, 2004.

'Κατάνυξις: Compunction as the Context for the Theology of Tears in St John Climacus.' *Κληρονομία* 17, no. 2 (1985): 131–36.

'A Spirituality of Imperfection: The Way of Tears in Saint John Climacus.' *Cistercian Studies Quarterly* 37, no. 4 (2002): 359–71.

Conomos, Dimitri E. *Byzantine Hymnography and Byzantine Chant*. Brookline, MA: Hellenic College Press, 1984.

Byzantine Trisagia and Cheroubika of the Fourteenth and Fifteenth Centuries: A Study of Late Byzantine Liturgical Chant. Thessaloniki: Patriarchal Institute for Patristic Studies, 1974.

'C. S. Lewis and Church Music.' In *Rightly Dividing the Word of Truth: Studies in Honour of Metropolitan Kallistos of Diokleia*, edited by Andreas Andreopoulos and Graham Speake, 213–34. Oxford: Peter Lang, 2016.

The Late Byzantine and Slavonic Communion Cycle: Liturgy and Music. Washington, DC: Dumbarton Oaks, 1985.

Constas, Maximos. *The Art of Seeing: Paradox and Perception in Orthodox Iconography*. Alhambra, CA: Sebastian Press, 2014.

Cooper, Adam G. *The Body in St Maximus the Confessor: Holy Flesh, Wholly Deified*. Oxford: Oxford University Press, 2005.

Holy Eros: A Liturgical Theology of the Body. Tacoma, WA: Angelico Press, 2014.

Corrigan, Kevin. *Evagrius and Gregory: Mind, Soul and Body in the 4th Century*. Farnham: Ashgate, 2009.

Costache, Doru. 'Byzantine Insights into Genesis 1–3: St Andrew of Crete's Great Canon.' *Phronema* 24 (2009): 35–50.

'Living above Gender: Insights from Saint Maximus the Confessor.' *Journal of Early Christian Studies* 21, no. 2 (2013): 261–90.

'Reading the Scriptures with Byzantine Eyes: The Hermeneutical Significance of St Andrew of Crete's Great Canon.' *Phronema* 23 (2008): 51–66.

Cunningham, Mary B. ' Andrew of Crete: A High-Style Preacher of the Eighth Century.' In *Preacher and Audience: Studies in Early Christian and Byzantine Homiletics*, edited by Mary Cunningham and Pauline Allen, 267–93. Leiden: Brill, 1998.

'Byzantine Views of God and the Universe.' In *A Companion to Byzantium*, edited by Liz James, 149–60. Chichester: Wiley-Blackwell, 2010.

'Dramatic Device or Didactic Tool? The Function of Dialogue in Byzantine Preaching.' In *Rhetoric in Byzantium: Papers from the Thirty-Fifth Spring Symposium of Byzantine Studies, Exeter College, University of Oxford, March 2001*, edited by Elizabeth Jeffreys, 101–13. Aldershot: Ashgate, 2001.

'The Impact of Pseudo-Dionysius the Areopagite on Byzantine Theologians.' In *A Celebration of Living Theology: A Festschrift in Honour of Andrew Louth*, edited by Justin A. Mihoc and Leonard Aldea, 41–58. London: Bloomsbury, 2014.

'The Reception of Romanos in Middle Byzantine Homiletics and Hymnography.' *DOP* 62 (2008): 251–60.

Dailey, Patricia. ' The Body and Its Senses.' In *The Cambridge Companion to Christian Mysticism*, edited by Amy Hollywood and Patricia Z. Beckman, 264–76. Cambridge: Cambridge University Press, 2012.

Daley, Brian. 'Finding the Right Key: The Aims and Strategies of Early Christian Interpretation of the Psalms.' In *Psalms in Community: Jewish and Christian Textual, Liturgical, and Artistic Traditions*, edited by Harold W. Attridge and Margot Elsbeth Fassler, 189–205. Leiden: Brill, 2004.

The Hope of the Early Church: A Handbook of Patristic Eschatology. Cambridge: Cambridge University Press, 1991.

Daniélou, Jean. 'Le mystère du culte dans les sermons de Saint Grégoire de Nysse.' In *Vom Christlichen Mysterium*, edited by Anton Mayer and Johannes Quasten, 76–93. Düsseldorf: Patmos-Verlag, 1951.

Davies, Stephen. 'Emotions Expressed and Aroused by Music.' In *Handbook of Music and Emotion: Theory, Research, Applications*, edited by Patrik N. Juslin and John A. Sloboda, 15–43. Oxford: Oxford University Press, 2010.

Derrida, Jacques, and Julian Wolfreys. *The Derrida Reader: Writing Performances*. Lincoln, NE: University of Nebraska Press, 1998.

Desby, Frank. 'The Modes and Tunings in Neo-Byzantine Chant.' PhD dissertation, University of Southern California, 1974.

Díaz-Vera, Javier E. 'Exploring the Relationship between Emotions, Language and Space: Construals of Awe in Medieval English Language and Pilgrimage Experience.' *Studia Neophilologica* 88 (2016): 165–89.

Dixon, Thomas. *From Passions to Emotions: The Creation of a Secular Psychological Category*. Cambridge: Cambridge University Press, 2003.

'Revolting Passions.' *Modern Theology* 27, no. 2 (2011): 298–312.

Driscoll, Michael S. 'Compunction.' In *Catholic Dictionary of Spirituality*, edited by Michael Downey, 193. Collegeville, MN: Liturgical Press, 1995.

Dubowchik, Rosemary. 'Singing with the Angels: Foundation Documents as Evidence for Musical Life in Monasteries of the Byzantine Empire.' *DOP* 56 (2002): 277–96.

Dyck, Andrew R. 'On Cassia, Κύριε ἡ ἐν πολλαῖς ...' *Byzantion* 56 (1986): 63–76.

Elsner, Jaś. 'Iconoclasm as Discourse: From Antiquity to Byzantium.' *The Art Bulletin* 94, no. 3 (2012): 368–94.

Engberg, Sysse Gudrun. 'The *Prophetologion* and the Triple-Lection Theory – the Genesis of a Liturgical Book.' *Bollettino della Badia Greca di Grottaferrata* (Series 3) 3 (2006): 67–91.

Eriksen, Uffe Holmsgaard. 'Drama in the *Kontakia* of Romanos the Melodist: A Narratological Analysis of Four Kontakia.' PhD dissertation, Aarhus University, 2013.

Essary, Kirk. 'Passions, Affections, or Emotions? On the Ambiguity of 16th-Century Terminology.' *Emotion Review* 9, no. 4 (2017): 367–74.

Fernández, Tomás. 'Byzantine Tears: A Pseudo-Chrysostomic Fragment on Weeping in the *Florilegium Coislinianum*.' In *Encyclopedic Trends in Byzantium? Proceedings of the International Conference Held in Leuven 6–8 May 2009*, edited by Peter van Deun and Caroline Macé, 125–42. Leuven: Peeters, 2011.

Florovsky, Georges. *Aspects of Church History: Volume Four in the Collected Works of Georges Florovsky*. Belmont, MA: Nordland Publishing Company, 1975.

Foskolou, Vassiliki A. 'Mary Magdalene between East and West: Cult and Image, Relics and Politics in the Late Thirteenth-Century Eastern Mediterranean.' *DOP* 65/66 (2011): 271–96.

Frank, Georgia. 'Crowds and Collective Affect in Romanos' Biblical Retellings.' In *The Garb of Being: Embodiment and the Pursuit of Holiness in Late Ancient Christianity*, edited by Georgia Frank, Susan R. Holman and Andrew S. Jacobs, 169–90. New York, NY: Fordham University Press, 2020.

'Dialogue and Deliberation: The Sensory Self in the Hymns of Romanos the Melodist.' In *Religion and the Self in Antiquity*, edited by David Brakke, M. L. Satlow and S. Wetzman, 163–79. Indianapolis, IN: Bloomington, 2005.

'The Memory Palace of Marcellinus: Athanasius and the Mirror of the Psalms.' In *Ascetic Culture: Essays in Honour of Philip Rousseau*, edited by Blake Leyerle and Robin Darling Young, 97–124. Notre Dame, IN: University of Notre Dame Press, 2013.

'Romanos and the Night Vigil in the Sixth Century.' In *Byzantine Christianity: A People's History of Christianity*, edited by Derek Krueger, 59–78. Minneapolis, MN: Fortress Press, 2006.

'Sensing Ascension in Early Byzantium.' In *Experiencing Byzantium: Papers from the 44th Spring Symposium of Byzantine Studies, Newcastle and Durham,*

April 2011, edited by Claire Nesbitt and Mark Jackson, 293–309. Farnham: Ashgate, 2013.

Frevert, Ute. 'Defining Emotions: Concepts and Debates over Three Centuries.' In *Emotional Lexicons: Continuity and Change in the Vocabulary of Feeling 1700–2000*, edited by Ute Frevert et al., 1–31. Oxford: Oxford University Press, 2014.

Frøyshov, Stig Simeon Ragnvald. 'The Early Development of the Liturgical Eight-Mode System in Jerusalem.' *St Vladimir's Theological Quarterly* 51 (2007): 139–78.

'The Georgian Witness to the Jerusalem Liturgy: New Sources and Studies.' In *Inquiries into Eastern Christian Worship: Selected Papers of the Second International Congress of the Society of Oriental Liturgies, Rome, 17–21 September 2008*, edited by Bert Groen, Steven Hawkes-Teeples and Stefanos Alexopoulos, 227–67. Leuven: Peeters, 2012.

Gador-Whyte, Sarah. 'Rhetoric and Ideas in the Kontakia of Romanos the Melodist.' PhD dissertation, University of Melbourne, 2011.

Theology and Poetry in Early Byzantium: The Kontakia *of Romanos the Melodist*. Cambridge: Cambridge University Press, 2017.

Galadza, Daniel. 'Greek Liturgy in Crusader Jerusalem: Witnesses of Liturgical Life at the Holy Sepulchre and St Sabas Lavra.' *Journal of Medieval History* 43, no. 4 (2017): 421–37.

Liturgy and Byzantinization in Jerusalem. Oxford: Oxford University Press, 2017.

'"Open your Mouth and Attract the Spirit": St Theodore Stoudite and Participation in the Icon of Worship.' In *Church Music and Icons: Proceedings of the Fifth International Conference on Orthodox Church Music, University of Eastern Finland, Joensuu, Finland, 3–9 June 2013*, edited by Ivan Moody and Maria Takala-Roszczenko, 441–55. Joensuu: International Society of Orthodox Church Music, 2015.

Gavrilyuk, Paul L. 'Florovsky's Neopatristic Synthesis and the Future Ways of Orthodox Theology.' In *Orthodox Constructions of the West*, edited by George E. Demacopoulos and Aristotle Papanikolaou, 102–24. New York, NY: Fordham University Press, 2013.

Gertsman, Elina, ed. *Crying in the Middle Ages: Tears of History*. Abingdon: Routledge, 2011.

Getcha, Job. *The Typikon Decoded: An Explanation of Byzantine Liturgical Practice*. Yonkers, NY: St Vladimir's Seminary Press, 2012.

Giannouli, Antonia. 'Catanyctic Religious Poetry: A Survey.' In *Theologica Minora: The Minor Genres of Byzantine Theological Literature*, edited by Antonio Rigo, Pavel Ermilov and Michele Trizio, 86–109. Turnhout: Brepols, 2013.

Die Beiden Byzantinischen Kommentare zum Großen Kanon des Andreas von Kreta: Eine Quellenkritische und Literarhistorische Studie. Vienna: Verlag der Österreichischen Akademie der Wissenschaften, 2007.

'Die Tränen der Zerknirschung. Zur katanyktischen Kirchendichtung als Heilmittel.' In *'Doux remède ...' Poésie et poétique à Byzance. Actes du Quatrième Colloque International Philologique 'EPMHNEIA' Paris, 23–24–25 février 2006 organisé par l'E.H.E.S.S. et l'Université de Chypre*, edited by Paolo Odorico, Panagiotis A. Agapitos and Martin Hinterberger, 141–55. Paris: Centre d'études byzantines, néo-helléniques et sud-est européennes, 2009.

Golitzin, Alexander. *Mystagogy: A Monastic Reading of Dionysius Areopagita.* Edited by Bogdan G. Bucur. Collegeville, MN: Liturgical Press, 2013.

Grosdidier de Matons, José. 'Liturgie et hymnographie: kontakion et canon.' *DOP* 34/35 (1980–81): 31–43.

Romanos le Mélode et les origines de la poésie religieuse à Byzance. Paris: Beauchesne, 1977.

Gross, Daniel M. *The Secret History of Emotion: From Aristotle's Rhetoric to Modern Brain Science.* Chicago, IL: University of Chicago Press, 2006.

Haldon, John F. *Byzantium in the Seventh Century: The Transformation of a Culture.* Cambridge: Cambridge University Press, 1990.

Hannick, Christian. 'The Theotokos in Byzantine Hymnography: Typology and Allegory.' In *Images of the Mother of God: Perceptions of the Theotokos in Byzantium*, edited by Maria Vassilaki, 69–76. Aldershot: Ashgate, 2005.

Harkianakis, Archbishop Stylianos. *On Prayer.* Athens: Armos, 1999.

Harl, Marguerite. 'Les origines grecques du mot et de la notion de "componction" dans la Septante et chez ses Commentateurs.' *Revue des Études Augustiniennes* 32 (1986): 3–21.

Harris, Oliver J. T., and Tim Flohr Sørensen. 'Rethinking Emotion and Material Culture.' *Archaeological Dialogues* 17, no. 2 (2010): 145–63.

Harrison, Carol. *The Art of Listening in the Early Church.* Oxford: Oxford University Press, 2013.

'Augustine and the Art of Music.' In *Resonant Witness: Conversations between Music and Theology*, edited by Jeremy S. Begbie and Steven R. Guthrie, 27–45. Grand Rapids, MI: Eerdmans, 2011.

'Enchanting the Soul: The Music of the Psalms.' In *Meditations of the Heart: The Psalms in Early Christian Thought and Practice. Essays in Honour of Andrew Louth*, edited by Andreas Andreopoulos, Augustine Casiday and Carol Harrison, 205–24. Turnhout: Brepols, 2011.

Harrison, Verna E. F. 'Male and Female in Cappadocian Theology.' *Journal of Theological Studies* 41, no. 2 (1990): 441–71.

Harvey, Susan Ashbrook. *Scenting Salvation: Ancient Christianity and the Olfactory Imagination.* Berkeley, CA: California University Press, 2006.

'2000 NAPS Presidential Address. Spoken Words, Voiced Silence: Biblical Women in Syriac Tradition.' *JECS* 9, no. 1 (2001): 105–31.

'Why the Perfume Mattered: The Sinful Woman in Syriac Exegetical Tradition.' In *In Dominico Eloquio/In Lordly Eloquence: Essays on Patristic Exegesis in Honour of Robert Louis Wilken*, edited by Paul M. Blowers, 69–89. Grand Rapids, MI: Eerdmans, 2002.

Hatfield, Elaine, Megan Carpenter and Richard L. Rapson. 'Emotional Contagion as a Precursor to Collective Emotions.' In *Collective Emotions*, edited by Christian von Scheve and Mikko Salmela, 108–22. Oxford: Oxford University Press, 2014.

Hausherr, Irénée. *Penthos: The Doctrine of Compunction in the Christian East.* Kalamazoo, MI: Cistercian Publications, 1982.

Hemmerdinger-Iliadou, Démocratie. 'Éphrem Grec.' In *Dictionnaire de Spiritualité, Vol. 4,* 800–15. Paris: Beauchesne, 1960.

Hinterberger, Martin. 'Autobiography and Hagiography in Byzantium.' *Symbolae Osloenses: Norwegian Journal of Greek and Latin Studies* 75, no. 1 (2000): 139–64.

'Emotions in Byzantium.' In *A Companion to Byzantium*, edited by Liz James, 123–34. Chichester: Wiley-Blackwell, 2010.

'Tränen in der Byzantinischen Literatur. Ein Beitrag zur Geschichte der Emotionen.' *JÖB* 56 (2006): 27–51.

Hollingsworth, Paul A., and Anthony Cutler. 'Iconoclasm.' In *ODB*, 975–77.

Hunt, Hannah. *Joy-Bearing Grief: Tears of Contrition in the Writings of the Early Syrian and Byzantine Fathers.* Leiden: Brill, 2004.

'The Monk as Mourner: St Isaac the Syrian & Monastic Identity in the 7th C. & Beyond.' In *Orthodox Monasticism Past and Present*, edited by John A. McGuckin, 331–42. Piscataway, NJ: Gorgias Press, 2015.

'The Tears of the Sinful Woman: A Theology of Redemption in the Homilies of St Ephraim and His Followers.' *Hugoye: Journal of Syriac Studies* 1, no. 2 (1998): 165–84.

James, Liz, ed. *Women, Men, and Eunuchs: Gender in Byzantium.* New York, NY: Routledge, 1997.

Jansen, Katherine Ludwig. *The Making of the Magdalen: Preaching and Popular Devotion in the Later Middle Ages.* Princeton, NJ: Princeton University Press, 2000.

Jeffreys, Elizabeth M. 'Kontakion.' In *ODB*, 1148.

'Sticheron.' In *ODB*, 1956.

'Troparion.' In *ODB*, 2124.

Jensen, Robin M. *The Cross: History, Art, and Controversy.* Cambridge, MA: Harvard University Press, 2017.

Juslin, Patrik N., László Harmat and Tuomas Eerol. 'What Makes Music Emotionally Significant? Exploring the Underlying Mechanisms.' *Psychology of Music* 42, no. 4 (2014): 599–623.

Kaldellis, Anthony. 'The Making of Hagia Sophia and the Last Pagans of New Rome.' *Journal of Late Antiquity* 6, no. 2 (2013): 347–66.

Kartsonis, Anna. 'The Responding Icon.' In *Heaven on Earth: Art and the Church in Byzantium*, edited by Linda Saffran, 58–80. University Park, PA: Pennsylvania State University Press, 1998.

Kaster, Robert. *Emotion, Restraint and Community in Ancient Rome.* Oxford: Oxford University Press, 2005.

Kazhdan, Alexander P. 'Germanos I.' In *ODB*, 846.

A History of Byzantine Literature (650–850). Athens: National Hellenic Research Foundation, 1999.

Kazhdan, Alexander P., and Anthony Cutler. 'Emotions.' In *ODB*, 691–92.

Kazhdan, Alexander P., and Elizabeth Jeffreys. 'Ekphrasis.' In *ODB*, 683.

Knight, Kimberley-Joy. '*Si puose calcina a' propi occhi*: The Importance of the Gift of Tears for Thirteenth-Century Religious Women and Their Hagiographers.' In *Crying in the Middle Ages: Tears of History*, edited by Elina Gertsman, 136–55. New York, NY: Routledge, 2012.

Knuuttila, Simo. *Emotions in Ancient and Medieval Philosophy*. Oxford: Clarendon, 2004.

Koder, Johannes. 'Imperial Propaganda in the *Kontakia* of Romanos the Melode.' *DOP* 62 (2008): 275–91.

Konstan, David. *The Emotions of the Ancient Greeks: Studies in Aristotle and Classical Literature*. London: University of Toronto Press, 2006.

'Rhetoric and Emotion.' In *A Companion to Greek Rhetoric*, edited by Ian Worthington, 411–25. Oxford: Blackwell Publishing, 2007.

Krans, Jan, and Joseph Verheyden, eds. *Patristic and Text-Critical Studies: The Collected Essays of William L. Petersen*. Leiden: Brill, 2012.

Krueger, Derek. 'Liturgical Instruction and Theories of Singing in Middle Byzantine Monasticism: From Constantinople to Athos.' Paper presented at Spatialities of Byzantine Culture, Uppsala University, 18–21 May 2017.

Liturgical Subjects: Christian Ritual, Biblical Narrative and the Formation of Self in Byzantium. Philadelphia, PA: University of Pennsylvania Press, 2014.

'Liturgical Time and Holy Land Reliquaries in Early Byzantium.' In *Saints and Sacred Matter: The Cult of Relics in Byzantium and Beyond*, edited by Cynthia Hahn and Holger A. Klein, 111–32. Washington, DC: Dumbarton Oaks Research Library and Collection, 2015.

'Romanos the Melodist and the Early Christian Self.' In *Proceedings of the 21st International Congress of Byzantine Studies: London, 21–26 August 2006*, edited by Elizabeth Jeffreys, 255–74. Aldershot: Ashgate, 2006.

'Scripture and Liturgy in the *Life of Mary of Egypt*.' In *Education and Religion in Late Antique Christianity: Reflections, Social Contexts and Genres*, edited by Peter Gemeinhardt, Lieve van Hoof and Peter van Nuffelen, 131–41. New York, NY: Routledge, 2016.

'The Transmission of Liturgical Joy in Byzantine Hymns for Easter.' In *Prayer and Worship in Eastern Christianities, 5th to 11th Centuries*, edited by Brouria Bitton-Ashkelony and Derek Krueger, 132–50. New York, NY: Routledge, 2017.

Writing and Holiness: The Practice of Authorship in the Early Christian East. Philadelphia, PA: University of Pennsylvania Press, 2004.

Lampe, G. W. H. *Patristic Greek Lexicon*. Oxford: Clarendon Press, 1961.

Largier, Niklaus. 'Inner Senses–Outer Senses: The Practice of Emotions in Medieval Mysticism.' In *Codierungen von Emotionen im Mittelalter/Emotions and Sensibilities in the Middle Ages*, edited by C. Stephen Jaeger and Ingrid Kasten, 3–15. Berlin: De Gruyter, 2003.

'Medieval Mysticism.' In *The Oxford Handbook of Religion and Emotion*, edited by John Corrigan, 364–79. Oxford: Oxford University Press, 2008.

'The Plasticity of the Soul: Mystical Darkness, Touch, and Aesthetic Experience.' *MLN* 125, no. 3 (2010): 536–51.

Larin, Vassa. '"Active Participation" of the Faithful in Byzantine Liturgy.' *St Vladimir's Theological Quarterly* 57, no. 1 (2013): 67–88.

Lauxtermann, Marc D. *Byzantine Poetry from Pisides to Geometres: Text and Context.* Vienna: Verlag der Österreichischen Akademie der Wissenschaften, 2003.

'Three Biographical Notes.' *BZ* 91 (1998): 391–405.

Leduc, Francis. 'Penthos et larmes dans l'œuvre de Saint Jean Chrysostome.' *Proche-Orient Chrétien* 41 (1991): 220–57.

Levy, Kenneth, and Christian Troelsgård. 'Byzantine Chant.' In *The New Grove Dictionary of Music and Musicians*, edited by S. Sadie and J. Tyrell, Vol. 4: 734–56. London: Macmillan, 2001.

Liddell, H. G., and R. Scott. *A Greek–English Lexicon.* Oxford: Clarendon Press, 1996.

An Intermediate Greek–English Lexicon. Oxford: Clarendon Press, 2002.

Lingas, Alexander. 'From Earth to Heaven: The Changing Musical Soundscape of the Byzantine Liturgy.' In *Experiencing Byzantium: Papers from the 44th Spring Symposium of Byzantine Studies, Newcastle and Durham, April 2011*, edited by Claire Nesbitt and Mark Jackson, 311–58. Farnham: Ashgate, 2013.

'How Musical Was the "Sung Office"? Some Observations on the Ethos of the Byzantine Cathedral Rite.' In *The Traditions of Orthodox Music: Proceedings of the First International Conference on Orthodox Church Music, University of Joensuu, Finland, 13–19 June 2005*, edited by Ivan Moody and Maria Takala-Roszczenko, 217–34. Joensuu: International Society for Orthodox Church Music, 2007.

'Hymnography.' In *The Encyclopedia of Greece and the Hellenic Tradition*, edited by G. Speake. Vol. 1, 786–87. Chicago, IL: Fitzroy-Dearborn, 2000.

'The Liturgical Place of the *Kontakion* in Constantinople.' In *Liturgy, Architecture and Art of the Byzantine World: Papers of the XVIII International Byzantine Congress (Moscow, 8–15 August 1991) and Other Essays Dedicated to the Memory of Fr John Meyendorff*, edited by C. C. Akentiev, 50–57. St Petersburg: Vizantinorossika, 1995.

'Medieval Byzantine Chant and the Sound of Orthodoxy.' In *Byzantine Orthodoxies: Papers from the Thirty-Sixth Spring Symposium of Byzantine Studies, University of Durham, 23–25 March 2002*, edited by Andrew Louth and Augustine Casiday, 131–50. Aldershot: Ashgate, 2006.

'Music.' In *Encyclopedia of Ancient Greece*, edited by Nigel Wilson, 484–86. New York, NY: Routledge, 2010.

'Performance Practice and the Politics of Transcribing Byzantine Chant.' *Acta Musicae Byzantinae* 6 (2003): 56–76.

'Sunday Matins in the Byzantine Cathedral Rite: Music and Liturgy.' PhD dissertation, University of British Columbia, 1996.

Lossky, Nicolas. *Essai sur une théologie de la musique liturgique.* Paris: Éditions du Cerf, 2003.

Lossky, Vladimir. *Essai sur la théologie mystique de l'Église d'Orient.* Aubier: Éditions Montaigne, 1944.

Louth, Andrew. 'Byzantium Transforming (600–700).' In *The Cambridge History of the Byzantine Empire c. 500–1492*, edited by Jonathan Shepard, 221–48. Cambridge: Cambridge University Press, 2008.

'Christian Hymnography from Romanos the Melodist to John Damascene.' *JECS* 57 (2005): 195–206.

Denys the Areopagite. London: Continuum, 1989.

'The Ecclesiology of Saint Maximus the Confessor.' *International Journal for the Study of the Christian Church* 4, no. 2 (2004): 109–20.

'Justinian and His Legacy.' In *The Cambridge History of the Byzantine Empire c. 500–1492*, edited by Jonathan Shepard, 99–129. Cambridge: Cambridge University Press, 2008.

'Mystagogy in Saint Maximus.' In *Seeing through the Eyes of Faith: New Approaches to the Mystagogy of the Church Fathers*, edited by Paul Van Geest, 375–88. Leuven: Peeters, 2016.

'Pagan Theurgy and Christian Sacramentalism in Denys the Areopagite.' *Journal of Theological Studies* 37, no. 2 (1986): 432–38.

St John Damascene: Tradition and Originality in Byzantine Theology. New York, NY: Oxford University Press, 2002.

Louw, Johannes P., and Eugene A. Nida. *Greek–English Lexicon of the New Testament: Based on Semantic Domains*. New York, NY: United Bible Societies, 1988.

Lust, Johann, Erik Eynikel and Katrin Hauspie. *A Greek–English Lexicon of the Septuagint*. Stuttgart: Deutsche Bibelgesellschaft, 1992.

Luzzi, Andrea. 'Synaxaria and the Synaxarion of Constantinople.' In *The Ashgate Research Companion to Byzantine Hagiography. Volume 2: Genres and Contexts*, edited by Stephanos Efthymiadis, 197–210. Farnham: Ashgate, 2014.

Maas, Michael. 'Roman Questions, Byzantine Answers: Contours of the Age of Justinian.' In *The Cambridge Companion to the Age of Justinian*, edited by Michael Maas, 3–27. Cambridge: Cambridge University Press, 2005.

Maguire, Henry. *Art and Eloquence in Byzantium*. Princeton, NJ: Princeton University Press, 1981.

Manolopoulou, Vicky. 'Processing Emotion: Litanies in Byzantine Constantinople.' In *Experiencing Byzantium: Papers from the 44th Spring Symposium of Byzantine Studies, Newcastle and Durham, April 2011*, edited by Claire Nesbitt and Mark Jackson, 153–71. Farnham: Ashgate, 2013.

Marinis, Vasileios. 'The *Historia Ekklesiastike kai Mystike Theoria*: A Symbolic Understanding of the Byzantine Church Building.' *BZ* 108, no. 2 (2015): 753–70.

Mathews, Thomas F. *The Clash of Gods: A Reinterpretation of Early Christian Art*. Princeton, NJ: Princeton University Press, 1999.

The Early Churches of Constantinople: Architecture and Liturgy. University Park, PA: Pennsylvania State University Press, 1971.

McEntire, Sandra J. *The Doctrine of Compunction in Medieval England: Holy Tears*. Lewiston: The Edwin Mellen Press, 1990.

McGinn, Bernard. '*Unio Mystica*/ Mystical Union.' In *The Cambridge Companion to Christian Mysticism*, edited by Amy Hollywood and Patricia Z. Beckman, 200–10. Cambridge: Cambridge University Press.

McGuckin, John A. 'Eschatological Horizons in the Cappadocian Fathers.' In *Apocalyptic Thought in Early Christianity*, edited by Robert J. Daley, 193–210. Grand Rapids, MI: Baker Academic, 2009.

'Poetry and Hymnography (2): The Greek World.' In *The Oxford Handbook of Early Christian Studies*, edited by Susan Ashbrook Harvey and David G. Hunter, 641–56. Oxford: Oxford University Press, 2008.

McKinnon, James, ed. *Music in Early Christian Literature*. Cambridge: Cambridge University Press, 1987.

McNamer, Sarah. *Affective Meditation and the Invention of Medieval Compassion*. Philadelphia, PA: University of Pennsylvania Press, 2010.

'Feeling.' In *Oxford Twenty-First Century Approaches to Literature: Middle English*, edited by Paul Strohm, 241–57. Oxford: Oxford University Press, 2007.

'The Literariness of Literature and the History of Emotion.' *PMLA* 130, no. 5 (2015): 1433–42.

Mellas, Andrew. 'Tears of Compunction in John Chrysostom's *On Eutropius*.' *Studia Patristica* 83 (2017): 159–72.

Meyendorff, John. *Byzantine Theology: Historical Trends and Doctrinal Themes*. New York, NY: Fordham University Press, 1983.

Imperial Unity and Christian Divisions. Crestwood, NY: St Vladimir's Seminary Press, 1989.

Miller, James. '"Let Us Sing to the Lord": The Biblical Odes in the Codex Alexandrinus.' PhD dissertation, Marquette University, 2006.

'The Prophetologion: The Old Testament of Byzantine Christianity?' In *The Old Testament in Byzantium*, edited by Paul Magdalino and Robert Nelson, 55–76. Washington, DC: Dumbarton Oaks, 2010.

Moller, Herbert. 'Affective Mysticism in Western Civilization.' *Psychoanalytic Review* 52, no. 2 (1965): 115–30.

Moore, Sophie V. 'Experiencing Mid-Byzantine Mortuary Practice: Shrouding the Dead.' In *Experiencing Byzantium: Papers from the 44th Spring Symposium of Byzantine Studies, Newcastle and Durham, April 2011*, edited by Claire Nesbitt and Mark Jackson, 195–212. Farnham: Ashgate, 2013.

Moran, Neil. 'The Choir of Hagia Sophia.' *Oriens Christianus* 89 (2005): 1–7.

Muraoka, T. *A Greek–English Lexicon of the Septuagint*. Leuven: Peeters, 2009.

Nagy, Piroska. *Le don des larmes au Moyen Âge. Un instrument en quête d' institution (V^e–XIIIe siècle)*. Paris: Albin Michel, 2000.

Nave, Guy D., Jr. *The Role and Function of Repentance in Luke–Acts*. Leiden: Brill, 2002.

Neil, Bronwen, and Lynda Garland, eds. *Questions of Gender in Byzantine Society*. Farnham: Ashgate, 2013.

Nellas, Panayiotis. *Deification in Christ: The Nature of the Human Person*. Translated by Norman Russell. New York, NY: St Vladimir's Seminary Press, 1997.

'The Mother of God and Theocentric Humanism.' In *Synaxis. Volume I: Anthropology, Environment, Creation*, edited by John Hadjinicolaou and translated by Liadain Sherrard, 129–40. Montreal: Alexander Press, 2006.

Nelson, Robert S. 'To Say and to See: Ekphrasis and Vision in Byzantium.' In *Visuality before and beyond the Renaissance: Seeing as Others Saw*, edited by Robert S. Nelson, 143–68. Cambridge: Cambridge University Press, 2000.

Nesbitt, Claire. 'Shaping the Sacred: Light and the Experience of Worship in Middle Byzantine Churches.' *Byzantine and Modern Greek Studies* 36, no. 2 (2012): 139–60.

Nesbitt, Claire, and Mark Jackson. 'Experiencing Byzantium.' In *Experiencing Byzantium: Papers from the 44th Spring Symposium of Byzantine Studies, Newcastle and Durham, April 2011*, edited by Claire Nesbitt and Mark Jackson, 1–16. Farnham: Ashgate, 2013.

Neu, Jerome. *A Tear Is an Intellectual Thing: The Meanings of Emotion*. New York, NY: Oxford University Press, 2000.

Nussbaum, Martha C. *The Therapy of Desire: Theory and Practice in Hellenistic Ethics*. Princeton, NJ: Princeton University Press, 2009.

Upheavals of Thought: The Intelligence of Emotions. Cambridge: Cambridge University Press, 2001.

Olkinuora, Jaakko. *Byzantine Hymnography for the Feast of the Entrance of the Theotokos: An Intermedial Approach*. Helsinki: Suomen patristinen seura ry, 2015.

'Revisiting the Great Canon by Andrew of Crete.' In *Proceedings of the 2016 International Congress of the Society of Oriental Liturgy in Armenia*, forthcoming.

Pantelakis, Emmanuel. 'Τα Σιναΐτικα χειρόγραφα των λειτουργικών βιβλίων της Ορθοδόξου Εκκλησίας [The Sinaite Manuscripts of the Liturgical Books of the Orthodox Church].' Δελτίον Χριστιανικής Αρχαιολογικής Εταιρείας 2 (1933): 129–57.

Papalexandrou, Amy. 'The Memory Culture of Byzantium.' In *A Companion to Byzantium*, edited by Liz James, 108–22. Chichester: Wiley-Blackwell, 2010.

'Perceptions of Sound and Sonic Environment across the Byzantine Acoustic Horizon.' In *Knowing Bodies, Passionate Souls: Sense Perceptions in Byzantium*, edited by Susan Ashbrook Harvey and Margaret Mullett, 67–85. Washington DC: Dumbarton Oaks Research Library and Collection, 2017.

Papanikolaou, Aristotle, and George E. Demacopoulos. 'Augustine and the Orthodox: The "West" in the East.' In *Orthodox Readings of Augustine*, edited by Aristotle Papanikolaou and George E. Demacopoulos, 11–40. Crestwood, NY: St Vladimir's Seminary Press, 2008.

Parpulov, Georgi R. 'Psalters and Personal Piety in Byzantium.' In *The Old Testament in Byzantium*, edited by Paul Magdalino and Robert Nelson, 77–105. Washington, DC: Dumbarton Oaks, 2010.

Patton, Kimberley Christine. '"Howl, Weep and Moan, and Bring it Back to God": Holy Tears in Eastern Christianity.' In *Holy Tears: Weeping in the*

Religious Imagination, edited by Kimberley Christine Patton and John Stratton Hawley, 255–73. Princeton, NJ: Princeton University Press, 2005.

Patton, Kimberley Christine, and John Stratton Hawley. *Holy Tears: Weeping in the Religious Imagination*. Princeton, NJ: Princeton University Press, 2005.

Pelikan, Jaroslav. *The Christian Tradition. A History of the Development of Doctrine, 2: The Spirit of Eastern Christendom (600–1700)*. Chicago, IL: University of Chicago Press, 1974.

———. *Imago Dei: The Byzantine Apologia for Icons*. Princeton, NJ: Princeton University Press, 2011.

———. *Mary through the Centuries: Her Place in the History of Culture*. New Haven, CT: Yale University Press, 1996.

———. 'The Odyssey of Dionysian Spirituality.' In *Pseudo-Dionysius: The Complete Works*. Translated by Colm Luibhéid and Paul Rorem, 11–24. New York, NY: Paulist Press, 1987.

Peltomaa, Leena Mari. 'Hymnography, Byzantine.' In *The Encyclopedia of Ancient History*, edited by Roger S. Bagnall, Kai Brodersen, Craige B. Champion, Andrew Erskine and Sabine R. Huebner, 3363. Malden: Wiley-Blackwell 2013.

Pentcheva, Bissera V., ed. *Aural Architecture in Byzantium: Music, Acoustics, and Ritual*. New York, NY: Routledge, 2017.

———. 'Hagia Sophia and Multisensory Aesthetics.' *Gesta: International Centre for Medieval Art* 50, no. 2 (2011): 93–111.

———. *Hagia Sophia: Sound, Space and Spirit in Byzantium*. Pennsylvania, PA: Pennsylvania State University Press, 2017.

———. 'Performing the Sacred in Byzantium: Image, Breath and Sound.' *Performance Research* 19, no. 3 (2014): 120–28.

———. *The Sensual Icon: Space, Ritual, and the Senses in Byzantium*. Pennsylvania, PA: Pennsylvania State University Press, 2010.

Pentiuc, Eugen J. *The Old Testament in Eastern Orthodox Tradition*. Oxford: Oxford University Press, 2014.

Petersen, William L. *The Diatessaron and Ephrem Syrus as Sources of Romanos the Melodist*. CSCO 475. Leuven: Peeters, 1985.

Pitra, J. B. *Analecta sacra Spicilegio Solesmeni parata. Vol. 1*. Paris: Jouby et Roger, 1876.

Pizzone, Aglae, ed. *The Author in Middle Byzantine Literature: Modes Functions and Identities*. Berlin: De Gruyter, 2014.

Plamper, Jan. *The History of Emotions: An Introduction*. Translated by Keith Tribe. Oxford: Oxford University Press, 2015.

Pott, Thomas. *Byzantine Liturgical Reform: A Study of Liturgical Change in the Byzantine Tradition*. Translated by Paul Meyendorff. Crestwood, NY: St Vladimir's Seminary Press, 2010.

Purpura, Ashley. 'Beyond the Binary: Hymnographic Constructions of Orthodox Gender Identities.' *Journal of Religion* 97, no. 4 (2017): 524–46.

Quasten, Johannes. *Music and Worship in Pagan and Christian Antiquity*. Translated by Ramsay Boniface. Washington, DC: National Association of Pastoral Musicians, 1983.

Quinlan, Andrew John. *Sin. Gr. 734–735. Triodion. Excerpta ex Dissertatione ad Doctorum*. Newberry Springs, CA: Pontificium Institutum Orientalium, 2004.

Raasted, Jørgen. 'Voice and Verse in a Troparion of Cassia.' *Studies in Eastern Chant, Vol. 3*, edited by Miloš Velimirović, 171–78. London: Oxford University Press, 1973.

'Zur Melodie des Kontakions Ἡ παρθένος σήμερον.' *Cahiers de l'Institut du Moyen-Âge Grec et Latin* 59 (1989): 233–46.

Ramelli, Ilaria. 'Tears of Pathos, Repentance and Bliss: Crying and Salvation in Origen and Gregory of Nyssa.' In *Tears in the Graeco-Roman World*, edited by Thorsten Fögen, 367–96. Berlin: De Gruyter, 2009.

Rapp, Claudia. 'Literary Culture under Justinian.' In *The Cambridge Companion to the Age of Justinian*, edited by Michael Maas, 376–97. Cambridge: Cambridge University Press, 2005.

Ray, Walter D. *Tasting Heaven on Earth: Worship in Sixth-Century Constantinople*. Grand Rapids, MI: Eerdmans, 2012.

Reddy, William M. *The Navigation of Feeling: A Framework for the History of Emotions*. Cambridge: Cambridge University Press, 2001.

Richter, Lukas. 'Antike Überlieferungen in der Byzantinischen Musiktheorie.' *Acta Musicologica* 70, no. 2 (1998): 133–208.

Riehle, Alexander. 'Authorship and Gender (and) Identity. Women's Writing in the Middle Byzantine Period.' In *The Author in Middle Byzantine Literature: Modes Functions and Identities*, edited by Aglae Pizzone, 245–62. Berlin: De Gruyter, 2014.

Rochow, Ilse. *Studien zu der Person, den Werken und dem Nachleben der Dichterin Kassia*. Berlin: Akademie-Verlag, 1967.

Rosaldo, Renato. 'Grief and the Headhunter's Rage.' In *Text, Play and Story: The Construction and Reconstruction of Self and Society*, edited by Stuart Plattner and Edward Bruner, 178–98. Washington, DC: American Ethnological Society, 1984.

Rosenwein, Barbara H. *Emotional Communities in the Early Middle Ages*. Ithaca, NY: Cornell University Press, 2006.

Runciman, Steven. *The Last Byzantine Renaissance*. Cambridge: Cambridge University Press, 1970.

'Women in Byzantine Aristocratic Society.' In *The Byzantine Aristocracy: IX to XIII Centuries*, edited by Michael Angold, 10–22. Oxford: British Archaeological Reports, 1984.

Rydén, Lennart. 'The Bride-Shows at the Byzantine Court – History or Fiction?' *Eranos* 83 (1985): 175–91.

Saradi, Helen G. 'Space in Byzantine Thought.' In *Architecture as Icon: Perception and Representation of Architecture in Byzantine Art*, edited by Slobodan Ćurčić and Evangelia Hadjitryphonos, 73–112. New Haven, CT: Yale University Press, 2010.

Schechner, Richard, and Willa Appel. *By Means of Performance: Intercultural Studies of Theatre and Ritual.* Cambridge: Cambridge University Press, 1990.

Scheer, Monique. 'Are Emotions a Kind of Practice (and Is That What Makes Them Have a History)? A Bourdieuian Approach to Understanding Emotion.' *History and Theory* 51, no. 2 (2012): 193–220.

Schibille, Nadine. *Hagia Sophia and the Byzantine Aesthetic Experience.* Farnham: Ashgate, 2014.

Schieffelin, Edward L. 'Performance and the Cultural Construction of Reality.' *American Ethnologist* 12, no. 4 (1985): 707–24.

Searle, John R. *Speech Acts: An Essay in the Philosophy of Language.* London: Cambridge University Press, 1969.

Sheldrake, Philip. 'Mysticism: Critical Theological Perspectives.' In *Blackwell Companion to Christian Mysticism*, edited by Julia Lamm, 531–49. Oxford: Wiley-Blackwell, 2012.

Silvas, Anna M. 'Kassia la Melode e il suo uso delle Scritture.' In *Fra Oriente e Occidente: donne e Bibbia nell' alto Medioevo (secoli VI–XI): greci, latini, ebrei, arabi*, edited by Franca Ela Consolino and Judith Herrin, 53–68. Trapani: Il Pozzo di Giacobbe, 2015.

'Kassia the Nun c. 810–c. 865: An Appreciation.' In *Byzantine Women: Varieties of Experience AD 800–1200*, edited by Lynda Garland, 17–39. Aldershot: Ashgate, 2006.

Smith, J. Warren. *Passion and Paradise: Human and Divine Emotion in the Thought of Gregory of Nyssa.* New York, NY: The Crossroad Publishing Company, 2004.

Sorabji, Richard. *Emotion and Peace of Mind: From Stoic Agitation to Christian Temptation.* New York, NY: Oxford University Press, 2002.

Špidlík, Tomáš. *La spiritualité de l'Orient chrétien.* Roma: Pontificium Institutum Orientalium Studiorum, 1978.

Spyrakou, Evangelia C. Οἱ Χοροὶ τῶν Ψαλτῶν κατὰ τὴν Βυζαντινὴ Παράδοση [*Singers' Choirs according to the Byzantine Tradition*]. Institute of Byzantine Musicology Studies, 14. Athens: University of Athens, 2008.

Stearns, Carol Z., and Peter N. Stearns. 'Emotionology: Clarifying the History of Emotions and Emotional Standards.' *The American Historical Review* 90, no. 4 (1985): 813–36.

Stewart, Columba. 'Evagrius Ponticus and the Eastern Monastic Tradition on the Intellect and the Passions.' *Modern Theology* 27, no. 2 (2011): 263–75.

'Evagrius Ponticus and the "Eight Generic *Logismoi*."' In *In the Garden of Evil: The Vices and Culture in the Middle Ages*, edited by Richard Newhauser, 3–34. Toronto: Pontifical Institute of Medieval Studies, 2005.

Suter, Ann. 'Tragic Tears and Gender.' In *Tears in the Graeco-Roman World*, edited by Thorsten Fögen, 59–83. Berlin: De Gruyter, 2009.

Taft, Robert F. *The Byzantine Rite: A Short History.* Collegeville, MN: The Liturgical Press, 1992.

'Christian Liturgical Psalmody: Origins, Development, Decomposition, Collapse.' In *Psalms in Community: Jewish and Christian Textual, Liturgical, and*

Artistic Traditions, edited by Harold W. Attridge and Margot Elsbeth Fassler, 7–32. Leiden: Brill, 2004.

'Commentaries.' In *ODB*, 488–89.

The Great Entrance: A History of the Transfer of Gifts and Other Preanaphoral Rites of the Liturgy of St John Chrysostom. OCA 200. Rome: Pontificium Institutum Orientalium Studiorum, 1978.

'Is the Liturgy Described in the *Mystagogia* of Maximus Confessor Byzantine, Palestinian, or Neither?' *Bollettino della Badia Greca di Grottaferrata* 8 (2011): 233–70.

'The Liturgy of the Great Church: An Initial Synthesis of Structure and Interpretation on the Eve of Iconoclasm.' *DOP* 34/35 (1980–81): 45–75.

The Liturgy of the Hours in East and West: The Origins of the Divine Office and Its Meaning for Today. Collegeville, MN: Liturgical Press, 1986.

'Mount Athos: A Late Chapter in the History of the Byzantine Rite.' *DOP* 42 (1988): 179–94.

'Orthros.' In *ODB*, 1539.

'"Thanksgiving for the Light": Toward a Theology of Vespers.' In *Beyond East and West: Problems in Liturgical Understanding*, edited by Robert F. Taft, 161–86. Rome: Pontifical Oriental Institute, 1997.

Through Their Own Eyes: Liturgy as the Byzantines Saw It. Berkeley, CA: InterOrthodox Press, 2006.

'Was the Eucharistic Anaphora Recited Secretly or Aloud? The Ancient Tradition and What Became of It.' In *Worship Traditions in Armenia and the Neighboring Christian East*, edited by Roberta R. Ervine, 15–58. Crestwood, NY: St Vladimir's Seminary Press, 2006.

Taft, Robert F., and Alexander P. Kazhdan. 'Cult of the Cross.' In *ODB*, 551–53.

Theodorou, Evangelos. Η Μορφωτική Αξία τοῦ Ἰσχύοντος Τριωδίου [*The Formative Value of the Prevailing Triodion*]. Athens: University of Athens, 1958.

Tkacz, Catherine Brown. 'Singing Women's Words as Sacramental Mimesis.' *Recherches de théologie et philosophie médiévales* 70, no. 2 (2003): 275–328.

Topping, Eva C. 'On Earthquakes and Fires: Romanos' Encomium to Justinian.' *BZ* 71, no. 1 (1978): 22–35.

Sacred Songs: Studies in Byzantine Hymnography. Minneapolis, MN: Light and Life Publications, 1997.

Torrance, Alexis. *Repentance in Late Antiquity. Eastern Asceticism and the Framing of the Christian Life*. Oxford: Oxford University Press, 2012.

Touliatos-Miles, Diane. *A Descriptive Catalogue of the Musical Manuscript Collection of the National Library of Greece: Byzantine Chant and Other Music Repertory Recovered*. Farnham: Ashgate, 2010.

Treadgold, Warren. 'The Historicity of Imperial Bride-Shows.' *JÖB* 54 (2004): 39–52.

Trembelas, Panagiotes N. Εκλογή Ελληνικής Ορθοδόξου Υμνογραφίας [*Selection of Orthodox Hymnography*]. Athens: Φοίνικος, 1949.

Tripolitis, Antonia. *Kassia: The Legend, the Woman and Her Work*. New York, NY: Garland Press, 1992.

Troelsgård, Christian. *Byzantine Neumes: A New Introduction to the Middle Byzantine Notation.* Copenhagen: Museum Tusculanum Press, 2011.

'Kanon Performance in the Eleventh Century, Evidence from the Evergetis Typikon Reconsidered.' In *Byzantium and Eastern Europe: Liturgical and Musical Links – In Honour of the 80th Birthday of Dr Miloš Velimirović*, edited by Nina Gerasimova-Persidskaia and Irina Lozovaia, 44–51. Moscow: State Conservatory of Moscow 'Piotr Tjajkowskij', 2004.

Tsironis, Niki. 'The Body and the Senses in the Work of Cassia the Hymnographer: Literary Trends in the Iconoclastic Period.' *Symmeikta* 16 (2003): 139–57.

Tsormpatzoglou, Panteleimon. ʿΟ Ανδρέας Κρήτης (660–740) και ο πιθανός χρόνος συγγραφής του Μεγάλου Κανόνος [Andrew of Crete and the Lkely Composition Date of the *Great Kanon*].' *Byzantina* 24 (2004): 7–42.

Turner, Victor W. *The Anthropology of Performance.* New York, NY: PAJ Publications, 1986.

The Ritual Process: Structure and Antistructure. Chicago, IL: Aldine, 1969.

Vailhé, Siméon. 'Saint André de Crète.' *Échos d'Orient* 5 (1902): 378–87.

Vermès, Géza. *Scripture and Tradition in Judaism: Haggadic Studies.* Leiden: Brill, 1961.

Ward, Benedicta. *Harlots of the Desert: A Study of Repentance in Early Monastic Sources.* Kalamazoo, MI: Cisternian Publications, 1987.

Ware, Kallistos. '"Forgive Us . . . As We Forgive": Forgiveness in the Psalms and the Lord's Prayer.' In *Meditations of the Heart: The Psalms in Early Christian Thought and Practice. Essays in Honour of Andrew Louth*, edited by Andreas Andreopoulos, Augustine Casiday and Carol Harrison, 53–76. Turnhout: Brepols, 2011.

'The Meaning of "Pathos" in Abba Isaias and Theodoret of Cyrus.' *Studia Patristica* 20 (1989): 315–22.

'The Meaning of the Divine Liturgy for the Byzantine Worshipper.' In *Church and People in Byzantium*, edited by Rosemary Morris, 7–28. Birmingham: Centre for Byzantine, Ottoman and Modern Greek Studies, University of Birmingham, 1990.

'"An Obscure Matter": The Mystery of Tears in Orthodox Spirituality.' In *Holy Tears: Weeping in the Religious Imagination*, edited by Kimberley Christine Patton and John Stratton Hawley, 242–54. Princeton, NJ: Princeton University Press, 2005.

'The Orthodox Experience of Repentance.' *Sobornost* 2 (1980): 18–28.

'Symbolism in the Liturgical Commentary of St Germanos of Constantinople.' In *Seeing through the Eyes of Faith: New Approaches to the Mystagogy of the Church Fathers*, edited by Paul Van Geest, 423–42. Leuven: Peeters, 2016.

Webb, Ruth. *Ekphrasis, Imagination and Persuasion in Ancient Rhetorical Theory and Practice.* Aldershot: Ashgate, 2009.

'Imagination and the Arousal of the Emotions in Greco-Roman Rhetoric.' In *The Passions in Roman Thought and Literature*, edited by Susanna Morton

Braund and Christopher Gill, 112–27. Cambridge: Cambridge University Press, 1997.

'Spatiality, Embodiment and Agency in Ekphraseis of Church Buildings.' In *Aural Architecture in Byzantium: Music, Acoustics, and Ritual*, edited by Bissera V. Pentcheva, 163–75. New York, NY: Routledge, 2017.

Wellesz, Egon. *A History of Byzantine Music and Hymnography*. Oxford: Clarendon Press, 1961.

Whitby, Mary. 'The Occasion of Paul the Silentiary's Ekphrasis of S. Sophia.' *The Classical Quarterly* 35, no. 1 (1985): 215–28.

'Rhetorical Questions.' In *A Companion to Byzantium*, edited by Liz James, 239–50. Chichester: Wiley-Blackwell, 2010.

White, Andrew Walker. *Performing Orthodox Ritual in Byzantium*. Cambridge: Cambridge University Press, 2015.

Index

CPSIA information can be obtained
at www.ICGtesting.com
Printed in the USA
BVHW052105010322
630337BV00008B/52

9 781108 720670